THE
EVERYTHING
Guide to
C. S. Lewis & Narnia

Dear Reader,

Though while still in high school I chose the intellectual course and a life of inquiry into the philosophical and theological underpinnings of things, and though I had been an evangelical believer most of those years, it's ironic that I didn't get into C. S. Lewis until my fifties. In fact, except for an earlier unsuccessful stab at reading *The Screwtape Letters*, it was the landmark 1993 feature film, *Shadowlands*, that awoke my appetite for a more fulsome encounter with Lewis.

That movie, not because of its production values but the thinking and reading it inspired, changed my life. Though always a reader, my passion for books has been redoubled since then, in part directly because of a line in *Shadowlands*, not even attributed to Lewis, that proposes, "we read to know that we are not alone."

In a sense my life has been radically refocused and reordered through my encounter with Lewis. A major aspect of that encounter is the journey into and through the fantasy world of Lewis, especially as portrayed in *The Chronicles of Narnia*. And that journey is greatly benefited by an understanding of Lewis's Christian conversion and his deepening appreciation of myth and truth. It's my hope that *The Everything® Guide to C. S. Lewis & Narnia* will enable you to enter that same understanding and experience the joy.

Jon Kennedy

Welcome to the EVERYTHING Series!

Welcome to the EVERYTHING® Profiles line of books—
an extension of the bestselling EVERYTHING® series!

These authoritative books help you learn everything you ever wanted to know
about the lives, social context, and surrounding historical events of fascinating
people who made or influenced history. While reading this EVERYTHING® book
you will discover 3 useful boxes, in addition to numerous quotes:

Fact: Definitions and additional information
Question: Questions and answers for deeper insights
They Said: Memorable quotes made by others about this person

Whether you are learning about a figure for the first time or are just brushing up
on your knowledge, EVERYTHING® Profiles help you on your journey toward
a greater understanding of the individuals who have shaped and enriched our
lives, culture, and history.

Editorial

Director of Innovation: Paula Munier

Editorial Director: Laura M. Daly

Executive Editor, Series Books: Brielle K. Matson

Associate Copy Chief: Sheila Zwiebel

Acquisitions Editor: Lisa Laing

Development Editor: Brett Palana-Shanahan

Production Editor: Casey Ebert

Production

Director of Manufacturing: Susan Beale

Production Project Manager: Michelle Roy Kelly

Prepress: Erick DaCosta, Matt LeBlanc

Design Manager: Heather Blank

Interior Layout: Heather Barrett, Brewster Brownville, Colleen Cunningham

---

Visit the entire Everything® series at www.everything.com

THE
EVERYTHING®
GUIDE TO
C. S. LEWIS
& NARNIA

Explore the magical world of Narnia
and the brilliant mind behind it

Jon Kennedy, M.A.
Foreword by Lee Oser, Ph.D.

Avon, Massachusetts

To my brother, Bob, and my lifelong friends (with the years we met):
John Golias (1958), Clarence Deffenbaugh (1962), Larry Miller
(1964), and Michael Masterson (1972).

An Everything® Series Book.
Everything® and everything.com® are registered trademarks of F+W Publications, Inc.

Published by Adams Media, an F+W Publications Company
57 Littlefield Street, Avon, MA 02322 U.S.A.
www.adamsmedia.com

ISBN 10: 1-59869-427-8
ISBN 13: 978-1-59869-427-7

Printed in the United States of America.

J   I   H   G   F   E   D   C   B   A

Library of Congress Cataloging-in-Publication Data
is available from the publisher.

This publication is designed to provide accurate and authoritative information with regard to the subject matter covered. It is sold with the understanding that the publisher is not engaged in rendering legal, accounting, or other professional advice. If legal advice or other expert assistance is required, the services of a competent professional person should be sought.

—From a *Declaration of Principles* jointly adopted by a Committee of the American Bar Association and a Committee of Publishers and Associations

Many of the designations used by manufacturers and sellers to distinguish their products are claimed as trademarks. Where those designations appear in this book and Adams Media was aware of a trademark claim, the designations have been printed with initial capital letters.

This book is available at quantity discounts for bulk purchases.
For information, please call 1-800-289-0963.

Contents

Acknowledgments

Grateful thanks is due my editors at Adams Media, Lisa Laing and Brett Palana-Shanahan, for their support and help in making this project possible. Also of immense help was the editorial review, suggestions, and comments of my friend and fellow parishioner at St. Stephen's, Gary Yee.

The Top Ten Things You'll Learn about C. S. Lewis & Narnia

1. Though one of England's top writers of the past century, Lewis was Irish by birth and of Welsh lineage.

2. Originally a poet, his bestselling children's novels are accompanied by well-known writings in religion, science fiction, and medieval literature.

3. Though widely considered the most effective defender of Christianity of his time, he spent his young adult life as an atheist.

4. He was self-taught in many languages in order to read original works, and he memorized some books in order not to have to buy them.

5. His original plan to write *The Lion, The Witch, and the Wardrobe* was expanded into the seven-book *The Chronicles of Narnia* because his publisher preferred a series of children's books to a single title.

6. Though a bestselling author during his lifetime and a professor at both of England's most venerable universities, he was never wealthy.

7. Lewis gave away up to two-thirds of his income.

8. Lewis didn't marry until near the end of his life, and that was to save the woman he married from being deported.

9. While otherwise fully employed, Lewis not only produced a stream of books over his lifetime, but also answered most of his admirers' mail and answered those who wrote for help.

10. Though his writing lifestyle was solitary and he felt himself an outsider at Oxford, he considered his friends the most precious aspect of his life.

Introduction

▶ SO MANY BOOKS, movies, and television presentations have appeared about C. S. Lewis in recent years that it's not likely that anything new, other than points of view or speculations about debated facts of his life, will emerge. But as new movies like 2008's planned release of *Prince Caspian* appear, awareness and interest in Lewis will continue to rise. Consequently, fresh takes on his life and his contributions to literature and Christian apologetics (defense of the faith) will continue to be in demand.

Though C. S. Lewis became well known in his adopted country of England as a religion speaker on the BBC, as a bestselling author of books (partly based on his radio talks), and later as a successful author of the children's fantasy series *The Chronicles of Narnia*, his fame has continued to widen and deepen since his death, in no small part because his writings have influenced Christian thinking more than any other twentieth-century writer. Some have even mused that although there are few points of agreement among Catholic, Protestant, and Eastern Orthodox Christians, most of them do agree upon the influence and the contributions of C. S. Lewis.

The Everything® Guide to C. S. Lewis & Narnia introduces C. S. Lewis as a man of great imagination, integrity, and intellect, capable of seeing and articulating a way through the thickets of modernity challenging religious faith. This book provides a look at Lewis the man, the people in his life, and the motivations and worldview behind his commitment to literature in general and the fantasy fiction world of Narnia in particular. Most of Lewis's best known books are reviewed and discussed in some detail throughout this book with a view to making them more accessible and understandable to today's readers. A chapter is devoted to each of the short Narnia volumes. Though this book follows C. S. Lewis's life from birth to death feel free to enter at any point where your interest in Lewis has been raised. May this overview baptize your imagination, whet your appetite for more, and inflame a desire to journey further up and further in that will change your life.

Foreword

MURDER! FASCISTS! LIONS! It isn't fair.
—*The Silver Chair*

In *The Return of Christian Humanism*, I focused a critical spotlight on G. K. Chesterton, T. S. Eliot, and J. R. R. Tolkien, reserving C. S. Lewis for a supporting role. Here the order is reversed, with Lewis taking center stage and the others swelling the ranks of the chorus. But like a shared musical theme, the movement known as Christian humanism runs through both books.

To people who associate humanism with secular humanism, the notion of a Christian humanism may seem as oxymoronic as Shakespeare's "heavy lightness." Lewis himself was censorious of Renaissance humanism, regarding it as pedantic scribbling unfaithful to the church. As he very well knew, the term *humanism* is a late coinage. It comes, by way of England and Germany, from the nineteenth century and was never used during the Renaissance. It has been shuffled in some peculiar markets. But if you were to say to Lewis (who so often figures in imaginary conversations) that you meant to include among the humanists thoroughgoing churchmen like the Elizabethan poet Edmund Spenser, I think you would establish some common ground.

The author of *The Chronicles of Narnia* takes from Spenser's *The Faerie Queene* the lesson that nature and reason should serve as guides to a good life. That lesson defines the humanist side of Christian humanism. The Christian side is foreshadowed but not completed by *The Faerie Queene*. In George Sayer's paraphrase of Tolkien (who adopted the idea from Chesterton), the Christian side is a revelatory myth, "the Christian story was a myth invented by a God who was real." If the Christian God is real, the goods of nature and reason are cosmically validated. The chaos of total relativism yields varying degrees and approximations of truth. History becomes a romance.

The strong connection in Lewis between truth and imagination gives him a distinctly modern pedigree, which has been little appreciated by professors at places like Oxford, Cambridge, Harvard, and Yale. When I attended the latter institution some fifteen years ago, I was the first scholar in a generation to write a dissertation on Eliot. Chesterton was heard from now and then as a shrewd English critic; Lewis was permitted as a distinguished medieval and Renaissance scholar; Eliot was a universal whipping boy; Tolkien a philologist who strayed. You would hardly have known that these men were blessed with superb creative gifts. We were operating, it seemed, under the influence of the Head at Experiment House.

How much has changed? Chesterton is, at least, a name to reckon with. Eliot is widely recognized as the leading poet-critic of the last century. Tolkien is becoming established as a serious author. And Lewis continues to astonish the world. These four men are at the heart of Christian humanism. Because of them, there is a chance the tradition will survive.

—Lee Oser, Ph.D.

Chapter 1

All of His Roads Before Him

Clive Staples Lewis was born November 29, 1898, in his family's home in Dundela Villas, overlooking the Belfast Lough (an inlet from the strait dividing Ireland from Scotland) in Belfast, in County Down in what is now Northern Ireland. Clive was the second of two sons to Flora Hamilton Lewis and Albert James Lewis, a successful Belfast attorney. The infant Clive was looked after by servants in the style common in professional-class British homes of the time, and he played mostly indoors because of Ireland's wet weather and the dangers of diseases that took a high toll on young children of the time.

Childhood in Victorian Ireland

C. S. Lewis's first friend and playmate was his brother Warren, called Warnie, who was three years old when Clive was born and to whom he remained close the rest of his life. The grandson on his mother's side of a rector in the Church of Ireland (as the Anglican Church is called there) and great-grandson of a Methodist minister on his father's, his family regularly attended Saint Mark's Church in Dundela, where his parents had met. The northern Ireland weather and their long periods of playing inside surrounded by a well-stocked family library are thought to have ignited the Lewis brothers' literary imaginations.

FACT

Though imagination and fantasy play were common for children before the age of TV kids' networks and computer games, it must have been an especially strong factor for boys living in Ireland with its surfeit of storytellers and fantastic characters like selkies (human by night and seals by day) and "little people," including leprechauns.

All of Ireland in the closing years of Queen Victoria's reign (1837–1901) was part of the British Empire, the world's major superpower at the time on which it was frequently said into the 1940s that the sun never set. From London to Hong Kong to India and colonies in Africa, the sun, indeed, was shining on some part of the empire at all hours.

Home rule for Ireland was already being debated, with several of the Queen's prime ministers and parliaments taking divergent stands back and forth, but when Lewis lived as a child in Ulster, Ireland's northeast province, the island was not yet partitioned between the Irish Republic and the six-county region of Northern Ireland as it now is. But special initiatives, "plantings" by Oliver Cromwell (who ruled England from 1599 to 1658) and King William III (1672–1702, known as William of Orange,) gave Scottish

Presbyterians and English Puritans and Anglicans land to develop and, indirectly, "Protestantize" Ulster. These efforts resulted in Ulster being Ireland's only Protestant-majority province.

Religious Rivalry

Unlike most cities in Britain and Ireland, Belfast is a relatively new development. Belfast was founded in 1609, less than twenty-five years earlier than the original settlements at New Amsterdam (New York) and Boston, Massachusetts, and two years *after* the establishment of the first permanent English settlement (Jamestown) in Virginia. Belfast and the six counties of Northern Ireland are still known as the site of the most intense and often violent rivalry in the world between Protestants and Roman Catholics. And it was into that milieu that the author of the most influential book promoting peace based on mutual respect among disparate orthodox Christian communions—C. S. Lewis's *Mere Christianity*—was born and spent his childhood in a strongly Protestant family.

"If aesthetic experiences were rare [in my childhood], religious experiences did not occur at all. Some people have got the impression from my books that I was brought up in strict and vivid Puritanism, but this is quite untrue. I was taught the usual things and made to say my prayers and in due time [was] taken to church."

The House of Lewis

On his father's side of the family, Lewis told his friend and later biographer, George Sayer, that he was descended from a Welsh farmer and it was the Welsh genes he considered his most characteristic ethnic line. Richard Lewis, Clive's great-great-grandfather, born in 1775, had owned a farm south of the border of England and Wales and was atypical in that he was Anglican when most Welsh had become chapel, or Methodists.

Richard Lewis's fourth son, Joseph, Clive's great-grandfather, settled near Chester, across the border from Wales in central England, and apparently fell out with his Anglican vicar over the limited role he was allowed to take in services. He subsequently joined the local Methodists and eventually became their minister. He is recalled as a "powerful preacher." Though C. S. Lewis omits mentioning his paternal great-grandfather's Methodist ministry in his 1955 biography, *Surprised by Joy*, Sayer attributes to this ancestor Clive's "religious enthusiasm, fine resonant voice, and real rhetorical ability."

Grandfather Richard

Joseph's fourth son (of a family of eight), also named Richard, joined the ship-building trade in Liverpool, England's "second city," and from there moved to Cork, Ireland, to continue that trade. In Cork he and his wife Martha Gee had six children, the youngest of whom was Albert, Clive's father, born in 1863. Richard took the family from Cork to Dublin, where he joined John H. MacIlwaine and moved with him to establish MacIlwaine and Lewis Boiler Makers, Engineers, and Iron Ship Builders in Belfast.

Though initially prosperous, the business relationship was eventually dissolved, with Richard falling into hard times after his children were grown. His sons, especially Albert, helped sustain him in his older years, until his death (in 1908) at age seventy-six when Clive was nine years old. Grandfather Richard was remembered as both boorish (for example, having bad table manners) and snobbish, and was known for mood swings ranging from extreme optimism to extreme depression, a trait that some biographers say Clive's father Albert inherited.

Among uncles on the Lewis side, Clive and Warnie were fondest of their eldest uncle, Joseph, Richard's first son, remembered as the most balanced Lewis of Albert's generation. But he died in Clive's tenth year.

Richard's second son, William (1858–1946) was remembered by Clive and Warnie as the least amiable of their paternal uncles. He was the first Lewis to send his sons to English boarding schools, an example that Albert followed by sending Warnie and Clive abroad in their preteens.

The Mother's Side

Clive considered his mother's side, the Hamiltons, as "Southern Irish" because, though originating in Scotland, they had been landed (given land) in County Down (south and east of what is now Belfast), Ireland, in the seventeenth century, under King James I. From their first home in Ulster, the line migrated to Dublin (southern Ireland), where Clive's great-great-grandfather was a fellow of Trinity College and later a bishop of the Church of Ireland.

> ## FACT
> Though *Scots-Irish* (or *Scotch-Irish*) is the term used to describe families like the Hamiltons who emigrated to northern Ireland from Scotland, not as well known is the fact that most Scottish families are descended from Irish immigrants who flooded Scotland following St. Columba (or, in Gaelic, Colm), a sixth-century Irish monk who evangelized the sparse population of Picts then inhabiting the Scottish highlands. "Scotland," *Scotia*, is actually the Latin name for Ireland.

Clive and Warnie held more affection for their Hamilton ancestors and were disinclined to like the Lewis side, though biographers see both sides as flawed. The Hamilton grandparents are recalled as poor parents who openly favored their elder two children, Lilian and Cecil, at the expense of the younger pair, Flora and younger brother Augustus. Grandmother Mary Warren Hamilton, the vicar's wife, was active in politics, especially advocating home rule for Ireland (meaning a local parliament but not separation from the British Empire). She also irked parishioners and Protestant neighbors by hiring Catholic Irish servants rather than the Protestant ones preferred by most northern Ireland non-Catholics. Mary's parental family, the Warrens, landed in Ireland during the reign of Henry II (1154–1189).

Mary Hamilton is said to have kept an untidy vicarage, presumably evidencing a calling higher or more cerebral than housekeeping. The house was overrun by cats whose presence was said to assault the olfactory senses of visitors when the door was opened by the family's maid.

Grandfather Thomas

The vicar of St. Mark's is remembered as a preacher often carried away by his own sermons and shedding tears in the pulpit, which embarrassed parishioners including members of his family

Flora Lewis. Used by permission of The Marion E. Wade Center, Wheaton College, Wheaton, IL.

and the Lewises. Sayer attributes to him Clive's strong devotion to his principles as well as the kind of bravery Clive would later show while serving in the First World War.

After graduating from Dublin's Trinity College where he took top marks in theology, Thomas volunteered as a navy chaplain for the duration of the Crimean War (1854–1856) and ministered in camps where cholera was as likely as combat to take sailors' lives. He considered swearing a deadly sin and openly reprimanded officers for using bad language in front of their troops. His preaching, not unusual in Ulster Protestant pulpits then and for generations afterward, was often virulently anti-Catholic, even referring to Catholics as demon-possessed or agents of Satan.

The aunt and uncles on the Hamilton side of their family were remembered by Clive and Warnie as bad-tempered and unkind. The eldest, Uncle Cecil, was recalled as "insolent" and always sarcastic with his sister, Lilian. Aunt Lilian was always "at war with as many members of the family as possible," Sayer claims in *Jack*, and was accused by a servant of having driven her short-lived husband to a lunatic asylum. Uncle Augustus, or Gussie, a late bloomer, was called selfish and mean, but with a sense of humor and "an original thinker." Despite his shortcomings and frequent requests for financial assistance, Albert considered him a close friend.

Parents' Marriage

Clive's father Albert turned to Flora after his older brother, William, had been rebuffed in attempts to court her. Though Albert had earlier maintained a long correspondence with a previous love interest, from age sixteen to twenty-two, he was more persistent through ups and downs with Flora. Albert, whose sons thought he could have had a career in politics, may have plied both the skill and the interest in befriending Flora's mother by being a willing and ready sounding board for her opinions about home rule and other social reforms. It seems a safe assumption that his alliance with his future mother-in-law helped him win Flora's affections.

THEY SAID

"Flora's father also found a way to make use of Albert's love for his daughter. He had Albert arrange and pay for a series of short holidays that he felt he needed, probably as a change from the unhappy and untidy life at the vicarage."

—George Sayer, *Jack*

Biographer Sayer insinuates that by this time Flora, who had finished her bachelor of arts from Queen's College, Belfast, in mathematics and logic in 1881, was approaching spinsterhood and may have feared remaining an unclaimed treasure. Albert and Flora were united in marriage in 1894 by her father in St. Mark's Church, when he was thirty-one and she thirty-two.

Child's Play and Fantasy

Lewis writes that his brother Warnie was his ally and confederate from the start. He never perceived him as an older brother, and they played and plotted together. From the earliest times Clive could remember, they were captivated by stories. They enjoyed creating their own characters and settings in which to play out their own fantasies and heroic feats. Though Warnie gravitated toward ships, trains, and stories of battles, Clive was more interested in magic and magical beings like elves, fairies, and classical heroes. Though they played indoors during inclement weather, as they became more independent they were able to explore the nearby countryside by foot and their bicycles.

"Jacksie," Then Jack

At about age four, Clive started insisting on being called "Jacksie" and refused to answer by any other name. Though George Sayer, who titles his biography simply *Jack*, doesn't provide an origin for the boy's preference, an encyclopedia entry on Lewis claims Jacksie was the name of his beloved dog who died at that time. After he outgrew the childish "Jacksie," family and friends ever after called Clive "Jack," and thus from this point on so will he be called here.

FACT

With the release of the film *The Lion, The Witch, and the Wardrobe*, the Northern Ireland Tourist Board introduced a C. S. Lewis Trail in East Belfast, featuring a sculpture of the author as a young man, the home of his paternal grandfather, the sites of his first and second homes, St. Mark's Church, and other related sites. See Appendix A for the tourist board's Internet address.

Jack's Ireland

Though Sayer makes more of Jack's claim to Welsh roots than his Irish birth and childhood, a historian claims Lewis showed a strong affinity for the Irish part of his past, returning to it as home throughout his life. Not only were views overlooking Belfast Lough instrumental in feeding the boys' imaginations, but from other windows they could see the Mourne Mountains in the distance and the Holywood Hills in the foreground. Later, when on holidays, they often hiked the hills and mountains near Belfast. Among Jack's most lyrical and romantic writings is a lengthy passage in Chapter 8 of *Surprised by Joy* extolling the beauty and inspiration to be found in the scenery of Northern Ireland's County Down and County Antrim.

A vignette in Sayer's biography illustrates another aspect of the Irish influence on Jack's young childhood. Hearing the legend from Irish mythology of the pot of gold buried at the end of the rainbow, Jack was sure that one day the rainbow ended in the middle of the front yard of his house. So there he dug a deep hole in the quest of treasure into which his father, arriving home from work after dark, tripped and fell, dirtying his business suit. An incensed Albert insisted the boys had laid a booby trap for him.

Jack's and Warnie's imaginations were even more enhanced by a move the family made when Jack was six, from Dundela Villas to a new house, called Little Lea, which was so large he says it seemed more like a city than a house to him and Warnie. Built especially for the family and about two miles farther out in what was then the countryside, Little Lea had what seemed endless corridors and rooms to explore.

The attic at Little Lea provided one room that Jack made into his own study, and it became the hub of activity for the boys in which they explored and where Warnie looked on admiringly while Jack turned out stories and pictures. Pictures were Jack's first creative endeavors in the plotting of stories, before he had developed the ability to write. Warnie first introduced his own drawings, but before long the younger brother was able to match Warnie's proficiency. Jack says that though their childhood art had many qualities, it showed no traces of beauty. His first memory of thinking something beautiful was a model of a

"To me, the important thing about the move was that the background of my life became larger. The New House is almost a major character in my story. I am a product of long corridors, empty sunlit rooms, upstairs indoor silences, attics explored in solitude, distant noises of gurgling cisterns and pipes, and the noise of wind under the tiles."

–*Suprised By Joy*

garden Warnie created in the lid of a biscuit tin, using moss and fungi to represent grass and trees.

Animal-Land and India

Jack's first stories were about Animal-Land and featured dressed-up animals and knightly mice and rabbits. They were probably inspired mainly by his nursery books, the first of which he recalls as *The Three Bears*, read to him at age two-and-a-half by his beloved nurse, Lizzie Endicott. Also introduced early were books by E. Nesbitt (*Five Children and It, The Phoenix and the Wishing Carpet*, and *The Amulet*), an illustrated edition of Swift's *Gulliver's Travels*, and the animal fantasies, especially *Squirrel Nutkin,* by Beatrix Potter, creator of the Peter Rabbit series. Potter's animal stories inspired in Jack what he describes as his first taste of literary beauty. Jack developed an exhaustive history for Animal-Land, and Warnie's stories were always set in India, his country. Warnie's first story, Jack recalled, was *The Young Rajah*.

Literary Awakenings

Both of Jack's parents wrote short stories, but neither had been published. Jack recalled that his father encouraged his interest in creating stories, though he was not much engaged in other ways. Though up to this point the boys were educated in what now would be called home schooling, shortly after the family's move into Little Lea, Jack says in *Surprised by Joy*, "my brother was packed off to an English boarding school and thus removed from my life for the greater part of every year."

"Neither [my father] nor my mother had the least taste for…that kind of literature to which my allegiance was given the moment I could choose books for myself. Neither had ever listened for the horns of elfland. There was no copy either of Keats or Shelley in the house and the copy of Coleridge was never…opened."

But rather than interrupting their writing, the separation after Warnie was shipped off to boarding school may have enhanced it. The brothers wrote to each other, and part of their writing was keeping their stories alive by discussing new turns in their characters' lives and circumstances. When Warnie returned to Little Lea for holidays, they resumed their drawing and writing together as though there had been no interruption, and Jack says they merged Animal-Land and India in a single map. India was turned into an island bordered by the Himalayas and was linked to Animal-Land by steamship lanes.

Not being able to create cardboard castles because of a joint in his thumb that he couldn't bend (a trait his father and Warnie shared), Jack said that learning how to create castles and the stories built around them through writing turned out to be much better. Creating Animal-Land was preparation for becoming a novelist, even if his childhood animal characters share little in common with those in the Narnia tales published in his adult life.

Any Child's Worst Nightmare

Though it was his nurse, Lizzie Endicott, rather than his mother, who read and told stories to Jack in his early childhood, he refers to his mother in *Surprised by Joy* as "everything that had made our house a home" and "all that was tranquil and reliable" in his life. In 1907, Flora, Jack, and Warnie traveled together to the French vil-

"What drove me to write was the extreme manual clumsiness from which I have always suffered...Nature laid on me from birth an utter incapacity to make anything...It was this that forced me to write. I wanted to make things... [so] I was driven to write stories instead."

lage of Beneval, Normandy, by way of London, where Flora took the boys to the zoo. There, Jack's main fascination was a cage of white mice. Probably inspired by that encounter, Warnie recorded that on that holiday Jack, then age eight, began writing a new book, *Living Races of Mouse-Land*, and Warnie thought it would be good when finished.

When Warnie was off at Wynyard School, Flora taught Jack French, Latin, and math. And his increased solitude without his big brother at his side probably enhanced Jack's desire to read even more voraciously than before. He recalls in *Surprised by Joy* that Little Lea was stocked with books that both of his parents bought. Some of them were appropriate for children and some were absolutely not, but he had access to them all, he says. Besides Flora's teaching, Jack also had the services of private tutors who were also part of the household retinue.

Seaside Holidays

It wasn't unusual in Victorian times for mothers in Flora's circumstances to take their children on summer holidays, often for all three summer months, at seaside resorts. In that tradition Flora took extended trips with the boys to the northern coastal village of Castlerock in County Derry, a few hours' train ride from Belfast, accompanied by a nursemaid and one or two other servants. Even from age two, his biographer says, Jack loved the sea, though his mother didn't allow him to go into the water.

QUESTION
How did Lewis explain why his childhood prayers for his mother's healing didn't work?
According to Lewis, "I had approached God, or my idea of God, without love, without awe, even without fear. He was, in my mental picture of this miracle, to appear neither as Savior nor as Judge, but merely as a magician."

It may have been while on the beach at Castlerock that Jack and Warnie first discovered what he later wrote about as a feeling of and for "Northern-ness," part of the longing (*sehnsucht*) that Jack used to describe the experience of joy that came to characterize his decades-long quest that ended in his finding Christian faith.

Passing

Flora had been suffering from headaches and fatigue for several years, and in early 1908 she was diagnosed with abdominal cancer, for which doctors performed surgery on her on February 15, at Little Lea. A time of improved health followed, with one more trip to the seaside with Jack in

May, but in June she had to take to her bed again. Late at night on August 21, Albert's birthday, she passed away with, "What have we done for Him?" recorded as her last words in Albert's journal. Jack says in *Surprised by Joy*, "then my father, in tears, came into my room and began to try to convey to my terrified mind things it had never conceived before."

To him and Warnie, Jack says, the bereavement began even before their mother's death, because her declining health had taken her away from them more and more over the months preceding her death. Jack said his father never recovered from Flora's death, and an evil consequence of her passing was that, in it, the boys lost both of their parents.

Chapter 2

Life with Father and Warnie

A romantic take on Albert's loss of his wife of fourteen years might suggest that after the formal mourning period the father and his sons would draw closer. But this wasn't to be in the Lewis family. Life after Flora was never the same for any of the three Lewis men. Perhaps in the Victorian era men as the heads of households were so unfamiliar with the needs of children that Albert never considered keeping the boys close to him at Little Lea. Perhaps his elder brother William persuaded him that men of their time were best forged in the preparatory and public schools (as privately owned boarding schools were then called). Whatever the case, when the school year started a few weeks after Flora's funeral, Jack was sent off with Warnie to what he refers to as "Concentration Camp."

Albert Lewis

Sayer believed that Albert was motivated by the boys' best interests in sending both of them to Wynyard School and that Jack's being sent just after losing his mother may have hastened what would have been an inevitability in any case. Warnie, after all, was about the same age as Jack now was when he'd been sent to Wynyard. It's also a strong possibility that Albert and Warnie both thought Warnie would be a better companion to Jack than his grieving father could be. Finally, prep school, as the type of school Wynyard was called, followed by public school seems to have been the preferred route into first-tier universities like Cambridge and Oxford at the time.

Poor Man or Rich Man?

Jack says that his father Albert represented adulthood to him as a life of unending drudgery, tinged by constant fear of financial ruin. Perhaps it was an Irish trait of their generation that men like Albert often referred to closing out their days in the poorhouse or workhouse, something Albert

C. S. Lewis (right) with his father, Albert. Used by permission of The Marion E. Wade Center, Wheaton College, Wheaton, IL.

frequently predicted despite the fact that the Lewises and Hamiltons had both prospered from one generation to the next. When most Irish people were living in farm cottages with thatched roofs and clay floors, Albert's expansive made-to-order Little Lea must have seemed a palace by comparison, even if, as Jack says in *Surprised by Joy*, the workmen who built it took advantage of Albert's immense "capacity to be cheated" by doing substandard work in many parts of the house.

THEY SAID

"Albert [was] a man of commanding presence, formally dressed, good-looking, but with a disapproving and slightly sulky air. He was a kind man all the same, generous to the poor and unfortunate...in gifts, money, and in legal work, which he often [did, unpaid]. Both [Albert and Jack] were generous, in spite of a fear of being bankrupt."

—George Sayer, *Jack*

But the imposing house was no longer a home, much less a palace, to Albert or his sons after Flora's departure. (That same year Albert lost his father, who had lived with them at Little Lea toward the end of his life, and his brother Richard.) Having been meant mainly for her, the house must have seemed indeed empty and forlorn, despite the presence of the household staff.

Albert is also remembered for having social connections outside his profession in literary societies in Belfast, as a writer of mostly unpublished short stories and poems, and as a political speaker. Sayer believes that if Albert had persevered as a writer he would have succeeded as a novelist. Jack calls his father "the best *raconteur* I have ever heard," a storyteller who acted out all the characters, freely embellishing his presentations with gestures, pantomime, and grimaces. Nothing pleased Albert more than being with his brothers and brothers-in-law telling stories that they called "wheezes."

Though Jack thought he'd lost his father when his mother died, Sayer reports that later in their school years Albert took an interest in vaudeville shows in order to share them with the boys, who had learned to like them.

Though Albert was remote in many ways, he did encourage Jack's writing of stories. He also read books that interested Jack, in order to encourage that interest, and sent Jack lengthy and frequent letters when he was off at school.

Exiled with Warnie

Jack recalls that Warnie had said little to prepare him for the horrors of Wynyard School, the "Concentration Camp," as he calls it in the title of Chapter Two of *Surprised by Joy*. There he lived "under the eye of a certainly brutal and probably insane tyrant of a headmaster," as Sayer puts it in *Jack*. But nevertheless, understandably, the mood was somber when Albert accompanied the boys, dressed in Eton collars that scratched, heavy boots, knickerbockers (a kind of trousers that buttoned tight at the knees), and bowler hats that seemed to Jack as made of iron, to the boat that would take them to England. Albert, moved by their parting, bid them farewell after some moments with them on the vessel, but Jack was mainly embarrassed and relieved to get away from his father's awkward and, undoubtedly grieving, presence.

"No Englishman will...understand my first impressions of England... I found a world to which I reacted with immediate hatred. The flats of Lancashire...The strange English accents... like the voices of demons. But what was worst was the English landscape...The flatness!"

It's ironic that Warnie, the lover of ships, got seasick on the rough night crossing from Belfast to Fleetwood, on central England's west coast north of Liverpool, while Jack turned out to be the better sailor of the two. Wynyard, which Jack disguises as Oldie's School or Belsen (which he also uses for the name of the town in which the school was located in *Surprised by Joy*), was across the country in Watford, a northwest suburb of London. Sayer recounts evidence of considerable research Albert had done to find a suitable school for both sons but concludes that it's hard to imagine how he could have chosen "a school quite as bad" as Wynyard.

Oldie's School

Consisting of only about sixteen to eighteen boys, half living nearby and half boarding, Wynyard was led by a headmaster, the Rev. Robert Capron, an Anglican clergyman, whom Warnie describes as a physically powerful man about sixty years old at the time. The school building was one semi-detached room, with a dormitory with only one washbasin. Baths were allowed only once a week, and the lavatories were remembered as primitive and so unsanitary they would not have passed inspection, if there had been one, even in 1905. In hot weather their stench permeated everything.

There were no fields attached to the school, with the only play area a flinty gravel lot on which Jack said "endless rounders" (a primitive form of baseball) were played. The school had no library and Jack says he had been doing the same kind of Latin exercises under his mother's tutelage that he still was on when he left the school two years later. There were only three faculty members—the headmaster, his son Wyn (nicknamed Wee Wee), and an usher (an assistant teacher). Jack says they called the headmaster Oldie. Mrs. Capron (the usher) is remembered as "a little, timid, faded woman," and at meals the only person bold enough to start a conversation was Wee Wee, who directed his comments only to his father. Boys could be punished for not finishing their meals, and the headmaster was described as eating "wolfishly" despite meals that were often nauseating. Sayer suggests that Jack's lifelong habit of eating quickly may have been developed under the scornful eye of Oldie.

Punishment and Protection

Learning lessons by rote was the preferred pedagogic method at Wynyard, an approach that Warnie called intellectually stupefying and brutalizing. The most stimulating aspect of an Oldie School education was the canes (long rattan or birch rods) that hung on the classroom walls and were used to whip boys who failed to give correct answers and in the correct way. Jack mentions many such cruel punishments, with Oldie holding the cane in position and running the length of the classroom to apply it to the offending boy's backside. Jack says that despite himself he became one of Oldie's favorites and does not mention any corporal punishments being applied to him directly.

Warnie protected Jack against bullies and hazing in his first two terms at Wynyard, but after that Warnie left for another school, Malvern College in Worcestershire. (Wynyard, in student age, is the equivalent of an American middle school, or in older terminology, a grammar school. So by fourteen Warnie had moved on to the college, which was, in age equivalency, a high school.)

Wynyard's Fall and the Aftermath

Each term that Jack spent at Wynyard, it steadily declined. Though he surmised in *Surprised by Joy* that in his past Oldie had no doubt accumulated an impressive academic record, by the time Jack got to Wynyard, Oldie and his school were in free fall. There were fewer students each term, the use of ushers was discontinued, one of Oldie's three adult daughters filled the teaching slots, and Oldie's wife died. In Jack's second year only five boarders remained and he was among the last holdouts. Oldie let it be known that he was going out to find a cure for souls and then he shut down the school.

Though most of his time at Wynyard was wasted (he even guessed that another two years there would have ruined his chances of ever having an academic career), Jack did allow that Oldie actually liked geometry and taught it well, so much so that Jack could claim in later life that there was not a day in which he didn't use some of the rational processes he had learned in that course. But his literary progress, advancing so well when he was on his own at Little Lea, was reversed, he felt, with his reading reduced mainly to boys' stories in magazines. He says that because the school had no library he couldn't fault Oldie for the lack of good reading material, but it's not clear why Oldie wouldn't be expected to provide a proper library. But Sayer says that it was at Wynyard that Jack began to appreciate historical fiction like *Ben Hur* and the science fiction of H. G. Wells, both of which tastes influenced novels he produced decades later.

Jack writes that a neighbor of the school reported later that it was believed in town that Oldie had gone insane, and an anonymous Lewis biographer confirms that "headmaster Robert 'Oldie' Capron was soon after committed to an insane asylum."

But the asylum stay must have been of short duration, because Sayer adds that Capron became vicar of a little parish in Radstock, where he died in 1911, only a year after he closed Wynyard. Sayer also says that Jack resented Oldie for the next fifty years, remaining unable to forget the harm his first headmaster's dominating ways had wrought and forgiving him finally only while he was ill a few months before his own death.

THEY SAID . . .

"In conversation with me, [Jack] once defended the school by saying, 'It taught all of us at least one good thing. It taught us to stick together, to support each other in resistance to tyranny.'"

—George Sayer, *Jack*

Taking the philosophical approach, Jack could say Wynyard had done him more good than harm. He appreciated the fact that the school had no organized sports or games, pastimes he had never been taught to enjoy, nor did he feel he needed. Instead, the boys were sent on long walks in the English countryside, during which time he admits he began to improve his opinion of Hertfordshire. And on these times away from school the boys did more talking than walking, and their talking was usually more serious than would be expected of ten- to thirteen-year-olds. Though Jack made no life-long friends among his Wynyard acquaintances, it was there that he began to appreciate the importance of friends and to develop the characteristics that would make him a loyal long-term friend.

He remembered one of the country walks with his schoolmates as the source of his first metaphysical conversation, a type of discourse he would engage in extensively in his adult career. The metaphysical topic was whether the future is more like a line you cannot see or more like one that is not yet drawn. When he wrote *Surprised by Joy,* he couldn't remember which side of the question he took, but it must have been something of a turning point for him.

Surprised by Faith

Also at Wynyard, and perhaps most surprisingly, Jack says he first came face to face with Christian faith and began to comprehend and accept the church's teachings. The school required church attendance twice every Sunday. Although his early impression of St. John's Church of Watford was that it was encumbered with unnecessary High-Church accretions that he wasn't used to in his grandfather's relatively Puritanical parish—like use of incense and kneeling to sing hymns—the message was getting through.

FACT

Jack does not mention recognizing any connection between his awakening to spiritual answers and the grieving process he would have still been in over the loss of his mother, though often the death of a person greatly loved turns the survivors' thoughts to the afterlife.

Jack calls this discovery of faith the most important thing that happened to him at Oldie's School. His childish innocence had no skepticism, so he became an effective believer. Religion was among the many topics discussed in the boys' walks away from school, and the religious effects included reading his Bible, praying regularly, and attempting to obey the promptings of his conscience.

Back to Belfast

Jack was not old enough when Wynyard folded to move to Malvern College with Warnie, so after the school's demise he stayed back in Belfast with his father. And alas, he recalls, the partial estrangement he felt with his father seemed to increase. Albert was too generous to strike a child, and too impulsive to punish spontaneously, so he employed the tools he was best at using, the rhetoric and even the vocabulary of the courtroom, lecturing the boys with much strength and many dramatic embellishments like facial expressions. Though the boys were at first intimidated, even terrified, by this approach to discipline, a point came when their father looked ludicrous and nothing less than comedic during his recriminations. The first time they perceived it as farcical, they had to hide their faces behind their hands to conceal not remorse or tears but convulsive laughing. Sometimes Albert became so engrossed in elaborating his case that he forgot what infraction the boys had made to elicit it.

FACT

Most of the time that summer after the demise of Wynyard the boys, who Jack admits were noisy, mischievous, and inclined to trust each other exclusively, were alone at Little Lea while Albert was gone for work from 9 A.M. to 6 P.M. They were still so occupied with "the endless drama of Animal-Land and India" that this distraction, which only they could understand, further distanced them from their father.

On the Other Hand

Yet Jack also remembers times when Albert was the best of companions, heartily joining into their fun without regarding "his own dignity," an occasional turn of events that Jack considered sheer delight. Warnie writes that when Albert had visitors at Little Lea the conversation was all politics, and unlike engaging political discussion, which requires at least two opposing points of view, all of Albert's visitors shared the same Protestant Unionist and anti-Catholic Nationalist positions on Irish governance as their host, something that Warnie believed led Jack to regard most adult conversation as stifling one-sided political ranting.

Jack and Warnie resented neighborhood attempts to entertain them. Especially bothersome, the boys thought, were neighborhood parties that were actually adult dances that children of the guests were also expected to participate in. These, he felt, were grownup activities that in effect mocked childish innocence and strained their shyness, all exacerbated by the dress-up clothing they were required to wear.

He also recalled that he was often encouraged to perform for adults in such gatherings, who found his extensive vocabulary unusual for a child, though it came naturally to him from his extensive reading. He didn't realize their game at the time, but he realized later that the adults who engaged him in conversations to amuse themselves considered him to be showing off, when to him it would have been showing off to use his schoolyard slang in their presence.

Belfast Life

Life back in Belfast was also full of other members of the family circle and, at this age of emerging from childhood, characteristics of the Lewises and Hamiltons became apparent to Jack in a new way. Grandmother Mary Warren Hamilton, for example, was now an eccentric, politically heterodox, unconventional, and outspoken widow, living alone with fifty felines.

He remembers A. W. Hamilton, "Uncle Gussie," as being the only adult who spoke to him face to face like a real person. Gussie imparted as much science as Jack could absorb, providing him much of the background for his later appreciation and criticism of H. G. Wells and "scientifiction," as Jack calls science fiction. Gussie probably cared about him less than his father's brother, Uncle Joseph Lewis, who also gave him lots of attention, but Jack preferred the man-to-man approach Gussie employed.

Sir W. and Lady E.

But the most important character among the extended family cast was a first cousin of his mother's, whom he calls Lady E., who may have been his mother's closest friend. She undertook, he believes for his mother's sake, to civilize Warnie and Jack. She did this mainly by giving them a standing invitation to have lunch at her home, which Jack calls Mountbracken, any time they were at home, during which times she plied them with sophistication and "*savoir faire.*" Not only Cousin Mary (Lady E.) but her family participated in the conspiracy to make gentlemen from the unruly Lewis orphans. Tools of their subterfuge included trips in motorcars (exciting novelties so early in the twentieth century), picnics, walks, and theater outings.

Sir W. E. (Cousin Mary's husband) and several of his brothers are described as owning one of the most important commercial concerns in Belfast at the time. Cousin Quartus, as Jack calls Sir W., made one of the strongest impressions on Jack of any man in his youth. Strikingly handsome

"Friends of our own age—boy and girl friends—we had none. In part this is a natural result of boarding school; children grow up strangers to their next-door neighbors. But much more it was a result of our own obstinate choice...Our lives were already full, and the holidays too short."

with a gray beard, he was humbly religious, generous, gracious, and practiced charity and a high level of responsibility on behalf of his dependents.

Only a mile from Little Lea, Mountbracken was the largest house Jack had ever been in at the time. In many ways it was like Little Lea in having endless corridors, attics to explore, and books in the family library to read. Life there, he recalls in *Surprised by Joy*, "glided like a barge" while their lives at Little Lea "bumped like a cart."

Campbell College, Belfast

At the end of that summer, buoyed for Jack by the sinking of Wynyard, he was delighted to hear that his father was enrolling him in Campbell College, a prep school in the public school system only a mile from Little Lea. Campbell had been created in 1883 by a wealthy Belfast linen merchant to provide opportunities for Belfast youths comparable to ones they would otherwise have to travel to England to get.

Farmers and Tradesmen

Jack says that while he was going to Campbell, "the population [there] was socially much more 'mixed' than at most English schools. "I rubbed shoulders there with farmers' sons." And the Campbell boy he got closest to was a tradesman's son who had been making rounds of his father's customers before the start of school. Jack makes these statements in what seems pleased egalitarianism, but Sayer maintains that both Flora and Albert had seen public schooling as a means of bettering the fortunes and further securing the status of gentlemen for their sons.

Jack boarded at Campbell in the fall of 1910 despite its being within walking distance of Little Lea, because one of the strong selling points of public schools is the independence they instill by providing experience in living away from home and learning to cope with life among peers. In mid-November, Jack was taken home because he'd developed a bad cough. He stayed at Little Lea for the rest of the term, sharing his father's bedroom at night and recalling cherished solitude in the house during those days. In those weeks, he later recalled, he and his father were closer than at any other time in Jack's life.

FACT

Campbell College is still going strong on a 100-acre campus in East Belfast. It has nine residences (schools within the college) for boys between age eight and thirteen. A landmark on the C. S. Lewis Trail, visitors who want to enter the campus are advised to make arrangements before arriving.

Albert, apparently concluding that northern Ireland's weather wasn't good for what he thought of as Jack's "weak chest," didn't send him back to Campbell but instead made arrangements for him to begin the next term in the same town, Malvern, in which Warnie's public school was located, at a prep school called Cherbourg.

Chapter 3

Back to England to Stay

Though Jack would revisit Ireland many times, and would think of it as home for the rest of his life, he probably couldn't have guessed that in 1911 when he sailed for Liverpool with Warnie en route to Malvern he was beginning his permanent transition from Irish boy to English man. He would not reside in Ireland again. Now thirteen, he was also permanently passing from a boy to a teenager. Already having begun smoking behind Albert's back, he would soon be introduced to a variety of other rebellious youthful behaviors. His recently won faith was already being tested, and he had virtually forgotten his childhood pursuit of "Joy."

Cherbourg School

Not long after their first overnight cruise from Belfast to Liverpool, Jack and Warnie learned that, instead of taking the first train to Malvern, they could go to the Lime Street Hotel near the train station and spend the morning, presumably in the lobby or ground-floor common areas, smoking and reading magazines to wait for the latest possible train that would get them to Malvern before the school arrival deadline. Jack's prep school was just up the hillside from Warnie's Malvern College (which he disguises as Wyvern in *Surprised by Joy*, and he calls Cherbourg "Chartres"). Jack's impressions of Malvern, the town and also of its geographical setting below scenic hills, were much more positive than his first takes on the relative flatness of Watford and Hertfordshire. He calls Malvern "one of the nicest English towns I've seen yet" in a document found in *The Lewis Papers*.

Probably even in that era it would not have been considered cool for Jack and Warnie to fraternize despite their close residential proximity. Biographies describe how much they both liked traveling together at the ends and beginnings of school terms, and Jack describes how reluctantly they parted company upon arriving in the Malvern station and how they met there again for the trip back home. This kind of enjoyment of each other's company is another reason, it can be assumed, that the brothers spent as much time as possible in Liverpool waiting for the last train to Malvern. And on the return trip they would regularly have supper of poached eggs in Livermore and stop at the Empire Music Hall in Belfast for vaudeville entertainment before getting back to Little Lea.

Though enrolling only about the same number of pupils as Wynyard had in the beginning of Jack's time there, Cherbourg had educational and relational qualities that far exceeded Wynyard's, and he had few complaints against it. And though Jack was often required to do hundreds of "impots"—impositions—as punishment for failing to do assignments or for breaking school rules, he quickly caught up with his peers academically.

Losing His Religion

If finding Christian faith was the best thing about Jack's time at Wynyard, losing it would later seem the worst part of his two years at Cherbourg. But he relates that by this time he was eager to leave it behind.

> ## THEY SAID . . .
> "Cherbourg was generously staffed. The headmaster…was a good teacher of Latin and English, and there were three other masters for the seventeen boys. Nevertheless, it was quite a feat on their part to have brought Jack in two years up to the Malvern College entrance standard, considering how little he…learned at Wynyard."
>
> —George Sayer, *Jack*

Sayer faults Cherbourg's headmaster for not dealing more proactively with emotional problems that led to disciplinary problems for Jack, but Cherbourg was not entirely lacking in caring and helpful staff members. One of these, the school matron called Miss C in *Surprised by Joy* and Miss Cowie in *Jack*, may have been overly attentive to his needs.

Sayer relates that according to other students at the school at the time, Miss Cowie was fired for "holding Jack in her arms," though the fellow students considered this more motherly than anything inappropriate. Jack was still, at thirteen, a small boy on the chubby side, so it's likely that he appeared to Miss Cowie more as a needy orphan child than as an erotic interest.

Jack says no school ever had a better matron than Miss C, so skilled at comforting sick boys or cheering healthy ones. Besides holding Jack in her arms, the school cited Miss Cowie for supporting Jack's complaints against Cherbourg's policy of censoring students' correspondence to their parents. Even Wynyard hadn't been that repressive about student communications, he said.

Spiritualism

Despite his love for Miss Cowie, Jack admits she indirectly played a major role in his abandoning his recently won Christian faith soon after his arrival at the new school. He calls her a seeker after religious answers who had found occult teachings that had won wide followings in Britain and America during that period. Though she never challenged his simple Christian theology and he thought her incapable of intentionally subverting his beliefs, things he heard her say about the spirit world of the occult, a world Jack had never conceived, shook his conceptions of God.

Sayer, however, while affirming Miss Cowie's spiritualism (suggesting that she was studying theosophy), attributes Jack's loss of religion to his having taken up masturbation and, unsuccessful in attempts to stop what was then widely preached against as a vice, felt his faith was not working. "He prayed, too," for deliverance, Sayer writes in *Jack*, "and, because his prayers were not answered, he soon lost his faith."

> "I remember summing up what I took to be our destiny, in conversation with my best friend at Chartres, by the formula, 'Term, holidays, term, holidays, till we leave school, and then work, work, work till we die.' Even if I had been free from this delusion, I think I should still have seen grounds for pessimism."

Considering that Jack's account of his changing beliefs in *Surprised by Joy* varies considerably with Sayer's take on the subject, it's unfortunate that Sayer fails to document his source, though it's possible that it came from conversations with Jack and/or Warnie that took place after Jack's early life autobiography was published.

Pogo

Jack was influenced both by new interests and styles being adopted by Warnie and Warnie's peers at "the Coll" (as his section of Malvern College was called) and by a new master who came to Cherbourg when Miss Cowie left. The new master, whom Jack calls Pogo, a recent university graduate, was not much older than the students under his charge and he considered part of his job enlightening the boys about all the worldly knowledge he had acquired. His dressiness and man-about-town ways immediately appealed, so Jack says that after getting to know Pogo's temper, "we fell at his feet and adored." Pogo's dress, in what Jack calls in *Surprised by Joy* "hobbledehoy fineries" and "knuttery," was quickly imitated by Jack and the other boys.

FACT

Hobbledehoys are defined as awkward young fellows, and Jack describes "the knut" as including such fashion statements as wide ties with pins, pressed trousers worn high to show off gaudy socks, "brogue shoes with immensely wide laces," and ("filthy habit," Jack says), plastering the hair with oil. It was only 1911, but it appears that the Roaring Twenties had come early in Midshire England.

Religion in Classic Literature

Jack also thought at this time that allusions to religion in classic literature seemed to complement Miss Cowie's spiritualist ideas. Virgil, especially, spoke of hundreds of religious ideas, none of which were given any credence by the teachers. Even saying that other religions were the work of devils might have given him something to think about, Jack writes, but no one brought up the idea. Moreover, though he was far from depressed at the time, Jack says a kind of pessimism, reinforced by his father's references to the endless drudgery of adult life followed by the workhouse, pervaded his life and the thinking of friends at Cherbourg.

Jack admits that it was only years later that he looked back at his extended family and realized what comfortable lives they had been living through such pessimistic times. Even boys, he says, can tell it's desert all around even if they're in a lush oasis.

Also reinforcing his pessimism was his fondness for the writings of H. G. Wells and Robert Ball, who had given him a conception of the coldness and vastness of space coupled with modern science's argument against design. Their pessimism about meaning or purpose in the universe underscored an argument for atheism he found in Lucretius that he considered a powerful argument for atheism:

Had God designed the world, it would not be
A World so frail and faulty as we see.

Years later, Lewis would be the author of the most effective English language antidote ever to Lucretius's faithless confession, *Mere Christianity*.

Failure in Prayer

Jack also writes of a failure in his prayer life that he presents as the major factor in his readily abandoning Christianity at age fourteen. Jack's prayer life failed because he had become too morbidly conscientious about it, to the point that after he prayed he would feel he had failed to consider an element of the prayer seriously enough and so would repeat it, and that attempt to perfect his prayers started to make him dread the night, his prayer time, because he was unable to let go of his misgivings. He was becoming unable to sleep and feared going mad over it.

Jack's rejection of faith was not a moment he consciously recognized, but with all of these factors coming into his life, it quickly and entirely faded away and was not noticeably missed. After a while he was comfortably affirming total atheism.

Rediscovery of Joy

The young teenager Jack Lewis comes across in chapter four of *Surprised by Joy* as something of a lout and, as he says of Pogo, something of a "lad," a dresser and a smoker out to impress anyone he could attract by his new-found mixture of vulgarity and *savoir faire*. Though his rebellions may seem mild in postmodern times, in his family and his time and place he must have mildly embarrassed and perplexed his elders. It probably embarrassed him to look back on that time himself, considering how sensitive he was as a child and how conservative as an adult. So he devotes a whole chapter—the second chapter devoted to his two years at Cherbourg—to rehabilitating his image, as it were. He's assuring his readers that the real Jack has not permanently vanished behind the argyle socks, slicked and oiled hairdo, and immensely wide shoelaces.

He titles the chapter "Renaissance" and devotes it to two major developments in those years that pointed back to older ways and ones that would stay with him after the fads had faded:

- He and Warnie recommit themselves to Animal-Land and India, recasting it in more mature terms and renaming it Boxen, but not drawing back from its original purpose of pushing the frontiers of their creativity.
- The real renaissance is Jack's return to and rediscovery of Joy.

Jack makes a clear-cut distinction between childhood, the age of self-absorbed innocence or indifference, from which he had started emerging when moving to Wynyard, and boyhood, the dark ages of the formative years. Both childhood and boyhood were mingling in his first year at Cherbourg with Miss Cowie as his surrogate mother.

FACT

It's ironic that one of Lewis's best-known books is *A Grief Observed*, considering that he fails to observe the role the grief over their mother's death played in his and Warnie's boyhood. He continues to notice that Albert is another man after Flora's loss but misses that the loss also colored everything he and Warnie experienced for years afterward.

But Miss Cowie's departure, his new friends, and Pogo challenged him to leave childish things behind and be more manlike and more independent from family and the past. To further emphasize the difference, he says he still found his favorite childhood reading worthwhile as an adult, while his boyhood reading was all pulp fiction or dross.

Déjà Vu

The stabbing pain and elevation of Joy in Jack's unique definition of it had been missing for at least three years when he stumbled on a

THE EVERYTHING GUIDE TO C. S. LEWIS & NARNIA

literary magazine. The headline that caught his eye was "Siegfried and the Twilight of the Gods," under which was a picture by Arthur Rackham that Jack describes only to say it turned the sky around for him.

THEY SAID . . .

"[The] review of Margaret Armour's recently published translation of *Siegfried and the Twilight of the Gods*...included an Arthur Rackham illustration of Siegfried, sunlit against a background of dim and distant mountains, gazing in wonder and astonishment at the sleeping Brunhilde."

—George Sayer, *Jack*

Jack says he knew nothing at the time of Richard Wagner, the German composer whose opera, *The Ring of the Nibelung*, contains *Siegfried and the Twilight of the Gods* as Part Four. Nevertheless, he says "Pure 'Northernness' engulfed me: a vision of huge, clear spaces hanging above the Atlantic in the endless twilight of Northern summer, remoteness, severity." He immediately recognized this as something, some place he had been before, and the memory of Joy, "almost like heartbreak," flooded back.

Sayer refers to Jack's flashes of Joy as religious experiences, and in that light, though he was not aware of it that way, it was a kind of conversion for Jack: conversion from the vulgar distractions he'd lost himself in for the past year or more, conversion back to culture, and conversion to a quest for Joy that would ultimately lead him back to Christ.

And this moment was followed by many reinforcing coincidences that seemed transcendent and led him on. He discovered Wagner's music and was able to get it for the gramophone his father had given him and Warnie. While spending a couple of weeks of the next summer holidays with the eldest of Lady E.'s daughters, he found the book that had been reviewed in the literary magazine and had turned him back toward Joy. He had to have a copy of his own and, despite Warnie's failure to comprehend Jack's fascination with the whole phenomenon, he suborned his brother to go halves in buying a less expensive edition of his own.

Boxen

Perhaps the least likely thing that happened to both Jack and Warnie in this phase of their lives was the continuation of their interest in and playing at, and writing on, Animal-Land and India, which were now combined into an empire they named Boxen. The stories grew and matured as they cast the kings of their respective kingdoms in images of their own alter egos. Both kings continued to rule jointly under a single parliament that met wherever was convenient. The coregents depended on the tutelage and counsel of Lord Big, a frog who strongly resembled their father Albert.

Jack assures his readers that though it was play, Boxen and its antecedents were not fantasies. They were its creators, so they could not be in it, which would have been a condition of their being fantasies.

Bloods, Fags, and Tarts

After the summer term of 1913, Jack passed the entrance examinations into Malvern College. Starting Malvern College, Jack says, was the most exciting thing to happen in his "outer life," the term he uses to describe all the events during his residency in the town of Malvern as opposed to those in his and Warnie's "inner lives," his pursuit and experience of Joy and Boxen and their family life back home. While at Cherbourg the boys had often attended sports events and marveled at the maturity and sophistication of the older (high-school-age) young men of the Coll.

No boy ever went there more ready to worship these "mortal gods," he writes at the beginning of Chapter 6 of his early years autobiography. That chapter, entitled "Bloodery," is all about the Bloods (boys who have seniority and excel at sports) and the fags (subservient, lower-rung "slave-class" boys).

Would-be Bloods wore the right clothes, used the right slang, and laughed at the right jokes, all things that suggest overlaps with voluntary gangs of boys probably anywhere in any time period, at least in the English-speaking world. New boys at school aspiring to eventually become Bloods are inclined to worship the highest ranks at school. Jack says that he was the only new student among the twelve new-term enrollees who knew much about the inner workings of the system, having been briefed by brother Warnie.

The third class of students in Malvern, and, as Jack confirmed, in such schools throughout England, were Tarts, whom he describes as effeminate-looking boys who were used as catamites (homosexual slaves) to one or more senior boys, usually Bloods. The Tarts were never forced into their service (they considered it an honor), were usually treated more like mistresses (valued love interests) than as prostitutes, and were rewarded at least in the form of favor in the sight of the Blood or Bloods they were attached to. Jack says that at Malvern fags constituted a general labor pool for the use of the Bloods, but at some schools a Blood pairs with a specific fag, which system he thought offered certain advantages, like offering the protection of a powerful senior student.

Malvern College

Jack's general feeling at Malvern after he got beyond orientation was that he was always tired. Fagging allowed almost no time to do the academic work expected, and being forced to go out for sports teams was a source of tremendous conflict. He hated sports, but for the sake of his hopes for advancing in the system and impressing the Bloods, he had to pretend enthusiasm.

Malvern, he reports in *Surprised by Joy*, turned him into a prig, "a highbrow," which is directly opposed to the whole purpose of fagging, which was to keep the new students from assuming superiority. After discovering Richard Wagner, Jack chose literary writing and classical music, and after taking as much abuse as he could stand from loutish Bloods, he rebelled by turning to snobbery.

In describing the relations between Bloods and Tarts, he emphasizes that he "is sure such practices no longer take place at Wyvern," a clear indication for why he disguises Malvern and the other schools and the personnel involved, except for himself and Warnie. Surprisingly to those who think of Lewis as a moralist, he refuses to condemn the pederasty at Malvern, saying that other practices there were no doubt worse, like condoning cruelty and duplicity. And he adds that he has little to say of homosexuality because it is one sin that he has never been tempted, in the least, to fall into.

Jack listed two blessings he received from Malvern. First was an unforgettable teacher, his form master, whom he calls Smewgy. He gave Jack an appreciation of the classics that would influence his work for the rest of his life and added Greek and Celtic mythologies to his already beloved Norse or Northern, Wagnerian, mythology. The second blessing was the school library, which proved to be an oasis offering many delights.

Great Bookham and the Great Knock

Chapter Eight of *Surprised by Joy* consists mostly of Jack's debates with his father to persuade him to let him leave Malvern. Finally, Albert calls again on his own tutor from his public school days at Lurgan College, William T. Kirkpatrick, whom he had earlier consulted regarding both Warnie's and Jack's prep and public schools. More recently, Kirkpatrick, known by the Lewises as the Great Knock, had undertaken to repair the damage to Warnie's education sustained at Malvern and was so successful that Warnie not only passed the exams for Sandhurst, the Royal Military College, but placed in the top of the list of candidates. So after months of pleading by Jack, Albert agreed to send him to the village of Great Bookham in Surrey, southeast England, to read for the university entrance examinations with Kirkpatrick.

"The greatest service we can do to education today is to teach fewer subjects. No one has time to do more than a very few things well before he is twenty, and when we force a boy to be a mediocrity in a dozen subjects we destroy his standards, perhaps for life."

The Great Knock began logically challenging everything Jack said, from a minute after they shook hands at the train station, and Jack conversationally threw out the comment that he had expected Surrey to be "wilder." Kirkpatrick wanted to know what information he had based that opinion on, and without observing any conversational niceties, after twenty questions he had destroyed Jack's ego by concluding that without any information on which to base such a comment he had no grounds for commenting at all. Though it was disconcerting the first time, because he had never encountered anyone who preferred conversation based on logic, once he got used to it Jack greatly appreciated Knock's approach.

QUESTION

What does Sayer see in Jack's teenage writings that Jack himself missed?

Though he could not have put a name to it, he was aware of holiness...Jack found [George MacDonald's] book *Phantastes* at the bookshop in Great Bookham Station...and wrote...to [his friend] Arthur, describing it as "a great literary experience." ...Not until years later did he call it "Holiness."

—George Sayer, *Jack*

For the next two and a half years, as the storm clouds of the First World War gathered and broke into continent-wide war, Jack studied with Kirkpatrick at Great Bookham, taking his entrance scholarship exams for Oxford on December 4, 1916, days after his eighteenth birthday. In his application he listed Malvern as his public school, omitting his cramming years at Knock's. He asked Warnie, who was already serving at the war's western front, to keep this a secret as he feared that if Knock found out he might have called it a lie and informed Oxford.

Chapter 4

First Friend, War, and Oxford

Jack had visited his next-door neighbor in Belfast, Arthur Greeves, while on holidays before going to Great Bookham, because Arthur had sent a note saying he was sick in bed and would like a visit. Jack says he didn't know why he accepted, as Arthur, who was actually Warnie's age, had tried to break into the Jack/Warnie alliance earlier and had been rebuffed. But when he got to Arthur's room Jack saw a copy of H. A. Grueber's *Myths of the Norsemen*, one of Jack's favorite books, on a bed table and, discovering that Arthur liked that book and many smaller coincidences in their tastes, a new, immediate, and permanent bond was formed. Jack and Arthur would continue influencing and providing support for each other over nearly fifty years.

Telltale Correspondence

Shortly after that meeting, Jack left for his years with Kirkpatrick at Great Bookham, and he started a correspondence with Arthur. This correspondence sheds light on some parts of Jack's private life that would be unknown if those letters and others had not been collected in *The Lewis Papers*, compiled by Warnie after Jack had gained some international fame. Even so, not all of the correspondence is in the collection. Jack reportedly censored some passages in the letters, saying they might reflect negatively on Arthur, and other letters appear to have been destroyed by Jack or Arthur.

Arthur's family was even more religious than Jack's—Puritanical or fundamentalistic to such an extreme that all of the children rejected their religion as adults. The Greeves were members of a British sect, the Plymouth Brethren, which emphasizes *dispensationalism*, a doctrine that believes God works at different ways in different dispensations or provisions of his grace, both in history and toward various chosen peoples. There are varied applications of this teaching, with some of the more extreme Brethren holding that Jesus's teachings were all for the Jewish people only, not the church.

The pattern of friendship that Jack established with Arthur would be repeated in other bonds he forged with peers like J. R. R. Tolkien, Charles Williams, Owen Barfield, Hugo Dyson, and others once he got to Oxford. He wrote from experience about friendship as one of the most vital and satisfying aspects of life.

Lurid Details

In their letters, Jack and Arthur shared details about their sexual fantasies and likings, including discussion of masturbation which Jack calls "IT" and "THAT" in some of the letters. When Arthur, who had a heart condition that caused his mother to coddle him, said that he had never masturbated, Jack began addressing him as "Sir Galahad," a reference to what he called his "purity." Jack even intimated that he was excited by sado-masochistic stimulations and signed at least one of the letters as "J. Philom.," short for "Jack Philomastix," Greek for "lover of the whip." He alluded to fantasizing about flagellating (whipping) beautiful women, which may have some bearing on his remaining single until late in life. Some "psychologizing" biographers have speculated that Jack's sado-masochism stemmed from the harsh treatment he witnessed in terror at Wynyard under the abusive Rev. Robert Capron.

Whisked Away

Though his correspondence with Warnie was now less frequent than letters between him and Arthur, the letters that the brothers exchanged were longer. And at the time Warnie, "with all the glory of a young officer," would suddenly appear on leave for reunions and whisk him from Surrey to Belfast, by first class rail and ferry, a level of luxury Jack had never experienced in his commuting six times a year to Ireland and back since age nine.

FACT

It's ironic that Disney is filming *The Chronicles of Narnia*, because Jack negatively cites Walt Disney in *Surprised by Joy* as an artist who betrays beauty. He disliked Dickens's novels, for example, because the illustrations in them that he pored over before he was able to read represented, like Disney's art, "simpering dolls intended for our sympathy which really betray the secret."

Jack says Arthur probably influenced him more for the better than the other way around. He tried without much success to increase Arthur's sparse appreciation for poetry, but Arthur more than anyone else instilled in Jack an appreciation for the "good, solid, old books" from authors such as Thackeray, Dickens, the Brontes, Jane Austen, and Hans Christian Andersen. And Arthur added to Jack's native romanticism an appreciation of the beauty and transcendence in the domestic commonplaces of their surroundings that he called "homeliness."

Into Officers' Training via Oxford

Jack writes that even after he realized that the war would probably continue until he was of military age, he refused to think much about it, discuss it, or read about it in newspapers (which he avoided all his life). In his officer's role, Warnie was in what was considered a relatively safe place even while he was on the western front, so there was not constant fear for his safety. When he was on leave, Warnie tried to recapture the former interests and preoccupations that characterized their relationship rather than telling war stories. In the service, his closest friend was a fellow officer whose interests were like his and Jack's, literary and philosophical, rather than profane banalities.

Jack was of the opinion that it was not even a good idea to encourage youngsters to read newspapers in peacetime, for reasons similar to those cited in his opposition to war reporting: doing so would give them a taste for irrelevant vulgarities and multiple "facts" that would be contradicted in the next report and would retain little long-term importance. Nevertheless, *The Lewis Papers* includes the news in a letter from Jack to Albert in 1921 that he had read of William T. Kirkpatrick's death in the *Times* of London.

Though Jack had been accepted for a scholarship at University College in December 1916, based on a brilliant performance in the examinations for study of classics, this did not guarantee the right to matriculate to Oxford University. For that he had to pass a more general set of exams, called Responsions, which included mathematics, a field Jack never mastered. To prepare, he went back to Kirkpatrick in January 1917 for several weeks of additional cramming. The Great Knock also failed where others had to impart mathematical mastery to Jack, an irony considering that math had been his mother's best subject in college.

"To read without military knowledge or good maps accounts of fighting which were distorted…and further distorted…and then 'written up' out of all recognition by journalists, to strive to master what will be contradicted the next day, to fear and hope intensely on shaky evidence, is surely an ill use of the mind."

Jack failed Responsions in March, after which he spent a month at Little Lea, where in April he was invited to move into his rooms at Oxford in preparation for the summer term. Though he failed the Responsions again in June, this period was one of the happiest he'd ever experienced. His rooms were like a dream come true—even including a grand piano—and Oxford, where he began making new friendships immediately, seemed like paradise. He was soon enrolled in the Officers Training Corps (OTC) at Oxford, and by his nineteenth birthday he was with the infantry on the front in France.

Mrs. Moore

Jack gives short shrift to his service in World War I in *Surprised by Joy*, saying at several points that those events have little to do with his purpose in writing the autobiographical account of his early life (to retrace his spiritual journey).

Autobiographical Omissions

He dismisses as not worth mentioning, other than as a joke, that sixty enemy combatants surrendered to him, a "crowd of field-gray figures who suddenly appeared from nowhere, all [with] their hands up." He includes only passing references to his wounding (by "an English shell" that embedded shrapnel into his body at three points), but through correspondence between Jack and Arthur, Albert, and Warnie, George Sayer reassembles the larger story. Of five comrades who were together when Jack came to the infantry, he was the only one to survive the war.

New friendships Jack had formed at Oxford OTC included his roommate, Paddy Moore, a fellow Irish native who shared many of Jack's interests. Paddy's mother, Mrs. Janie King Askins Moore, invited Jack and several other officers in training to spend time at the furnished rooms she had rented in Oxford to be close to her son before his leaving for combat.

Jack immediately took a liking to Mrs. Moore, whose Irish hospitality seemed to match his homesickness for Ireland. When the OTC training was over, he chose to spend the first half of a month's leave before shipping out to France with Paddy, Mrs. Moore, and her eleven-year-old daughter, Maureen, at her home at Bristol (one of southern England's largest cities) rather than spending it all with his father in Belfast. Biographers see this as a strong indication that Mrs. Moore, then forty-five, was becoming a surrogate mother to eighteen-year-old Jack. Others wonder if she and Jack may have been lovers for a time, a speculation for which the major support comes from two references by Jack in letters to Arthur Greeves in 1918 that he was now in love. Mrs. Moore is the only woman being mentioned in his correspondence at the time.

FACT

As a concession to Ireland's quest for more independence from England at that time, Parliament had exempted it from supporting the war against Germany. Warnie, Jack, Paddy, and others from Ireland were not required to serve, but presumably because they desired to study at England's major university and later make careers in England, they felt a duty to do so.

Wounded in Action

Jack was sent to the front lines in November 1917, just before his nineteenth birthday, undertrained and only twelve days after arriving in France. The same happened to Paddy Moore, who Sayer says was much more physically fit for the role of soldier than Jack. Paddy went missing in action and his death was not confirmed for a month afterward.

Jack's first hospitalization in the war resulted from trench fever, three months after getting to the front. After twenty-seven days in the hospital, he was released for what he called "a four days tour of the front." He received the wounds previously described on March 4, from a shell that killed "one or two" of his best friends, including one he had known since Malvern. Warnie, hearing of Jack's wounds, bicycled 50 miles one way to visit him in the Etaples hospital, apparently fearing he might die.

Jack said in a letter to his father from the hospital in France that he had been wounded in his left arm, but in fact shrapnel had also entered his underarm and his chest besides his wrist. The shell fragment in his chest could not safely be removed so it stayed with him the rest of his life, without being troublesome, but the hand and wrist wound gave him life-long discomfort.

Back in Bristol

Jack might have had another stint of residency in Belfast if his request to be sent to a convalescent home there after he was fit to leave the hospital had been granted, but the military said that wasn't possible. His second choice was Bristol, so he could visit and be visited in the convalescent home by Mrs. Moore and another acquaintance, "Perrott of the Somersets," a member of the same unit in which Jack served and a schoolmate from Malvern. In a letter to Albert, replying to an expression of thanks from Albert for the hospitality she'd shown his son, Mrs. Moore reveals that Jack had promised Paddy he would look after her if Paddy didn't return from the war, a promise he kept until Mrs. Moore's death in 1951.

Oxford Scholar at Last

Jack says he arrived back at a "demobbed" Oxford two months after the war's end, probably a reference to university establishment fears that Oxford would be flooded by radicalized veterans after the war. The Responsions (which Jack had never passed) were waived for veterans; it appears the university and a grateful nation were doing what they could to repay the men who had offered their lives to save England from German rule under Kaiser Wilhelm II. Waiving the requirement with its mathematics component may have been the only way Jack could ever have become an Oxford scholar.

The Bolshevik revolution in Russia that followed almost immediately after the world war ended could have been described as being born in England (Karl Marx having lived in London for years before his death in 1883) and, along with the growing violence in the struggle for independence in

Ireland, may have influenced English fears. Even Warnie's correspondence indicated that he feared Jack had been more radicalized by the war than he ever was, and the fact was that the veterans who came to Oxford were generally conservative. They were looking forward to returning to the Oxford they had known before going to war.

The Oxford that Jack had barely started studying at the summer before his OTC training had been a ghost of the real thing, most of the students having already been called away by the war and the campus's main occupants then being military units undergoing training. One downside after the war that Jack noted in correspondence, however, was that breakfast was no longer served to the students in their rooms; they had to go to the dining hall.

FACT

"Kaiser Bill," Wilhelm II, the emperor of Germany and king of Prussia, was widely considered the instigator of the First World War and was epitomized as the stereotypical German by Allied forces and their anti-Axis propaganda. Historians have since debated whether his role was in fact central. Like his contemporary the Czarina Alexandra of Russia, his maternal grandmother was the United Kingdom's late Queen Victoria.

Published Poet

In March of that first year as a full-fledged Oxford scholar, Jack's first published book was released by William Heinemann. *Spirits in Bondage: A Cycle of Lyrics* was a collection of poems in three parts: "The Prison House," "Hesitation," and "The Escape." The publisher listed Jack, who published under the pseudonym Clive Hamilton, as one of the house's "soldier poets." Jack had written the poems from 1915 on, many of them when he was at Malvern College and Great Bookham, beginning when he was sixteen. One poem in the collection, "Death in Battle," was published in the literary magazine *Reveille* alongside works by some of England's most highly regarded poets.

Jack wrote to Arthur Greeves that the collection reflected his religious worldview at the time, that "matter (=nature = Satan, remember) [must not] get too great a hold on me, and dull the one spark I have." One of the poems has Satan claiming to be the creator of the material world, indicating that the author is not an atheist, Sayer observes in *Jack*, "but…a Manichee, a dualist" torn between good and evil gods. Jack's philosophical leanings at the time, including a rejection of his mentor Kirkpatrick's rationalistic atheism (which left little room for imagination or romanticism) come through in several of the poems. One of these, "Our Daily Bread," affirms the frequent appearance in life of spiritual "nourishment."

Good reviews of *Spirits in Bondage* in top publications failed to effect significant sales, so eventually most of the copies were destroyed, making copies of the edition rare items.

Warnie offered his opinion in a letter to his father that Jack had erred in publishing the book at age twenty under the banner of an atheist. Though he agreed with Albert that some poems in the book were excellent, he argued that "a profession of a Christian belief is as necessary a part of a man's mental make-up as a belief in the King, the Regular Army, and the Public Schools" (*Jack*). Jack wrote back to his father's inquiries on this that he was continuing daily Christian practices at the university but failed to mention that these were part of the university's requirements for all students.

Years in Poverty

After his first full term as an Oxford student, on the holidays Jack helped Mrs. Moore move from Eastbourne, Sussex, on the south coast of England, to Bristol, considerably farther west, not far from the southern border of Wales. Jack's delayed return to Belfast gave rise to speculative and critical letters between Warnie and Albert about the mystery of young Jack's seeming infatuation with or manipulation by a woman old enough to be his mother. Jack's time with Mrs. Moore was making his visits to Belfast less frequent and, when they occurred, shorter.

Albert had learned that Mrs. Moore was separated from her husband, who still lived in Ireland. She was in poor circumstances and had been known to receive occasional £10 notes from Jack. As Jack was still depending on a regular allowance from his father for his living expenses as an Oxford student, this concern by Albert worried Jack. He tried his best to keep his dealings with Mrs. Moore secret from Albert, but Albert was adept at spying on both of his sons, directly asking them probing questions, looking at their mail, and even going across the road to Arthur Greeves to find out what he could from him.

Dishonoring Father

After helping Mrs. Moore move in 1919, Jack finally went to Little Lea, where Albert confronted him about his bank balance. Jack lied, saying he had about £15, whereas Albert had already found out that Jack's account was overdrawn. They quarreled and Albert later complained to Warnie that he didn't know where he had failed Jack or why he would lie to him and insult him.

But the correspondence between Jack and Warnie over the war and postwar years indicates that both brothers were generally frustrated and fed up with their father's interference, meddling, and always having to know the details about their lives now that they were adults.

FACT

George Sayer says that of all the people he knew who were acquainted with Mrs. Moore—by all accounts a good-hearted woman—Warnie was the only one who did not like her. He suggests this was because when their mother died, Warnie tried to take her place, and he was hurt by Jack's choosing Mrs. Moore for his substitute mother.

At the end of the summer term, Jack helped Mrs. Moore move again, from Bristol to the village of Headington, just outside Oxford. After this move, he shared Mrs. Moore's and her daughter Maureen's rented residences, which changed at least nine times over the next eleven years.

Mother or Mistress

Though Jack regularly referred to Mrs. Moore as "Mother," even introducing her to George Sayer this way, questions like the ones that mystified Warnie and Albert also have nagged at other Lewis biographers and aficionados. Sayer was persuaded that Mrs. Moore and Jack did not have a sexual relationship. *The Lewis Papers* finds no proof of such an arrangement, and it is known that they had separate bedrooms. Owen Barfield, one of Jack's closest friends at Oxford in the 1920s, thought the likelihood was only fifty-fifty. Perhaps the clincher was that when a woman of Jack's age visited him at Mrs. Moore's house and showed interest in developing a relationship with him, he told her that he was in no circumstance to consider marriage, which Mrs. Moore told him later had been an overreaction to the young woman's expression of interest. Mrs. Moore would never have said this to Jack if she had been his mistress, Sayer concludes, and just as likely, if she had been Jack's mistress he would not have described the exchange to her as he did or have mentioned it at all.

Jack has written that becoming a university don (the title used for heads, tutors, and fellows at colleges of Oxford and Cambridge) was the only profession he could imagine would be suitable for him, but his student and early teaching years were marked by poverty. He looked for employment even as a master at one of the public schools like Malvern, but despite his stellar performance in his chosen academic path, his only money-earning success as a student came from poorly paid tutoring. He could not have afforded a residence off the campus by himself, and he was undoubtedly motivated, at least in part, to share residence with Mrs. Moore for reasons of economy for both of their sakes, as well as keeping his promise to Paddy. A diary that he kept for a while in 1922 indicates that he enjoyed the domestic side of his life then, and it is agreed among those who knew him that he thrived on the role of Oxford student.

New Friends

Jack made new lifelong friends quickly at Oxford, the first two of whom were A. K. Hamilton Jenkin and Owen Barfield. Jenkin, he recalls, continued

Arthur Greeves's progress in educating him, taking him beyond appreciating homeliness to finding beauty even in ugliness, like the natural surroundings on rainy-day walks.

QUESTION
Why did Jack consider Arthur Greeves and Owen Barfield examples of every man's first and second best friends?
Arthur, the first, represented Jack's alter ego; they saw everything alike. Owen, though sharing most of Jack's interests, disagreed with him about everything and was more an antiself than alter ego.

Jack refers to Owen as having read all the right books, but he invariably got the wrong thing about all of them, always nearly right but missing the mark. He describes all of his close Oxford friends as good so far as pagan standards can define that. By this, he says in *Surprised by Joy*, he means they strived for "veracity, public spirit, chastity, and sobriety," hallmarks of secular goodness that Jack mentions several times.

Financial Aid

Despite their frequent disagreements, his father continued to send Jack £30 at the beginning of each term, which was the equivalent of about $1,000. Mrs. Moore apparently received sporadic child support from her estranged husband for Maureen, though it could not be depended on. Her house was always receiving visitors, who must have been a drain on the tight resources. The only other source of income was Jack's scholarship and the winning of several student awards, including the vice-chancellor's essay prize in 1921.

Jack failed to win a fellowship that he applied for at Magdalen College, Oxford, for 1923, which may have been a blessing as it forced him to continue his studies for another degree, in English Language and Literature, which enabled him to continue receiving scholarship funds and was important to his eventual employment as a university don. When he finished that course, he had won three degrees with honors. But now his scholarship support ceased, making the household financial situation even more dire. Only Albert's £85 (about $1,700) remained to depend upon. Warnie was able to contribute only about £5 now and then, as all of his savings from his war years had been spent. Jack and Mrs. Moore had to dismiss the household maid, and Jack earned extra money from grading examinations and tutoring one student. He became depressed and began to show physical symptoms of it like indigestion, sleepless nights, and nightmares.

Chapter 5

A Career in Oxford

In 1924, nearly a year after completing his third degree, Jack was offered a substitute teaching position at Oxford's University College. Jack didn't hesitate to accept University College's offer, though it paid only £200 for the year and was for that year only, filling in for a permanent philosophy tutor, E. F. Carritt, who was spending the year as a guest lecturer at the University of Michigan. But £200 was the equivalent of about $4,000 at the time, more than most salaried people were making, and more importantly, it was a door to teaching at Oxford that might open on to better opportunities in the future.

5

Lecturer at University College

Choosing "The Moral Good—Its Place Among the Values" as the topic of the course, Jack described his preparation for the fourteen hours of lectures in the first term as the best job he'd ever had. He wrote to his father that he didn't know how he would fill fourteen hours, as probably everything he knew could be covered in five. He joked that he would have to learn the "slow deliberate method" he had heard so many times not only from his own Oxford course lecturers but by many curates (preachers) who often seemed to "slowly deliberate" to fill twenty minutes.

As C. S. Lewis is best remembered as a professor of medieval literature and English language, in which he would later publish his scholarly works, it's a little ironic that he was hired because of his degree in philoso-

C. S. Lewis in the late 1930s. Used by permission of The Marion Wade Center, Wheaton College, Wheaton, IL.

phy (Greats, as it was called at Oxford). Knowing that many of the lecturers he had heard as a student used the "slow deliberate method," Jack worked hard to avoid taking the easy way one of his new colleagues recommended, to make the first lecture introductory. That approach was the reason, he told his father, that he had not attended that colleague's lectures.

THEY SAID . . .

"[Jack] had done some shopping for her 'and was immediately sent back into Headington with another message.' When he got home, she turned on him 'rather savagely for having forgotten to take Pat [the dog] out with me.' He found self-control very difficult and did not reply because he feared he might say 'regrettable things.'"

—George Sayer, *Jack*

Once Jack reached his stride in the 1930s and 1940s, his lectures were consistently the best attended at the university. The first term, however, he was not popular. An error in the college's class listings had his students going to a wrong lecture hall, and for much of the term he had only two regular attendees, so he invited them to meet at his college rooms, which were more intimate. But he made a mistake by saying that to keep the lecture time informal the two regulars were welcome to interrupt him at any time. One of them, an older clergyman, interrupted so often that Jack said he soon found it hard to get a word in edgewise.

Domestic Discord

Jack's appointment to fill in for Professor Carritt was not all good news for his domestic life, especially before the funds began coming in. Without a maid, Mrs. Moore had come to depend on Jack's help around the house, which became less available once he had to prepare for lectures. He began to learn that family life is a crucible for learning the virtues, especially through forbearance. In a diary entry after getting the appointment, he wrote of a quarrel with Mrs. Moore in which he found it hard not to get hysterically angry. It must have seemed to him that he was bearing the lion's share of supporting Mrs. Moore, her daughter, and her constant stream of guests, and that she was less than enthusiastic about the fact that he had finally won an important job for which he had to do much preparation.

After his first term on the other side of the lectern began, Jack spent weekends and holidays at Mrs. Moore's house and went there after morning lectures for lunch, returning to the college where he met students in evening tutorials and had dinner in the college dining hall, a formal and ceremonial affair, and stayed the weekday nights in his college rooms, where he was served breakfast. From the beginning Jack read all the philosophy texts he would use but made notes only, not writing his lectures out. He explained to his father, "read lectures send people to sleep and I think I must make the plunge from the very beginning and learn to talk not to recite," (*Jack*), adding that he practiced his lectures in front of imaginary audiences.

Job Search

Jack applied to all openings being listed in English and philosophy at the Oxford colleges through the year he spent at University College. His last application, Sayer says, was a long shot, a fellowship at Magdalen College (one of Oxford University's thirty colleges) where competition for the post included professors with proven track records at Oxford. But as in his winning the replacement opening at University College in 1924, his degree in the Greats proved to be his strong suit. English was a relatively new subject and Magdalen was playing it safe in case English didn't draw many students, so the college hoped to find a man who could handle both English and philosophy. Jack was just the man.

On to Magdalen College

At £500 a year, with a pension plan and rooms in the college, the pay for the fellowship of, initially, five years was considerably better than his substitute salary at University College. Jack celebrated by taking a two-week holiday with Mrs. Moore and Maureen in Somerset, in England's southwest peninsula, most likely traveling by train and charabanc (an open-top touring bus) to Minehead and Porlock. Though Sayer says Jack took some driving lessons, he never became a driver.

Despite their sometimes estrangement (which George Sayer probably makes too much of, perhaps from misconstruing the Irish temperament), on receiving Jack's telegraphed good news, "Elected fellow Magdalen. Jack," Albert recorded in his diary, "I went to his room and burst into tears of joy. I knelt down and thanked God with a full heart. My prayers have been heard and answered." Little did he know.

Breakfast Friends

Unlike some other colleges, like University (where Jack had been served breakfast in his rooms), the Magdalen fellows served themselves breakfast in the college dining room. An early arriver, Jack usually sat with Paul Victor Mendelssohn Benecke, J. A. Smith, and Adam Fox, all of whom Sayer recalls "liked to talk," as Jack did. (Later on, the fellows would vote for silence in the dining room during breakfast.)

Benecke, a senior fellow at Magdalen thirty years older than Jack and a grandson of Felix Mendelssohn, the composer, has been described as possessing unusual insight into holiness and living an ascetic lifestyle (practicing denial, including fasting, of many comforts of life to heighten spiritual sensitivity). As illustrative of Jack's orientation to holiness in this atheistic period of his life, he took up Benecke's cause when other fellows derided him for his near-monastic way of life.

THEY SAID . . .

"Benecke's holiness was revealed especially in his understanding of animals. He once told Jack that he understood why Indians perceived the deity in the elephant, and that the sadness in a dog's eyes arose from its pity for men...He drank nothing alcoholic...never missed a chapel service, and fasted on Fridays."

—George Sayer, *Jack*

Other breakfast companions and conversationalists were J. A. Smith, Wayneflete Professor of Moral and Metaphysical Philosophy and a philologist (a student of the root meanings of words), which study Jack found fascinating and which became more important to him as he matured, and Adam Fox, the dean of the divinity school and an influence on Jack's thinking toward Christianity and, after his conversion, an advisor.

Political Faux Pas

When E. K. Chambers, an elderly and dry lecturer, was nominated as a professor of poetry, Jack led a successful campaign to have Fox, who was not an academic, given the post instead. Though Fox may have been a better lecturer than Chambers, he was not stellar, and some fellows felt his lack of academic credentials should have disqualified him. Jack's campaign for him created some animosity among other faculty members, and it was a tactical error that he later regretted.

Jack the Tutor

"Many former Lewis pupils have commented on the bullying and impersonal style Lewis used in his tutorials, while many others have recalled the tutorial sessions with fondness," writes David Graham in *We Remember C. S. Lewis*, a collection of reflections by former acquaintances of Lewis that previously appeared in *The Canadian C. S. Lewis Journal*. Some former pupils of the new fellow in English at Magdalen College have said he could be aloof.

Jack apparently tried to adapt to his own personality some of the teaching techniques of William T. Kirkpatrick that worked so well on him and his father before him. But, understandably, many of his pupils, having done well in environments like Malvern College (where Jack floundered), were not prepared for the challenging they got when they used words they were not able to define, much less defend. "Just exactly what do you mean by the word *sentimental*, Mr. Sayer," George Sayer remembers Jack tossing back to him during tutorial. Jack worked diligently to be prepared for his tutorials, but some of his undergraduates did not, as his letters and diary comments attest.

Dom Bede Griffiths, one of the earliest of Jack's tutorial pupils, who went on to become a Catholic (Benedictine) monk in India and to publish books about intellectual and emotional wholeness (*The Golden String, Return to the Centre*), wrote in *The Canadian C. S. Lewis Journal*, "I never found him in the least degree 'aloof' in his attitude."

THEY SAID . . .

"[O]ur tutorials would sometimes go on for hours after we finished the real business...This was the beginning of a lasting friendship and we continued in the same spirit for the rest of his life...He may have been different with other people, but that may have been their fault."

—Dom Bede Griffiths

Another early student was John Betjeman, later a film critic who became England's poet laureate in 1972. He turned in an essay as part of his tutorial with Jack that, Jack wrote, was "a pure fake" because Betjeman was not able to discuss it in the one-to-one tutoring session. Jack wrote that he wanted to "get rid of the prig," a wish that came true when Betjeman later failed a divinity exam that ended his Magdalen College career.

Griffiths was the first of eight Oxford acquaintances of Lewis who wrote about his tutoring in *We Remember C. S. Lewis*. Martin Moynihan, who was taught by Lewis in 1938 and later authored *The Latin Letters of C. S. Lewis*, remembered him as contrasting with the image in the film *Shadowlands*, which depicts a don towering over a small group of tutorial pupils, seated on low stools as it were at his feet. Instead, both student (just one at a time in Moynihan's experience) and don sat in similar overstuffed chairs and, though students were taken to task about the material under discussion, each was treated like an equal and a friend.

In an introduction to the contribution in the recollections of Jack's tutorial style by Martin Lings, the book's editor says, "Lewis mentioned Lings and another undergraduate Adrian Hugh Paterson...in a letter to his friend Arthur Greeves, 'I wish you knew my two pupils, Lings and Paterson. Both are poets (quite promising I think) and fast friends of each other. They are just in the state you and I remember so well—the whole world of beauty opening upon them—and as well they share the same digs they must have a glorious time. One or other of them often accompanies me on my afternoon walk.

"'You can imagine how I enjoy them both. Indeed this is the best part of my job. In every given year the pupils I really like are in a minority; but there is hardly a year in which I do not make some real friend. I am glad to find that people become more and more one of the sources of pleasure as I grow older.'"

Joan O'Hare, who writes in the same collection, was one of the first two women pupils Jack tutored. She and another woman from St. Hilda's College went to tutorials together. "This was a great honor," she writes, and if this was the first time Jack tutored more than one pupil at a time, it may have had more to do with 1941 conceptions of decorum or proper appearances than efficiency. Another of Oxford's early coeds recalls that women always went to tutorials in pairs in those times. O'Hare characterizes Jack as "a great human being, and if I brought little of academic interest from him, I gained personally from his kindness and tolerance."

John Lawlor was one pupil who had a negative impression of Jack, speaking of "Lewis's determined impersonality towards all except his very closest friends" and thinking he must have hated teaching and would rather be working on his novels than tutoring. Even George Sayer says that Jack could seem impersonal, and it was not until he ventured to recommend a book he thought Jack would enjoy that Jack's "attitude toward me completely changed." The book was George MacDonald's *Lilith*, and when he heard the title, "he remarked at once, 'Holy Writ apart, I know of no book that is in a spiritual sense more deeply moving.'" The moment was the beginning of a lifelong friendship between Jack and Sayer, Jack even making many visits to Sayer and his wife at Malvern College when the latter was the Master in English there.

Lecturer and King

Another of the World War II–era women pupils, Rachel Trickett, writes, "When I was an undergraduate in Oxford between 1942 and 1945, Lewis was the uncrowned king not only of the English faculty but of the whole university" (from "Uncrowned King of Oxford," *We Remember C. S. Lewis*).

FACT
College campuses often have struggles between students in the sciences, math, and engineering, called "techies," and majors in liberal arts, theater, and journalism—"fuzzies." Oxford had a similar division between "hearties," players of rough English sports, and "aesthetes," whose tastes were artistic and sensitive. Though their interests were more aesthete, Jack and Warnie dressed as untidy hearties, Sayer says.

Meetings of the Socratic Society, which Jack had founded and presided over, drew large crowds of members of the university community as well as frequent celebrity debaters, which his participation assured. In that forum, Trickett says, Jack was "in his element," his debating style "Chestertonian," by which she means a disarming "gaiety and nimble command of paradox."

Jack feared that many Magdalen students were little different than a new level of Malvern and other public school Bloods, and in fact most of them were products of Malvern-type schools. He applied a line from Henry James that he thought captured the essential character of many of his most conceited pupils, as possessing "the cynicism of forty and the mental crudeness and confusion of fourteen."

The Private Man

Though Trickett saw Jack's tutorials as "combat" to be survived, she saw his private life as demonstrating humanity, loyalty, and "stealthy generosity." Jack pursued "doctrines of perfection," or what some Christians call sanctification, by contributing all of the royalties of his theological works to orphans, widows, or "any deserving case." But to be popular in the university was to be perceived as unscholarly, which became a cross Jack had to bear, as will be seen in Chapter 9.

The final essay on Lewis as professor in *We Remember C. S. Lewis* is by Roger Poole, who knew and sat under Jack at Cambridge after Jack had left Oxford to accept the chair in English that Cambridge offered and Oxford had denied him. His assessment of Jack as lecturer is concise and comprehensive. "What exactly was the magic element in Lewis's lecturing technique?" Poole asks. "It was the ability to ask questions no one had thought of, and to start towards an answer of them by reference to sources no one had read." This may have been an elitist approach to the subject matter, but for Jack there were two elements in every audience: "Those who were fascinated by the subject itself, and those who weren't. And to the latter, he had nothing to say."

Dymer

A year after Jack became a fellow at Magdalen College, on September 20, 1926, his book-length narrative poem, *Dymer*, was published by J. M. Dent and Sons under the pseudonym Clive Hamilton. Described as the book that Jack worked hardest to produce, and like *Spirits in Bondage*, well reviewed, it failed in the marketplace. A new trend in poetry, free verse, was on the ascendancy, with T. S. Eliot and Ezra Pound among its most popular authors, and Jack's classical rhymed and metered structure seems to have gone out of style. Sayer says that producing the book cured Jack of an excessive fantasy life, its themes being metaphors for such a struggle on the part of its hero, Dymer.

Synopsis

Dymer follows the protragonist of its title from his birth in a totalitarian Orwellian state, mockingly called "The Perfect City," to circumstances that culminate in his death at the hands of a monster he begot.

QUESTION

What obsession did Jack cure by writing *Dymer*?
George Sayer says Jack referred to fears that his fantasy life would so take over his personality that his true self would never emerge. He called such fantasies "Christina Dreams," named for Christina Pontifex from Samuel Butler's *The Way of All Flesh*. In a later letter, Jack compared Christina Dreams with masturbation.

After living his first nineteen years under the control of the state, Dymer, under the influence of spring and the sight of a songbird, rises in his lecture hall and murders the aged lecturer before his class, leaving the stunned civilians behind as he wanders outside of The City. Dymer then regresses to a more base state, casting off his clothing along with all strictures of civilization, and wanders in the forests until he comes upon an empty mansion where there was food prepared. After eating, he sees himself naked in a large mirror surrounded with many choices of clothing, and dressing himself again with finer apparel, verbally accepts any sin these stolen items may represent. Dymer encounters and has sex with a she-monster in the darkness of the mansion. On awakening, Dymer steps outside the palace, finds the creature he begot, then flees through the palace in terror.

In denial of the creature he encountered, Dymer calls out for his idealized lover. Hearing no returning cry, he searches the palace grounds for her. Instead, he encounters a tall, regal woman guarding a door that leads he knows not where, except that it is the only place in the palace he has not searched.

After pleading with her to "yield but one inch; once only from your law," Dymer approaches the woman intending to fight his way past her. What happens at this point is uncertain, but Dymer emerges wounded from the palace and limps into the woodlands.

It rains in the woods that night, and Dymer encounters yet another person he cannot see in the dark, this time a wounded man, a magician, also from The Perfect City. He tells Dymer that since his absence from the city a revolutionary named Bran used Dymer's example and name to foment an uprising among the citizens, who went on to sack and raze the city. Dymer is dumbfounded at this information and stays silent in the night until the magician's wounds prove fatal, then sets out again for the wilderness.

Looking back on his life and the "several Dymers" he has been, he realizes that he, a mortal, has begotten a monster by mating with an immortal. Realizing his duty, he seeks out the monster, knowing that whatever the outcome of their encounter it will redeem him.

Reviews

Hugh d'A Fausset, who reviewed *Dymer* for the *Times Literary Supplement*, wrote to Jack directly, "I have not read any poem recently which has so impressed me by its inevitability of expression and by the profundity of its metaphysics…[by which] your poem stands head and shoulders above most modern verse. But it is a metaphysic which is wholly…translated into terms of image and symbolism, and this seems to me the final test of greatness in poetry."

Another reviewer was "wholly delighted by the lyrical quality of many of the lines" (*The Poetry Review*), and *The Spectator* review called *Dymer* "a little epic burnt out of vital experience and given us through a poet's eye."

George Sayer writes that the final appraisal of *Dymer* has probably not yet been seen. It may, like some other works of literature, become more widely recognized for its genius after generations than it was at the time of its release. Its production enabled Jack to get over older fantasy obsessions and also drew him closer to a theistic worldview.

Chapter 6

Journey to Faith

According to George Sayer, Jack believed that study of the Greats (the ancient philosophers) should lead to belief. But in *Surprised by Joy*, Jack says that when he referred to philosophy as a "course," it was his friends Owen Barfield and Bede Griffiths who reminded him that Plato's definition of philosophy was as a way of life, comparable to religion, a seeming contradiction between Jack's and Sayer's accounts. Yet Jack's short autobiography does give much support for the idea that in his case, philosophical knowledge and thinking through to the truth were expected to lead to Truth—he even calls it a "theory of life."

A Slow Ascent from Atheism

Jack describes a change of perspective that took place during his first two years at Oxford after the war (1920–21) as his "New Look." The confluence of the entrance into his life of an Irish clergyman who had lost his faith but jabbered unceasingly about his quest for immortality; a two-week struggle with Mrs. Moore's brother, a physician, Dr. John Askins, who went mad while they looked on unable to help; the new Freudianism that everyone was talking about; as well as new conceptions of his maturity brought on and formed his new perspective.

The New Look cleansed him of all "fancies" and directed him to build safe boundaries around imagination, which Freudians (amateur or otherwise) were saying could get out of control and lead to breakdowns like the one that had affected Dr. Askins. (Jack later came to believe the breakdown had physical, not intellectual, causes, but the idea that wrong thinking led to madness was dominant at the time.) Even Joy, which he had once lived for, was relegated to the category of aesthetic experience and was seldom glimpsed in Jack's New Look.

Anthroposophy

But his New Look was soon challenged at its root by the conversion of two of his new close friends, A. C. Harwood and Owen Barfield, to anthroposophy, "a spiritual philosophy based on the teachings of Rudolf Steiner, which states that anyone who 'conscientiously cultivates sense-free thinking' can attain experience of and insights into the spiritual world."

Jack was never tempted to try anthroposophy for himself and allowed in later years that it had probably wrought good effects in the lives of his friends who embraced it. But at the time he found their "taking this plunge into the occult" (which he later called an overstated oversimplification)—just when he was in retreat from all superstitions and dependence on anything metaphysical—a great shock. Barfield, whom he walked and talked with frequently, became the object of a verbal "Great War" he waged to talk some sense into him. "And this Great War was a turning point in my life," Jack concludes in *Surprised by Joy*.

Newfound Idealism

Though not making him an anthroposophist, Barfield had been able to talk Jack out of his "chronological snobbery," which thinks (as younger generations generally assume) that whatever is out of date is inferior to what's "in" in their time.

Part of this realization was becoming aware that he and those peers who considered themselves realists were unconsciously operating on assumptions of theism that had never been examined, even if they considered themselves post-Christian or atheist, as Jack had recently claimed. Jack found that adopting the popular alternative to realism, behaviorism, was impossible for him. And being unwilling to give up the meaning he had found in his experiences forced him to conclude that "our logic was participation in a cosmic Logos."

But Jack was not alone in seeking the comforts of theism without believing in God, he recalls. Belief in the Absolute is another form of belief in God, as the late evangelical apologist Francis Schaeffer often famously preached and wrote. But many writers at the time when Jack was an Oxford undergraduate were defending the same position he found himself in: believing there was no god while professing to have roots in Absolute Truth.

"The emotion that went with all this was certainly religious. But this was a religion that cost nothing. We could talk religiously about the Absolute: but there was no danger of Its doing anything about us. It was 'there'; safely and immovably 'there.' It would never come 'here,' never (to be blunt) make a nuisance of Itself."

Books and Friends Turn Against Him

His course, English Literature and Language, in 1922, had another impact on the unstable foundations of Jack's belief structure. Not only did it happen that the one student, Nevill Coghill, among the dozen or so in the English lectures who appeared to be a man after Jack's heart, was "a Christian and a thoroughgoing supernaturalist," but Jack's deeper look into English literature itself seemed to be confronting him on every turn with supports for Christian faith.

Bees in Their Bonnets

George MacDonald (1824–1905), the Scottish parson who wrote some fifty-seven books ranging from poetry and fairy tales to contemporary novels, had influenced Jack from the time he had discovered *Phantastes* (MacDonald's best-known fairy tale) in the train station at Great Bookham. But Jack, as he mentioned in *Surprised by Joy*, had felt "it was a pity he had that bee in his bonnet about Christianity."

G. K. Chesterton, Jack had already concluded, made more sense to him than all of the other "moderns," but again, this was despite the Christian apologetic bee in Chesterton's bonnet. Chesterton's best-known books are *Orthodoxy* and *The Everlasting Man*, the latter of which profoundly affected Jack. When he read it in 1926, he remarked that it had driven him to admit that "Christianity was very sensible apart from its Christianity."

FACT

G. K. Chesterton, social critic and antagonist-debater-friend of George Bernard Shaw, had several weekly columns at this time. A contemporary of the early days of H. L. Mencken, the American journalist and author he somewhat parallels, Chesterton was an orthodox Christian in a country becoming more secular while Mencken was a freethinker in one becoming more Christian.

Among Jack's other most esteemed authors, Samuel Johnson (*Dictionary of the English Language*), Edmund Spenser (*The Faerie Queene*), and John Milton (*Paradise Lost*) shared the same profession of Christianity, and even the ancients—Plato, Aeschylus, and Virgil—were inclined to support religion. Those famous for their disdain and critiques of religion—like Shaw, H. G. Wells, Edward Gibbon, and Voltaire—struck Jack as "a little thin," or what he would have said as a boy, tinny. Writers Jack was being introduced to in this year of concentrated study, like Langland, Donne, Thomas Browne, and especially George Herbert, also drew their depths from their Christian foundations.

Sayer in several instances (especially in reviewing the published poetry of Jack's atheist period) indirectly suggests that Jack's religious foundation was never absent, only weakened or unacknowledged for what it was through the period of his apostasy. Still, both Jack and Sayer say that his retreat from his Cherbourg conversion had positive consequences in his later writing, making him aware of patterns of thinking and providing insights on how to effectively address them, that he would not likely have had if he had stayed true to that boyhood commitment.

The only writers not preferring religion who Jack considered as "knowing anything" were the Romantics, and even some of those were "tinged by something like religion, even at times with Christianity." In *Surprised by Joy* he offers a "perversion of Roland's great line in the *Chanson*, 'Christians are wrong, but all the rest are bores'" as seeming to capture the Romantics' skirting of religious confession.

Objections to Christianity

Though it had been a love-hate relationship thus far, Jack's objections to Christianity dated from early childhood, when he and Warnie were taken to church regularly but experienced it as a source of dissonance rather than harmony. Their maternal grandfather's preaching was overly emotional and embarrassing, they perceived the hymns as more grating than inspiring, and the most apparent reason for going to church appeared to be to keep up appearances in the community as good Protestants. As Jack was quoted in Chapter 1, "If aesthetic experiences were rare, religious experiences did not occur at all" in his and Warnie's childhood.

From *The Lewis Papers* it seems obvious that Albert and Flora Lewis's Christianity was more than something they put on for appearances' sake, but children tend to latch on to the easiest explanation for anything complicated. It's likely that show was a large component, more obvious than many others, of the multifaceted rationale for keeping the faith, or going through the motions of doing so, in the time of Jack and Warnie's parents.

Cosmic Chess

Throughout his first decade at Oxford, from beginning as a student and continuing in his teaching career, it seemed to Jack, as he put it in *Surprised by Joy*, that he was being outsmarted by a better chess player he calls his "Adversary." God was making moves that didn't alarm him until it was too late.

His discovery of the Australian-born philosopher Samuel Alexander enabled Jack to realize that he had been confusing the enjoyment and the contemplation of Joy, an awareness that made him feel that "parts of my experience were beginning to come together with a click."

And realizing that as a teacher of philosophy he was failing his students because he lacked a firm foundation of his own, he found himself moved from Hegelian idealism toward Berkeleyanism, which dared to identify the Absolute as God, though Jack was not yet ready to see this Berkeleyan God as anything like "the God of popular religion." Then he read Chesterton's *The Everlasting Man*, which produced the effect described previously.

But hardly had that wave washed over him than an even more decisive blow struck Jack's already weakened underpinnings. The "hardest boiled of all the atheists I ever knew," Jack writes in *Surprised by Joy*, made a throw-away remark in a meeting in 1926. Sayer identifies the hard-boiled atheist as T. D. ("Harry") Weldon, Magdalen's lecturer and tutor in Greats, a cynical scoffer that Jack wrote elsewhere "lives at rock bottom."

"All that stuff of Frazer's about the Dying God," Weldon mumbled, referring to writings about myth and religion by Scottish social anthropologist Sir James George Frazer, "rum thing. It almost looks as if it had really happened once."

Jack could not believe his ears, but when he pressed Weldon to say more, Weldon dodged, preferring to change the subject. But if he believed something like "God dying had taken place once," it behooved Jack to look more closely at whatever evidence Weldon and/or Frazer had to support such claims, and so he set out to see it firsthand.

Anger Management

Though the seeming lack of long-term grieving at the loss of their mother has been noted previously, anger—toward God—has not been considered in Jack and Warnie's atheism. On the subconscious level, it seems appropriate to wonder if withholding love toward God for what he seemed to do to them at such a vulnerable age had much to do with Jack and Warnie's years of professed faithlessness (especially if Sayer is right about the religious, but unacknowledged, motivations in the poetry Jack published in his atheist period). Or something having results like those of anger—fearing to hope against hope in the reality of God—may have been at work.

Even their antipathy toward their father after Flora's death may be connected to such unacknowledged anger. If many find it hard to believe in God because they have negative images of their biological fathers, some must find it difficult to believe in their biological fathers if they have felt let down by their spiritual one.

Political Religion

The childhood belief that church attendance was mostly a matter of politics was not mitigated by Jack's later exposures to required church attendance at Malvern College and church parades in the military. All of these church experiences came across as obligations that had little connection with Jack's real life, nor did they seem to be of much importance to anyone else involved. Though his contact with most members of the clergy were positive, like his friendship with Adam Fox, the dean of the Magdalen Divinity School, these didn't strike Jack as having much if anything to do with those men's connection to organized Christianity.

Despite these misgivings, Jack began regularly attending Sunday services at his Headington Quarry parish and weekday chapel services at Magdalen as a way of showing his colors, making the statement to anyone who cared to note it that he had become a believer in God—a theist if still not a Christian.

Albert's Death

Jack says in *Surprised by Joy* that his father's death "does not really come into the story I am telling," but Sayer says that "Albert's death affected Jack profoundly" just at the time he was beginning to confront the inconsistencies in theism without God. Albert had retired from his legal practice in

May 1928, had been lonely and unhappy in retirement, and his health was failing.

Jack spent most of August 1929 in Belfast doing as much as he could for Albert. After an operation in September, Albert's doctors confirmed that he had cancer but surmised that he might live a few years, so Jack returned to Oxford to get ready for the upcoming term only to be called back within two days. He got back to Belfast to the news that Albert had passed away the day before, September 25.

Though Jack immediately wired Warnie, who was stationed in Shanghai, his brother did not get home until more than six months later. The final arrangements for Albert and having to settle the estate were a great burden to Jack, who thought Warnie would be more suited for those tasks. Jack enlisted Mrs. Moore to help him sort through the contents of Little Lea and choose what to move to Oxford and what to leave at the house and deal with on Warnie's return.

THEY SAID . . .

"[Jack] felt bitterly ashamed of the way he had deceived and denigrated his father in the past, and he determined to eradicate these weaknesses in his character. Most importantly, he had a strong feeling that Albert was somehow still alive and helping him."

—George Sayer, *Jack*

The perception that his father was watching over him, Sayer says, gave Jack a new orientation to take seriously the immortality of the soul and to renew interest in Christian teachings about eternal life. This was reinforced when Warnie finally arrived back in England the following April and revealed that he also had been taking a serious new look at Christianity and was frequently attending church services. Warnie stayed in England for the rest of 1930 and up to December 1931, during which time the brothers frequently attended church services together, despite feeling dissatisfaction with the church and continuing to register reservations about Christianity.

Friends Indeed

Plato, Dante, MacDonald, Herbert, Barfield, Tolkien, Dyson—"Everyone and everything had joined the other side," Jack writes of the final days of his religious resistance. "Even my own pupil Griffiths—now Dom Bede Griffiths—though not yet himself a believer, did his share," Jack laments in *Surprised by Joy.* "Really, a young atheist cannot guard his faith too carefully."

Jack had finally fallen to his knees in prayer, "admitted that God was God," even if he had done so as "the most dejected and reluctant convert in all England." But though he was now a churchgoer, Jack still did not believe in the Gospel or the deity of Christ. Still, Weldon and the "rum thing" incident had driven him back to reading the Gospels and concluding that they were not myth. Their style was too artless. These were accounts written by men who believed they were retelling personal experiences and historical realities, not inspirational sagas. And if there had been a "dying God," who could it be? Such questions were haunting him.

An Important Walk

After dinner with Hugo Dyson and J. R. R. Tolkien at the Magdalen dining hall on a September 1931 evening, the three men walked on Addison's Walk and discussed mythology and the nature and purpose of myths. Though a lifelong fan of myths, and after reading Frazer's writings on myth and religion, Jack was not convinced he could *believe* in a myth. But Tolkien took the opposite position.

THEY SAID . . .

"Tolkien's view was radically different. He said that myths originate in God, that they preserve something of God's truth, although often in a distorted form. Furthermore, he said that, in presenting a myth… one may be doing God's work…[And] the Christian story was a myth invented by a God who was real."

—George Sayer, *Jack*

Jack reported that he heard wind rushing through the trees as Tolkien talked but checked his enthusiasm lest he be "carried away." Tolkien left Jack and Hugo to continue their discussion just before three o'clock the next morning. Dyson continued to talk about the experiential benefits of Christianity to believers, being able to get freedom from sin and spiritual peace.

A Step, Not a Leap

Jack took the next step, believing in Christ, two days later while riding in the sidecar of Warnie's motorcycle to the Whipsnade Zoo in Dunstable northwest of London, a recently opened 600-acre wildlife park and one of the largest in Europe. "When we set out I did not believe that Jesus Christ is the Son of God, and when we reached the zoo I did," Jack reports in *Surprised by Joy*. He adds that he didn't spend the ride to the zoo in thought (more likely he was thinking about whether Warnie was going to get them there without bodily injury, as he had mentioned in an earlier reference to a sidecar adventure), yet in the procession to Whipsnade his mind had changed.

The account seems to fit the consummate logician Jack had long been, but perhaps it says more about prevenient grace (divine grace that precedes human decision). Jack repeatedly mentions that one thing he feared was being "interfered with" or that the Absolute would "make a nuisance of Itself," but apparently God did not impose.

The Holy War

Once he committed to faith in Christ, Jack never wavered or held back on showing his colors, though students who knew him only as a professor rather than a friend were not likely to know he was a Christian. He was, his friend and executor of his literary estate, Walter Hooper, said, "the most thoroughly converted man I ever knew." He waited until Christmas Day, 1931, to receive the first communion after his conversion back to profession of Christ. Sayer says it was a coincidence (though it may have been a planned one) that Warnie, now serving back in Shanghai, also took his first communion in some years that Christmas.

The Pilgrim's Regress

Jack had learned from the writing and publishing of his first two books, both of which were poetry in classical styles that found little public acceptance, that writing worked as therapy to sort through and consolidate his thoughts and attitudes. So even from his conversion to theism, he had considered turning out another book. "Writing comes as a result of a very strong impulse, and when it does come, I for one must get it out," he told Shirwood Wirt in an interview for *Decision* magazine in May 1963. Possibly because he felt his thinking was still unsettled, he waited until his full conversion to produce his next book-length writing.

QUESTION

What does Jack reveal about his growth as a writer in the decade after *The Pilgrim's Regress*?

In the introduction to the second edition ten years after the book's first appearance, Jack says that two shortcomings of the book were its obscurity (mainly in using romanticism in a way no longer widely understood) and its sounding angry toward the leading character's adversaries.

Less than a year after his mind-changing motorcycle ride to Whipsnade Zoo, during a two-week visit with Arthur Greeves in Belfast, Jack produced *The Pilgrim's Regress: An Allegorical Apology for Christianity, Reason, and Romanticism*. Jack originally planned to call it *The Pilgrim's Regress, or Pseudo-Bunyan's Periplus: An Allegorical Apology for Christianity, Reason, and Romanticism*. This prose work of ten books comprised of seventy-nine short chapters is modeled after John Bunyan's classic *Pilgrim's Progress*. The protagonist is John, presumably a pseudo John Bunyan. John's *periplus* (from the Greek word meaning "a sailing around") takes place in the narrator's dreams through many roads, paths, and encounters crisscrossing the many shires of his "Mundi," or world, from his birthplace in Puritania to Mother Kirk, an obvious reference to the Church. Jack explains in the preface to the tenth anniversary third edition of the book that Mother Kirk was meant to refer only to general Christianity, not any denomination or ecclesial jurisdiction.

John is the son of tenants who try to follow the instructions of their property Stewards (a metaphor for the clergy), which have been codified in a list of rules that John is told as a boy to hang on the wall of his room. But after finding the rules on the front side of the rule card too hard to keep, he turns it over to find rules that contradict those on the front and are easy to follow. (A metaphor, perhaps, for the "do what we say, not what we do" approach to rules-based religion.)

The Stewards tell John and all residents of his shire that living by the rules pleases the Landlord (metaphor for God) and that breaching them forces the Landlord to throw rule breakers into a black hole "full of snakes and scorpions as large as lobsters" (metaphorical for hell). And though the Landlord is exceedingly kind and good to his tenants, any infraction will result, understandably, in their being tortured to death. After all, it's his land they occupy.

FACT

Jack's first prose book, *The Pilgrim's Regress*, first published in 1933 by J. M. Dent, sold only 600 copies in its first printing. But the Catholic publisher Frank Sheed liked it and because of its treatment of Mother Kirk assumed it to be by a Catholic author, so he asked permission to release it through Sheed and Ward, where it went through several editions.

As John gets older, he starts exploring his world and the untraveled territory of rule-breaking that he feels he's been forced to live in. One day he glimpses an island far out across the bay and wants to get closer, even to go there, but once the weather changes the island is no longer visible (possibly a metaphor for Jack's glimpses of and seeking Joy). Day after day he looks for it again and finds himself going farther and farther from home, into the woods, trying to get closer to the water, but can't see the island again. Traveling toward the eastern mountains, in the woods John finds a "brown girl" sitting naked in the grass, laughing and speaking. "And John rose and caught her," the narrator says, "all in haste, and committed fornication with her in the wood." Breaking this rule becomes habit forming and, before he knows it, John finds the woods full of little brown girls. When his brown girl partner tells him they are all offspring of their liaisons, he decides to change directions.

Going west, John "begins to think for himself and meets Nineteenth Century Rationalism, who can explain away religion by any number of methods—'Evolution' and 'Comparative Religion,' and all the guesswork that masquerades as 'Science,'" the narrator says in the top notes of Chapter 1 of Book 2. Jack soon meets Mr. Enlightenment, who tells him Puritania is a good place to be away from and that there is no Landlord, "There never has been and never will be." Mr. Enlightenment is an image of Enlightenment thinking in general, of course. And it is thus that Jack continues tracking John's progress or regress. All of Jack's own philosophical journeys are represented, along with more general descriptions of others who members of his generation are likely to encounter. In a sense, *The Pilgrim's Regress* is a fictitious account of the same journey that Jack traces years later in *Surprised by Joy*, and it sets up most of the subjects and subtexts of his later fiction including the Space Trilogy and *The Chronicles of Narnia*.

Chapter 7

Life at The Kilns and Oxford

The New York Stock Exchange crash in October 1929 is still remembered by most Americans as the beginning of the Great Depression, a time of poverty and struggles to survive for most Americans that continued through World War II. But neither C. S. Lewis's *Surprised by Joy* nor George Sayer's *Jack* concentrates on the 1930s as a decade of great economic depression for the United Kingdom. In fact, for Jack it was an era of relative affluence compared with the years of poverty as an Oxford student and his first year of substitute teaching for University College at Oxford.

Property Ownership

England was still recovering from the destruction of its economy wrought by World War I. But the death of Jack's father just a month before the Wall Street crash not only diverted Jack's attention from economic news (which he was not likely to have followed closely at any rate), but through the settlement of Albert's estate his own economic circumstances were being improved.

Though Albert's estate was considerably smaller than Jack and Warnie had expected, they decided to pool their shares and join with Mrs. Moore to buy a house where they could all live, along with Maureen. They collected the furnishings and personal effects of Little Lea and sorted them into sections of some to be moved to Oxford, some to be sold at auction, and others to be discarded. Among items sold at auction were the animal figurines Jack and Warnie had played with as the characters resident in their fictional land of Boxen. Albert had accumulated a massive collection of letters and personal papers that Jack suggested Warnie sort and organize as the beginning of *The Lewis Papers*, which Warnie undertook, putting together eleven volumes (presumably in loose-leaf binders).

FACT

Sayer reports that Albert's estate yielded about £3,000 for Little Lea (approximately $90,000), and Albert's holdings might provide only £100 ($3,000) in annual income. The brothers depended on Mrs. Moore putting a share provided by the trustees of the estate of her brother Dr. Askins to enable them to buy an adequate house. The trustees on her behalf and the Lewis brothers put in £1,500 each for the house they chose.

The Kilns

They found and bought The Kilns, a large house with outbuildings and about 8 acres of land, about a half mile from the village of Headington Quarry and 3 miles from the center of the city of Oxford. It was named for a brick kiln that operated on the property some years earlier and still stood there, though in ruins, grown up in weeds and ivy. The acreage included a woods and a pond that was on the site of the former clay pit that had been dug to make the bricks. The house had running water (its only modern convenience) supplied by a spring atop a rise above the pond. The property came with a generator for electricity, but it was in such disrepair that a fulltime handyman was needed to keep it running. Heat was provided by fireplaces. Despite its proximity to the village, The Kilns seemed entirely secluded when it was purchased, but a large lot adjacent to the front of it was developed in row houses not long after the Lewises and Moores bought it in 1930.

Entries in Warnie's diaries indicate that he was delighted by The Kilns, though he was still enlisted for a couple of years of service after the property's purchase, and Jack was also taken by it. They immediately set to work to improve the buildings, outbuildings, and features of the property like the pond. They hired maids, added adjoining work rooms or studies for Jack and Warnie, and hired a combination handyman-chauffeur-gardener, Fred Paxford, who became a fixture of The Kilns for years, even after Jack's death. Jack bought a used car that Paxford (and sometimes Maureen) used to drive him and Warnie into town and to pick Jack up when he was done with work on campus and ready to return to The Kilns for lunch, afternoon swims in the pond, or working on projects. He enjoyed planting trees, draining a swamp below the pond, making the pond more useful, and taking walks in the woods. Sayer says the household also added a couple of dogs and cats.

Jack becomes nearly rhapsodic in describing life at The Kilns in letters to Arthur Greeves, describing birds "thrilling and chuckling in abundance," trees in the woods turning golden yellow in fall, and moorhens with their chicks "half-swimming and half flying 'with a delicious flurry of silver drops'" when he would disturb their hiding places.

Jack was the main source of funding for the property as he was the main breadwinner among its occupants. Sayer says Jack paid Fred Paxford's salary, though the gardener considered Mrs. Moore his employer (she being much more consistently there than Jack) and held her in high regard. The property title was held in Mrs. Moore's name and she had provided in her will that it would be entrusted to Jack and Warnie at her death and would become Maureen's after Jack and Warnie passed on.

The Allegory of Love

Despite his great pleasure in the new home, Jack continued to spend week-nights during college terms in his rooms at Magdalen College where he was thriving in his teaching vocation. Becoming a Christian revitalized his sense of calling and he felt a mission to use his opportunities to make connections with his tutorial students. Sayer observes that from every generation of students, at least one became a personal longtime friend of Jack. His lectures were becoming considered among the best at Oxford, where he was admired for making dry subjects lively and engaging.

Publish, Don't Perish

But Jack didn't try to build his standing in academic life solely on the basis of his acceptance in lecture halls and tutorial sessions. On the advice of his tutor F. P. Wilson, Jack, while still a student himself in 1925, began working on a scholarly study of allegory in medieval literature that became a major part of his work from 1933 to 1935. It was published by Clarendon Press in 1936 as *The Allegory of Love.*

The work explores the medieval conventions of courtly love through literary criticism and a historical overview of works like *Le Roman de la Rose* (*The Romance of the Rose*), a French chivalric poem by Guillaume de Lorris, who composed the first 4,058 lines in 1237, and Jean de Meun, who added 17,724 lines in 1275. Jack presents this work, along with others by Spenser (*The Faerie Queene*), Chaucer (*Troilus and Criseyde*), Gower (*Confessio Amantis*), and Shakespeare (*Sonnets*) to show that the poems and the times that produced them were the roots of courtly love and romantic love. He credits Spenser in particular for introducing the theme of romantic love between married couples, thus revolutionizing humanity's oldest institution by re-establishing its base in romantic love rather than parental matchmaking.

Jack's treatment of the subject was so accessible to the students of Oxford that it became an immediate standard in the field of medieval literature and was said to have created a noticeable demand in literature from the medieval period at Blackwell's, Oxford's best-known booksellers. *The Allegory of Love* was also widely praised by critics, with the critic for the London *Sunday Times* calling it "a great book." Professor Ifor Evans writes in the *Observer,* "Out of the multitude of volumes on literary history there arises once or twice in a generation a truly great work. Such I believe is this study by Mr. C. S. Lewis."

Two of the early female students of Jack referred to *The Allegory of Love* in their reminiscences for *We Remember C. S. Lewis* as already established as an Oxford standard by the time they came to study with him. "Our English studies had required us to read his *Allegory of Love,*" wrote Patricia M. Hunt, adding that his lectures in Magdalen Hall "were always crowded out." And Rachel Trickett, who called Jack the "uncrowned king of Oxford," had the impression that it was "the book that brought Lewis to fame" and reflects that it had gone on to be regarded as "one of the most original works of scholarship of the twentieth century." Some critics of the work eventually and inevitably arose, she admits, but "which of his refuters ever persuaded a student actually to read Gower, or to take Spenser seriously, as Lewis had done? ...This was his triumph."

> "Years ago when I wrote about medieval love-poetry and described its strange, half make-believe 'religion of love,' I was blind enough to treat this as an almost purely literary phenomenon. I know better now. Eros by his nature invites it. Of all loves he is, at his height, most god-like; therefore most prone to demand our worship."
>
> —*The Four Loves*

In the book Jack describes allegory as inventing literary devices (characters, places, and ambiance) to express factual ones. So in his allegory *The Pilgrim's Regress,* "John" is the device, a character, that represents Jack himself to some extent, as well as every pilgrim through the antitheistic thickets of philosophy, history, and media reports to the truth found in God and his real creation. Lewis scholar Doris T. Myers, professor of English at the University of Northern Colorado and author of *C. S. Lewis in Context,* calls *The Allegory of Love* Jack's "first major work of literary scholarship" and describes the work as a survey of the "major documents of Christian humanism."

The Inklings

The Inklings were founded at Oxford in 1930 by student Edward Tangye Lean and continued after Lean's graduation in 1933 by Jack and J. R. R. Tolkien. It's safe to assume that this group has inspired the formation and imitation of more

The Inklings (left to right): Commander James Dundas-Grant, Colin Hardie, Dr. R. E. Havard, C. S. Lewis, and Peter Havard (Dr. Havard's son). Taken at "The Trout" outside Oxford, ca. 1940. Used by permission of The Marion E. Wade Center, Wheaton College, Wheaton, IL.

writers and literary discussion groups throughout the world than any other society ever. Though Lean's group was mostly students, with Tolkien and Lewis as regular faculty participants, in the beginning of their get-togethers after Lean left Oxford it was only Lewis and Tolkien. Warnie was added a bit later, and then another sixteen or seventeen members, most of them Oxford academics, joined over the next three decades.

Among the later members were Owen Barfield, Charles Williams, Adam Fox, Hugo Dyson, Robert Havard, Nevill Coghill, Charles Leslie Wrenn, Roger Lancelyn Green, Colin Hardie, James Dundas-Grant, John Wain, R. B. McCallum, Gervase Mathew, C. E. Stevens, J. A. W. Bennett, Lord David Cecil, and Christopher Tolkien (J. R. R. Tolkien's son). From its beginning in 1933, it continued meeting into the 1960s.

A Society of Two

Before Jack and Tolkien began meeting as the Inklings, Tolkien had hosted another literary group in his rooms, the Coalbiters, who studied Icelandic myths and the Icelandic language, which Jack regularly attended. At first Jack was leery of Tolkien, whom he described as "diffident and a private person," and he mentioned once that Tolkien was two things he had been long warned to hold suspect: a Roman Catholic and a philologist. But their discovery of a shared interest in "Northernness" prompted discussions that led Tolkien to offer a section of his work in progress, *The Silmarillion*, for Jack to critique.

Jack took the request seriously and gave Tolkien many suggestions on how to improve the work. Though Tolkien did not follow many of the suggestions, he was appreciative for the interest and proposed a weekly get-together to continue going through *The Silmarillion*. Those meetings grew into the new incarnation of the Inklings.

Though Tolkien and, by this time, Jack, were orthodox Catholic and Anglican Christians respectively, the Inklings was not limited to Christians. Though the works of most of its published members reflect Christian values, atheists and anthroposophists (notably Owen Barfield) were regular participants. Most members had come through invitation from Jack, who said one type of member they were *not* looking for was "the sort of fellow who uses language not to communicate thought but *instead* of thought."

Warnie wrote that "Properly speaking, the Inklings was neither a club nor a literary society, though it partook of the nature of both. There were no rules, officers, agendas, or formal elections."

Limitations and Purposes

As there were no female students in the Oxford of the 1930s, the Inklings' membership was all male. Though Dorothy L. Sayers, the well-known mystery writer and essayist, was a friend of Jack and Charles Williams and is one of the writers honored along with members of the Inklings at the Marion E. Wade Center at Wheaton College in Illinois, she never attended Inklings meetings.

Reading and discussing members' works in progress remained the main purpose of Inklings meetings. But informal fellowship and frivolity, like a contest to see who could read passages of the famously bad nonfiction of Amanda McKittrick Ros longest without laughing, were also highly valued. Jack's *Out of the Silent Planet*, Tolkien's *The Lord of the Rings*, and Charles

Williams's *All Hallows' Eve* were among the prepublication novels read to and critiqued by the Inklings. The fictional Notion Club in Christopher Tolkien's *Sauron Defeated* was based on his experiences with the Inklings.

Venues

Inklings readings and discussions were held usually on Thursday evenings in Jack's Magdalen College rooms until late 1949. The Inklings also got together at several Oxford pubs, with the Eagle and Child, long known in Oxford by the nickname the Bird and Baby, being the best known. But pub meetings were purely social, with manuscripts not read in that setting. Pub meetings were also held across the street at the Lamb and Flag in later years, but the Eagle and Child remains the principal pub stop for most Oxford literary tourists. It has framed photographs of famous Inklings and a plaque about the group in its back meeting room.

Tolkien spoke later about the succession of the Inklings from Lean's student club to his and Jack's of professional writers and academics. "Although our habit was to read aloud compositions of various kinds (and lengths!), this association and its habit would in fact have come into being at that time, whether the original short-lived club had ever existed or not."

FACT

J. R. R. Tolkien did not expect the stories he was working on in the 1930s to be popular, but on Jack's urging, he submitted *The Hobbit*, written for his own children, to a publisher in 1937. *The Hobbit* was so popular that its publisher asked Tolkien to write a sequel, which he did with the support of the Inklings.

Collections

The Marion E. Wade Center at Wheaton College, Illinois, is a collection of works, papers, and artifacts from seven British authors. Four of them, Jack, Tolkien, Barfield, and Williams, were Inklings. Two others, G. K. Chesterton and George MacDonald, were highly influential on the Inklings, and Dorothy L. Sayers was a friend of Jack and Williams who also wrote Christian essays. The Wade collection contains more than 11,000 volumes, including first editions and critical works, as well as letters, manuscripts, audio and videotapes, artwork, dissertations, periodicals, photographs, and other materials from and about its seven primary authors.

Science Fiction

From his childhood conversations with his uncle Gussie Hamilton on, Jack had been interested in science, and at Wynyard School he had begun reading and appreciating science fiction of the type produced by H. G. Wells and Jules Verne. Though he had indirectly referred to science fiction as pulp literature (when describing his loss of interest in classical literature during his Wynyard years), Jack came to regard it as a serious subset of romance fiction that could be a twentieth-century complement to the fantasy novels of George MacDonald and James Stephens (well-known for his rewrites of many Irish folk tales).

THEY SAID . . .

"[Jack] pointed out that the difficulties of the Christian writer or lecturer arose from the fact that the culture was not at all Christian. This meant that the influence of a Christian lecture or article would be undermined very quickly by the influence of [other media] in which an opposing point of view was taken for granted."

—George Sayer, *Jack*

Jack wrote to Ruth Pitter that finding a copy of David Lindsay's 1920 novel *Voyage to Arcturus* had excited him. Though he disagreed with Lindsay's "borderline diabolical" philosophy, the fact that the book exhibited a specific philosophy was one of the things about it that excited Jack. Just as reading George MacDonald had set him up to see the truth of

Christianity, Jack realized that his own writing could have similar effects on a new generation.

He proposed to Tolkien that the two of them endeavor to write books with philosophical underpinnings consistent with their Christian world-views, which Tolkien agreed to and which was instrumental in the development of their Inklings meetings. Jack and Tolkien also agreed that writing of this kind was rare in their generation in England and that "what was needed was not more 'little books about Christianity,' but more books by Christians on other subjects in which the Christianity was *latent*," as Jack put it in a lecture to a church convention. But not only did the science fiction genre have mass appeal, it also spoke to the serious interest Jack perceived in the then-current generation in space travel and colonizing other planets as a means of saving the human race, which was increasingly in serious competition with the salvation offered by Christianity.

Out of the Silent Planet

Jack's first attempt to reach a mass audience was *Out of the Silent Planet*, which he wrote in 1936 with Tolkien's encouragement. The book reflects much influence from Wells's *First Men in the Moon* but with the added dimension that Jack and Tolkien had agreed upon: a Christian worldview.

It is the first of three books about Elwin Ransom, an English philologist who travels through space to other planets, in this first instance against his will as a victim of a kidnapping by a former schoolmate of his, Devine, and Devine's coconspirator, Professor Weston. They travel to Malacandra, where his captors plan to use Ransom, presumably in exchange for some of the planet's plentiful gold.

But overhearing their plans, Ransom escapes to fend for himself in the strange planet inhabited by sorns, hrossa, and pfifltrigs, and led by eldila, angelic beings of light led by the Oyarsa, the archangel in charge of Malacandra. An eldil takes Ransom to meet their Oyarsa, from whom he learns that all planets are ruled by Oyarsa who are accountable to Maledil, the equivalent of Jesus to the Malacandrans, and that the Oyarsa assigned to Earth, known in Malacandra as Thulcandra, is in rebellion to Maledil.

And because of its rebellion, Thulcandra is known as the Silent Planet. Until the arrival of Ransom and his captors, it has not been heard from in the rest of the solar system lest its communication also lead the other planets into the Thulcandran's rebellion against Maledil and the Creator.

Initially, critics missed the Christian images in the book, considering it straight science fiction, and inferior in some ways to that of Wells and other established authors. It did not sell well until a few years later, after Jack became famous. Since then, however, it has remained in print and has become considered a classic of the genre.

Rehabilitations *and* The Personal Heresy

Based on the success of *The Allegory of Love*, in 1939 Jack approached Oxford University Press about publishing two more works of scholarship. Most likely because Jack was so highly regarded at that time, Oxford University Press released both volumes. They were *Rehabilitations and Other Essays*, a collection of nine critical essays Jack had produced in his teaching career thus far, and *The Personal Heresy*, a debate between Jack and E. M. W. Tillyard (1889–1962) about the consideration the personality of a poet or other writer should be given in literary criticism.

QUESTION
What was the meaning of "rehabilitations" in the title of Jack's first collection of published essays?
Professor Bruce Edwards, of Bowling Green State University in Ohio, says the title "characterized much of Lewis's work, as he attempted to bring the fading critical reputation of authors he revered back into balance."

The essays in *Rehabilitations* are "Shelley, Dryden, and Mr Eliot," "William Morris," "The Idea of an 'English School,'" "Our English Syllabus," "High and Low Brows," "The Alliterative Metre," "Bluspels and Flalansferes: A Semantic Nightmare," "Variation in Shakespeare and Others," and "Christianity and Literature." *Rehabilitations* has never been reprinted, but six of the nine essays have been reprinted in another collection of Jack's writing, *Selected Literary Essays* from Cambridge University Press in 1969. A seventh, "Christianity and Literature," was republished in 1967 by Geoffrey Bles, London, and Eerdman's, Grand Rapids, in *Christian Reflections*. Only "The Idea of an 'English School'" and "Our English Syllabus," both of which discuss how English was being taught at Oxford at the time and Jack's opinions regarding proposed curriculum changes, have not been reprinted.

THEY SAID . . .

"[To] his smart colleagues; nothing could be more outrageous...than that a man should not only talk religion, but should publish it, and be known and have a reputation way beyond theirs because of religion and not scholarship. Thus, his scholarship tended to be overlooked."

—James Houston, *We Remember C. S. Lewis*

The Personal Heresy grew out of a critical article Jack wrote about Tillyard's book, *Milton*, which claimed that *Paradise Lost* reflected John Milton's state of mind when he wrote it. Jack's article maintained that poetry transcends, rather than reflects, the poet's state of mind, which sparked an exchange of articles debating the point that were turned into the book. Though no bestseller, the book was credited with changing the way literature was taught and criticized, with many agreeing that personality profiles do not constitute literary critiques. And it may be the biggest irony of Jack's life that he argued this point so strenuously as his own literary fame has thrived on biographical details of his life. In fact, because the papers have been collected, many of them published and others made accessible to researchers at places like the Wade Center, most serious students of Lewis probably know more about his school years than they remember of their own.

The In and Out Lewis

That Jack's stellar performance in his first decade of teaching did not lead to his receiving a full professorship at Oxford is generally recognized as a major failing on the university's part, which even it acknowledged by attempting to make amends too late. It seems to have been a matter of institutional politics being allowed to get out of hand. Jack "felt isolated during his early years at Magdalen and under dialectical attack during the later ones," Sayer says.

Jack's devotion to his large circle of close friends, his participation in frequent evening social events like the Inklings and the Socratic Club, and regular dinner meetings described by Houston and others are generally seen by those who knew him as partially motivated by his feelings of isolation from the college's inner circle of policymakers. His Irish reticence, coupled with his Christian humility, prevented his promoting himself, despite the fact that the success and sheer volume of his work spoke so elegantly on his behalf.

Chapter 8

War and Writing

On September 1, 1939, Germany, under the totalitarian government of Adolf Hitler and the Nazi Party, invaded Poland. On September 3, the United Kingdom and France responded by declaring war on Germany. World War II, which would provide England both its darkest and its finest hours, was underway. Although Jack was described as being horrified by the development, he readily supported England's war declaration, believing in the long-standing Christian doctrine of justifiable war. Jack argued, in a talk he gave entitled "Why I Am Not a Pacifist," that historical experience demonstrates that some wars have been necessary and have produced good results, like overthrowing tyranny, stopping genocide, and saving lives of people caught in the middle of political struggles.

Justifiable Warfare

Jack spoke against the pacifist arguments based on "resist not evil...turn the other cheek" (Matthew 5:39) as applying to individuals and churches but not nations. In St. Paul's letter to the Romans, nations are described as wielding the sword on behalf of the people, who are to respect the nation's (or government's) authority and its right to exist.

Jack felt that although the war would be horrendous, it would also strengthen the country through its renewed unity of resolve and purpose. As a personal example, he wrote to Arthur Greeves, "For me, personally, it has come in the nick of time: I was just beginning to get too well settled in my profession, too successful, and probably self-complacent."

Though he did everything he could to support England's war effort, Jack feared that he might be subject to the draft at the beginning of the war, as the government proclamation said that men between eighteen and forty-one were considered draft eligible. Jack was forty. He also feared that, as he had seen during World War I, Oxford might be virtually deserted and that he would have no job even if he were not conscripted.

The War at Oxford

Magdalen College went so far as to declare that the New Buildings, where his rooms were located, would be taken over by the army, so Jack moved his extensive library of books from his rooms to the basement. Later the college said the buildings would not be used by the army after all, so Jack had to spend several days moving the books back upstairs.

Word came that students aged eighteen to twenty would continue being taught by the university and that Jack's teaching would be considered a reserved vocation (exempt from the draft). He offered to instruct cadets, an offer rejected with the suggestion that, because of his writing skill, he might join the Ministry of Information instead. Producing propaganda, however, Jack felt would be too hard on his conscience, so he did not follow through on that suggestion but joined the Oxford City Home Guard Battalion instead. The battalion was tasked with keeping watch for German invasions by air. This required him to report for duty in the wee hours of the morning once every nine nights.

War and Warnie, and Jack

Warnie, however, was not as lucky, being still enlisted as an officer in the reserves. He was called up several weeks before the war began but felt himself unfit to serve at his age and being given to binge drinking when under stress. He spent much time in the hospital during his tour of active duty and was discharged after eleven months for reasons never entirely revealed. Jack dismissed a tutorial he was giving when Warnie was scheduled to disembark at the local train station for active duty, in order to see him off, but he missed the train's departure. He wrote long letters every week to help Warnie stay upbeat and, Sayer suggests, force him to concentrate on replying, which would help him stay sober. The war was said to have given Jack a greater sense of urgency in his work, and also apparently led him to reflect more than he typically did on political theories and situations, feeling, Sayer says, that the war had made all in England residents of occupied territory.

Wartime Residents at The Kilns

Part of England's preparation for the war that was inevitably going to come to them from over the English Channel was to relocate as many children as possible outside London and other sites likely to be primary German bombing targets. Jack and Mrs. Moore supported this initiative by inviting children to The Kilns through the rest of the war.

Several students of Lewis have proposed that young girls living at The Kilns for the duration of the war gave insights and stirred memories of boyhood that were vital to Jack's writing of *The Chronicles of Narnia*, in which a young girl is one of the strongest protagonists. A brief scene in the film dramatization of Jack's late-in-life marriage to Joy Davidman, *Shadowlands*, gets at this by depicting colleagues of Jack's at Oxford teasing him about writing stories for children when, so far as they knew, he didn't even know any children.

"Our schoolgirls have arrived, and all seem to me—and what's more important, to Mint—to be very nice, unaffected creatures and all most flatteringly delighted with their new surroundings. They're fond of animals, which is a good thing (for them as well as for us)."

—*Letter from Jack to Warnie*

Charles Williams

A strange coincidence led to Jack's close friendship with Charles Williams, an editor at Oxford University Press who wrote in several genres, including plays, novels, theology, and poetry. (The stone on Williams's Oxford grave specifies "Poet," which was how he preferred to think of himself.)

Working for Oxford Press in London, he had been asked to read proofs of Jack's *The Allegory of Love* when it was being prepared for publication, and he was so impressed that he sent Jack a note praising it. (Clarendon Press, the publisher of Jack's *Allegory*, is an imprint of Oxford University Press.) Coincidentally, Jack had just read Williams's latest novel, *The Place of the Lion*, and had sent similar praise to Williams. The notes crossed in the mail and a new long-term friendship began. It was, in fact, Williams who suggested the final title for *The Allegory of Love*; Jack's working title had been *The Allegorical Love Poem*.

FACT

Jack described Charles Williams to Arthur Greeves as "ugly as a chimpanzee but so radiant (he emanates more love than any man I have ever known) that as soon as he begins talking he is transfigured and looks like an angel." In another letter to a former pupil he called Williams "friend of friends, the comforter of all our little set."

At the beginning of the war, Oxford Press moved its offices from London to Oxford, requiring Williams to move there in September 1939, which enabled him to become a regular participant in weekly meetings of the Inklings. Besides the Thursday evening meetings, he and Jack often met at the Eagle and Child pub on Tuesday mornings.

Williams, like Jack a devoted Anglican, has been called the greatest influence in Jack's life and literary output during the war, the period when Jack's talent blossomed or came of age, and Sayer calls him the friend that Jack loved the most. He was also remembered as an eloquent lecturer, and though he had completed no college-level degree, Oxford University gave him an honorary Master of Arts. Williams's death in May 1945 is described in several short biographies simply as sudden and unexpected.

The Problem of Pain

Jack's first bestseller was *The Problem of Pain*, which he worked on during the early days of the war and which came out in October 1940. Though reading it in the context of general Christian theology might suggest that he wrote it as an ingenious and popular approach to one of the classical questions addressed in theology, the problem of evil, Jack did not write it with that purpose in mind. Rather, Jack was asked to prepare a book on pain and suffering by Ashley Sampson, the editor of the Christian Challenge popular theology series of Geoffrey Bles Publishing. Sampson had been so impressed by reading Jack's *The Pilgrim's Regress* that he thought he'd found the right man for the task. Jack

> "What would really satisfy us would be a God who said of anything we happened to like doing, 'What does it matter so long as they are contented?' We want, in fact, not so much a Father in Heaven as a grandfather in heaven—a senile benevolence who, as they say, 'liked to see young people enjoying themselves.'"
>
> —*The Problem of Pain*

found his motif for the short discourse on pain and suffering in a profound but simple line from George MacDonald: "The Son of God suffered unto the death, not that men might not suffer, but that their sufferings might be like His" (*Unspoken Sermons*, First Series).

He begins by showing that pain and suffering are everywhere and always. Prior to the twentieth century all generations had to endure pain "without chloroform," yet every generation in human history before the then-current century believed in God, not because of the proofs to be seen in the natural world, which has more prickly coldness, dangers, and bleakness than fuzzy warmth and comforts, but because God showed himself to them. This he did through the human experience of the Numinous, the virtually universal awareness that there are spirits, ghosts, and beings deserving fear and awe, in life in all times and places ever recorded.

Universally Held Beliefs

Jack says that he writes from a perspective consistent with all "ancient and orthodox doctrines" and "I have tried to assume nothing that is not professed by all baptized and communicating Christians." He begins by giving a logical defense against the often-heard argument that a good and benevolent God would not allow pain and suffering in a world he had created.

In Chapter 2, "Divine Omnipotence," he demonstrates as fallacy the nonsense of proposing, as many detractors do, that if the Bible says "with God, all things are possible" (Matthew 19:26), then if it can be shown that there is something God can't do the Bible and its God are exposed as fictions. But God can't do anything contradictory to his own character, standards of justice, his word, and his nature as love, nor can he do nonsense. So he cannot create human beings with free will and yet prevent them from freely choosing actions that may lead to pain and suffering.

God's Pets

In Chapter 3, "Divine Goodness," perhaps Jack's most original proposal is that God's kindness to human beings is analogous to the kindness we show to animals, especially dogs, that we love. We know that training them, even though we know their own first choice would be to remain wild and undisciplined, is the more loving thing for them and for us. Though we are not their creators, we are their lords and masters and we know their lives will be better and most likely lengthened if they learn good behaviors. And we do this not mainly because they love us (any wild dog will love anyone who feeds it), but because we love them. Just so, God doesn't want us primarily because we love him but because he wants to love us. But first we must become lovable by yielding to his divine "training" and discipline.

Analogies between human-pet relationships and God's relationships with human beings are taken up again in Chapter 9, "Animal Pain," where Jack explores the idea that as God provides a way for us to enter his kingdom through Christ, it seems likely that through us our animal companions receive their personalities or spirits and any kind of life after death there may be for pets. Though he doesn't claim any religious support to believing in a pet heaven, he agrees that it is an attractive idea to all pet lovers.

Hell and Heaven

Chapter 8, "Hell," proposes that eternal estrangement from God, which is one definition of Hell, is always the conscious choice of whoever ends up there. If there is a game, it must be possible to lose, and if there is free will, it must be possible to choose to decline God's love and to have nothing to do with heaven. So it would be illogical to insist, as some preachers have, that all shall be saved whether they like it or not. Because if God imposed heaven on those who choose against it, where is free will? Where is love?

Finally, in Chapter 10, "Heaven," Jack argues that "either there is pie in the sky, or there isn't," and Christianity has always and everywhere confirmed through the Scriptures, tradition, and pulpit exhortation that there is a reward to come in the life beyond this one. And really, he argues in setting a theme that will resound through his later works, that heavenly realm is our real home and it is what we have always been nostalgic for. It is this that has intrigued us through all our favorite books, poems, and songs. It won't be the stereotypical mansions in the clouds often pictured, but heaven will be a place where new vistas will always be waiting for us to see, where new heights will always be waiting for us to scale.

The Screwtape Letters

Jack wrote in a wartime letter on July 20, 1940, to Warnie that he was working on an idea for a series of letters between devils in the service of "the Father below" (Satan). One of the devils, an uncle showing tricks of the temptation trade to a nephew novice, is an idea that occurred to Jack while attending a late-morning Sunday service at his local parish. Though his practice was to take communion at an earlier and shorter service, he had been feeling poorly so he decided to stay in bed a bit longer that Sunday.

From his working title of "From One Devil to Another," the collection of letters was first published one a week in the Anglican magazine *The Guardian*, the only magazine that Jack subscribed to. It eventually became *The Screwtape Letters* and was, until recent years when sales of *The Chronicles of Narnia* surpassed it, Jack's consistent bestseller. The concept of Screwtape, the uncle, instructing a young devil named Wormwood in the best ways to trip up a would-be follower of God's way, described only as "the patient," seemed to strike a familiar chord in people from all walks of life.

FACT

Despite their popularity from their publication in the church magazine, Jack said writing the letters—having to think the way a devil would—had been an ordeal he wouldn't want to repeat. Nevertheless, he wrote a sequel, "Screwtape Proposes a Toast," that first appeared in the *Saturday Evening Post* and has been included in subsequent editions of the book.

Screwtape's first letter to Wormwood notes that the patient is being pulled away from serving the Father below, meaning he is on the verge of converting to Christianity. By the second letter, it's apparent that the patient is now serving "the enemy," and Wormwood is on the brink of being punished in the House of Correction for failing in his mission. Screwtape tells Wormwood his only hope is to tempt the patient to fall away from his profession of Christian faith, suggesting that gradual small sins like anger and pride will be more effective to that end than big dramatic sins like adultery or murder. The sequel article, "Screwtape Proposes a Toast," is a critique of tax-supported education, especially in the United States, in the 1950s.

A Preface to Paradise Lost *and* Perelandra

A Preface to Paradise Lost is not, as some have assumed, a lengthy preface to a new edition of John Milton's *Paradise Lost*. It is a 154-page, eighteen-chapter stand-alone book published by Oxford University Press in 1943, based on the Ballard Matthews Lectures that Jack delivered at University College, North Wales, in 1941. As his first new scholarly published work following the disappointing reception in 1939 of *Rehabilitations* and *The Personal Heresy*, it became a must-read for any course on Milton's epic poem and restored Jack's reputation as the towering scholar in the field of medieval and Renaissance literature at that time. Republished by Oxford University Press in 1961, it has remained in print ever since.

Dedicating the book to Charles Williams (and citing Williams's influence on his own understanding of Milton), Jack addresses the then-current criticisms of Milton that had somewhat tarnished *Paradise Lost*'s standing as the greatest work of poetry ever published in the English language. Jack lays out the meaning and purpose of epic poetry, defending it especially from Ezra Pound and T. S. Eliot, the most highly regarded poets in the United States and England in that period and critics of Milton.

Part Two of the Space Trilogy

Perelandra, the second book in Jack's Space Trilogy (and Jack's personal favorite), takes Dr. Ransom to his second planet, Venus, which in the old planetary language is Perelandra (as Malacandra was Mars in the first, *Out of the Silent Planet*). Its writing was influenced by Jack's work on *The Preface to Paradise Lost*, as it is essentially the story of the losing (or nearly losing) of paradise on a second planet, Venus, comparable to its being lost in the early chapters of Genesis and in Milton's book.

THEY SAID . . .

Reviews for *Perelandra* were generally positive, though some thought it was "too Christian." "He should read more Verne and less Aquinas," said Alan Pryce-Jones in the *Observer*. But *Commonweal's* Leonard Bacon saw in it "the poetic imagination at full blast" with "whole passages of prose poetry...that suggest the sweep of Dante and of Milton."

Dr. Ransom is propelled from Earth (or Thulcandra) to Perelandra to try to dissuade the Green Lady (Perelandra's version of Eve) from succumbing to the tempter's efforts to lead her to sin. On Perelandra, the tempter is not a serpent but a physicist, the same Dr. Weston seen in *Out of the Silent Planet*. As Tal Cohen puts it in his online review, "it is only Weston's body that is present; Weston is clearly no longer human, being totally possessed by the Evil One himself."

Published in March 1943 by John Lane and reprinted as *The Voyage to Venus* in paperback by Pan Books in 1953, George Sayers says of *Perelandra* that "for many Christians this is likely to be the most rewarding of his novels."

The Abolition of Man

The Abolition of Man is an edited version of three lectures Jack gave at Durham University in 1942, a critique of an approach to language he found in a textbook for high-school-level English students, *The Control of Language*, by Alec King and Martin Ketley. Jack disguises King and Ketley in the lectures and book as Gaius and Titius because, he says, they surely meant no harm in propagating their faulty presuppositions.

Those presuppositions are that all value judgments are to be seen as subjective matters of opinion, with no objective or absolute guidelines to be followed in deciding, for example, whether a waterfall is pretty or sublime. "Pretty" may be correct if it is likely to reflect most people's opinion, King and Ketley propose, but "sublime" is an internal feeling about the waterfall, which cannot be verified by taking a vote of general reactions. Jack shows that "sublime" does not describe a feeling, but that the feeling that makes someone think an object is sublime is properly called veneration, not a sublime feeling.

Though the point seems simple, even simplistic, Jack goes on to construct one of the most important points found in his work, and one of its recurring themes: that ethics and values are not subjectively derived but are rooted in universal values the human race has generally agreed upon from the earliest examples of literary records available. Christianity, for example, does not give a new set of ethical principles, but it represents a new way of teaching the most generally held ethical principles of humanity from the earliest records of civilized societies. Educational philosophies that deny the "justice" of sentiments like finding a beautiful place sublime are pushing younger generations toward denying all sentiments and, eventually, destroying their hearts and creating "men without chests," which is the title of Jack's first lecture.

Jack traced literature from various civilizations to ancient times to show that all share most of the principles most people refer to as human or humane values. He sees the source of these in what he (and the church throughout the ages) calls "Natural Law." But to emphasize its universality in this context, he calls the source of these shared values part of the Tao, or Way, that has been taught in ancient Asian philosophies like Confucius's (sixth to fifth centuries B.C.), Lao Tse's (also rendered Lao Tsu and Laozi, sixth century B.C.), and in other philosophies or religions like ancient Jewish, Egyptian, Greek, and Hindu.

FACT

Hiermonk Damascene of the St. Herman of Alaska Brotherhood, a monastic-missionary Orthodox Christian brotherhood, took Jack's application of the Tao a step farther in his 1999 book, *Christ the Eternal Tao*, in which he shows numerous overlaps between Lao Tse's teachings and those of the Gospels. Christ the Way (Logos) is also the Tao, properly understood, in Damascene's view.

Though *The Abolition of Man* was perceived at first as difficult to understand, it has grown into one of Jack's most significant books. And to the extent that relativity and elimination of fixed standards of good, bad, right, and wrong in philosophy and in education is a cause opposed by social conservatives, it is also his most political nonfiction book.

Chapter 9

Mere Christianity

Though *Mere Christianity* did not appear in its permanent form until 1952, its origin dates from August 1941, when Jack began the first of four series of radio broadcasts about Christianity at the request of the director of religious broadcasting for the BBC, Dr. James Welch. Welch, who approached Jack on the basis of his positive impression of *The Problem of Pain*, thought that talks on Christianity would have a large audience in the uncertain days of the war. Though Jack had never been a fan of radio, he thought the opportunity to reach millions who would never read his books should not be lost, so he agreed. The talks were an immediate hit, with letters pouring in to Jack before the first four-broadcast series ended. Over the next two years, three similar series of talks were broadcast. Eventually, all were published in one volume as *Mere Christianity*.

Book One: The Case for Christianity

The first four talks, given in August and September 1942, and a fifth added to answer listeners' questions (and which generated even more letters), were published by Geoffrey Bles together with a second series of five talks as *Broadcast Talks*. The series was called "Right and Wrong as a Clue to the Meaning of the Universe" in the BBC program listings and its printed versions and comprises Book One of *Mere Christianity*.

THEY SAID . . .

"I remember being at a pub filled with soldiers on one Wednesday evening. At a quarter to eight, the bartender turned the radio up for Lewis. "You listen to this bloke," he shouted. "He's really worth listening to." And those soldiers did listen attentively for the entire fifteen minutes."
—George Sayer, *Jack*

The first of the five chapters in Book One, "The Laws of Human Nature," deals with standards, giving as examples the generally assumed ideas that taking another person's turn in a line or bullying someone of obviously inferior strength are wrong. He discusses how these ideas became standard behaviors and how they demonstrate a higher law. For most of human history, Jack argues, these standards have been regarded as laws of nature, but in the scientific age, people think of laws of nature as referring to things like gravity, thermodynamics, and the survival of the fittest. So he proposed they be called laws of human nature. This meshes closely with the development of the Tao in *The Abolition of Man*.

Instincts Versus Oughts

Chapter 2, "Some Objections," clears up misunderstandings of some of Jack's meanings in talking of the laws of human nature. They are not instincts, he argues to those who think they may be, because instincts often produce urges that should be resisted rather than followed, like pushing sexual intimacy on someone you consider attractive but who is uninterested. Nor are they social conventions, as social conventions can be in conflict. Saying Christian morality is better than Nazi morality assumes there is a higher or real morality or standard on which to judge moralities.

Chapter 3, "The Reality of the Law," stresses that Jack's job as broadcaster is not to fix blame or judge how much blame goes where but to seek and find the truth. And whereas laws of nature like gravity are not rules but observations about what always happens in nature, the laws of human nature are rules because they get at what ought to be rather than what always is.

Behind the Law, a Person

"What Lies Behind the Law," Chapter 4, compares and contrasts the materialist view and the religious view. Jack describes the materialist view as believing that matter and space have always existed and have "just happened" to have changed from their primordial forms to the present forms, including living creatures and self-conscious human beings. The religious view is that the force behind the universe is "more like a mind than it is like anything else we know." He cautions that he is not at all—yet—talking about the Christian God, but just the kind of entity which, logically, would have to under gird the universe if the materialist view is wrong.

Chapter 5, "We Have Cause to Be Uneasy," was, when Jack originally gave it, considered the end of his broadcast talks. He tries to allay fears of any who, after the previous talk, may think they've been tricked into just another "religious jaw." This he attempts to do by emphasizing the logical consistency of his arguments.

You may think it's too late to go back to religion: "the world has tried that and you cannot put the clock back," he said. But he counters that sometimes, as when a clock is fast, the best thing to do is set it back. And if you want to make progress you must know that where you're headed is where you want to be. If it's not, going ahead is not progress but, in fact, turning back immediately is the fastest way to get back to the right course.

If you accept that moral law is a given, there must be a mind behind it. Call it God if you like, but realize that does not mean God exists simply to forgive, as some Christians advocate thinking. Only a person can forgive, he argues, and the moral law includes the condition of obeying the laws. It's time, he says, to get over our religious wishful thinking. His conclusion strongly suggests that Jack is hoping for a sequel, or as they say in contemporary broadcasting, that his "series contract will be renewed."

Book Two: *What Christians Believe*

Based on the first lecture series's popularity, Welch asked Jack to renew his contract, and the second series of five talks, "What Christians Believe," was broadcast in January and February 1942 and was published with the first series later that year as *Broadcast Talks*. Book Two is the theological kernel of *Mere Christianity* in which Jack's conciliatory approach, not only to all "rooms of the Christian edifice" but even to other—non-Christian—religions, shines through.

Chapter 1, "The Rival Conceptions of God," begins by saying that before telling his readers what they should believe to be as Christians he will tell them something they do not have to believe: they don't have to believe that all other religions are false through and through. In the same paragraph he adds that as a Christian he thinks Christianity is the only entirely true religion. Just as in arithmetic an answer is either right or wrong but some answers are closer to right than others, so in religion one is right and some others are more nearly right than others.

Among believers in a God, some believe in a God who is good (Christians, Muslims, and Jewish believers). Others think everything that exists is "good" and therefore God is not about good and bad. Cancer is bad because it kills people, but a physician who killed a cancer would also be bad, this latter view claims when pushed to its logical roots.

In Chapter Two, "The Invasion," Jack says atheism is too simple because it refuses to answer how the universe has no meaning when we can logically talk about meaning. How would anything have developed eyes if there were no light in the universe? How is there any meaning in human thinking if the universe lacks any underlying meaning? Before he became a Christian he refused to hear arguments about how a good God could create such a messed-up world, Jack says, but eventually he realized his objections to attempts to explain this were based on his own conceptions of justice. Subsequently, he then had to confront how "justice" became such a universal standard that he found himself using it to argue against God. Even the power to be evil is derived from, or stolen from, a greater power, the power of good or to be good, which logically suggests a supreme intelligence, or God.

Chapter 3, "The Shocking Alternative," addresses why an absolute being would allow disobedience and disharmony in his created world. A good parent concludes that in the children's best interest they must be allowed to voluntarily keep their room tidy, so rather than forcing them to be tidy she tells them she's going to let them learn that necessity for themselves.

The devil, according to this logic, must have been the best of God's created beings to have gone so wrong. But the shock is that in history we encounter a man who goes around calling himself God, capable of undoing all the Evildoer's messes and forgiving the sins of any who will repent, something which, unless the speaker actually *is* God, would be ludicrous. Then follows Jack's famous "trilemma," that any man who would claim to forgive sins would be either a liar, a lunatic, or the Lord (God) himself. (Jack mentions elsewhere that he borrowed the "trilemma" argument from G. K. Chesterton, but it is more often credited to Jack because of the greater circulation of his works.)

> Somebody once asked me: "Why did God make a creature of such rotten stuff that it went wrong?" The better stuff a creature is made of—the cleverer and stronger and freer it is—then the better it will be if it goes right, but also the worse it will be if it goes wrong.
>
> —*The Invasion*

Atonement

Chapter 4, "The Perfect Penitent," is Jack's presentation of the Christian doctrine of atonement. Though all Christians believe that Jesus Christ is the one and only "perfect penitent," they disagree about the details of how it worked. But the details are not the essential matter in Christianity; the essence is in believing that it works, not believing in any one interpretation of how it works.

Some say the Father punished Jesus in order to be able to forgive mankind's sins; others say that this is untenable in any accurate understanding of the Father's character as the essence of Love. Jack refuses to engage in these and other disputes among denominations, saying they are not of the essence of what he calls "mere" Christianity.

Altar Call

"The Practical Conclusion," Chapter 5, is Jack's altar call, summoning listeners to put on the "new kind of life which began in Him." Baptism, belief, and the Eucharist (as Holy Communion is now commonly called but which in the time of the broadcast was not generally used) are the three ordinary methods of coming into that new life, he says.

He compares childhood ignorance of the pleasurable act of sexual congress as the means of bringing new physical human beings into life with a "natural" ignorance among human beings of how these three essential sacraments, ordinances, or "obediences" can be effective in bringing into being new spiritual life.

Book Three: Christian Behavior

The third of Jack's series of BBC lectures was broadcast in September and October 1942 and published in 1943. Originally written as fifteen-minute programs, the BBC cut them to ten minutes, but the text was restored to the original size for publication. Both in the broadcast listing and as Book Four of *Mere Christianity* they are called "Christian Behavior."

Chapter 1, "The Three Parts of Morality," takes up the New Testament requirement that Christians pursue perfection rather than ideals or generalities. Though it may be true that unaided no one may be able to draw a perfectly straight line or achieve any other routine activity to perfection, perfection is still the goal of the Christian life. Getting to the goal requires perfectly following the directions in the sense that any deviation will at the very least require an adjustment along the way. And adjustments—turning back—are allowed.

Chapter 2, "The Cardinal Virtues," discusses the four virtues that "all civilized people recognize": prudence (exercising common sense), temperance (enjoying pleasures to the right extent and no farther), justice (fairness, honesty, give and take, truthfulness, keeping promises), and fortitude (facing danger and sticking with it when in pain).

Chapter 3, "Social Morality," dispatches arguments for Christian politics in the sense of promoting the election of Christians only, then sets out what the New Testament clearly hints at about what a fully Christian society would be like. Jack stresses that charity is an essential of any Christian social organization, even to the point of having to sacrifice one's own pleasures in order to be able to afford to help others.

Chapter 4, "Morality and Psychoanalysis," backtracks to the subject of the previous chapter to say that the fact that a perfect social situation may not be achieved in our time should not lead us to give up working toward it. Then he addresses how psychological problems affect morality, and vice versa, and concludes with a lesson that saints have referred to through church history: "when a man is getting better, he understands more and more clearly the evil that is still left in him" and "when a man is getting worse, he understands his own badness less and less."

FACT

Francis Collins, current director of the National Human Genome Research Institute and a former atheist, became a Christian through *Mere Christianity*. "It was an argument I was not prepared to hear," he said. "I was very happy with the idea that God didn't exist, and had no interest in me. And yet…I could not turn away."

Jack begins Chapter 5, "Sexual Morality," by contrasting chastity and modesty and allows that "chastity is the most unpopular of the Christian virtues." Either the teaching must be wrong, he then says, or the sexual instinct must be flawed, and he comes down on the side of the instinct being flawed. He compares sex to eating, both of which are necessary for human survival. But while both come with rules concerning their proper limits, most people see the teachings about nutrition and gluttony as sound but are less willing to accept the Christian sex-in-marriage-only rule. He ends the discussion by cautioning that the center of Christian morality is not in sexual sins, calling them "the least," but worse infractions are backbiting, "putting other people in the wrong," hating neighbors, and selfishly exploiting others.

Chapter 6, "Christian Marriage," he says, is the positive version of the mostly negative talk of sex in Chapter 5, the virtue of faithfulness in marriage. Churches vary on whether divorce can be allowed and on what bases, but all teach that marriages are for life and that if divorce occurs it is always a serious failure of love. He argues against considering "being in love" or "remaining in love" as the only basis for keeping marriages going.

Chapter 7, "Forgiveness," begins by saying that loving our neighbors may be even more unpopular than chastity among the Christian virtues because, for Christians, neighbors include enemies as well as friends. Loving neighbors does not equate to "being fond of" them or finding them attractive, he says, and he goes on to discuss how "love thy neighbor like thyself" applies to both neighbor and self.

Chapter 8, "The Great Sin," treats pride, or self-conceit, and its opposite, humility. All other moral lapses he has addressed are, in comparison, "mere fleabites" compared with pride, which Christian tradition teaches caused Satan's fall from heaven and is behind every other kind of sin. Furthermore, it is the most deceitful sin, as people eaten up by pride often think themselves faithful practicing Christians.

Chapter 9, "Charity," considers the first of the three theological virtues. Charity is willed love, which Jack explains is required of Christians to people they don't find attractive or feel affection toward.

Chapter 10, "Hope," the second theological virtue, describes the Christian's expectation of the coming kingdom of God not as escape from reality but as a basis of what God says is truly real and worth living for.

Chapter 11, the first of two called "Faith," the third theological virtue, discusses faith as believing and believing as a virtue. How is something that is believed (a matter of concluding something is reasonable and worth trusting in) virtuous? Jack asks. He answers that when faith wavers, then "keeping the faith," "abiding in him," as Jesus taught, becomes a virtue, something sometimes practiced even through "force" of the will or what the New Testament calls violence (Matthew 11:12).

Chapter 12, the second on faith, discusses the higher sense of faith, of taking things on faith or keeping on in the Christian faith even when we encounter matters we don't understand or believe in. Leaving it to God, Jack says, is easier said than done, but in some cases in our walks toward Christian perfection that is the better part of virtue.

Book Four: Beyond Personality I

Subtitled "First Steps in the Doctrine of the Trinity," Book Four addresses the question skeptics sometimes raise concerning misgivings about thinking of God as personal or a person. Jack says they are right if they think of "person" in the human sense, for God is no more like us human persons than a statue, even the best likeness of one of us, is like us. There are observable similarities, but, in the essentials, the statue is more unlike than like us. Just so are human beings, though we are an image of God, more dissimilar to him than similar to him. Thus "Beyond Personality" looks beyond person, in the usual sense of the word, to what is vastly different regarding God.

Jack begins this final series of talks by admitting he is now examining theology despite his guess the public resists that academic specialization. The lectures were carried on the BBC from February to April, 1944, and were compiled as the book, *Beyond Personality*, published in England in 1944 and in the United States in 1945.

The Three-Personed God

Chapter 1, "Making and Begetting," introduces the new series and shows how things we beget are exactly like us, but things we make are essentially not like us. God's only begotten Son, then, is exactly like him, as our children are in all features just like us. But we, his "made" creatures, are less like him than similar to him, just as any likeness of our selves, our children, or anything, is less like than similar to us.

Chapter 2, "The Three-Personed God," explains why it was essential that God be three persons in order to love us by becoming, in one person, the Son, to remain in control of the universe without interruption as another, and also so that he could dwell with and in us throughout the history of the church-his-body through the third person, his Spirit.

Wrinkles on Time

Jack encourages readers to skip Chapter 3, "Time and Beyond Time," if they are not interested in speculations about the nature of God. But it has one of his most fascinating ideas and one that undoubtedly influenced his science fiction and fantasy writing. Understanding God as all-powerful and all-knowing implies that he is apart from time. To him, time must be somewhat like a line drawn on a sheet of paper, which he can see from beginning to end, from what we creatures perceive as past and future, but which to him all happen simultaneously.

Though time-bound creatures struggle on the line on the piece of paper, God has the whole sheet before him. One wonders if the late Madeleine L'Engle had Chapter 3 in mind when she wrote *The Wrinkle in Time*. Jack ends by saying there is no dogma or even theology here, just speculation about how time might be perceived from the perspective of eternity.

THEY SAID . . .

The point about reading C. S. Lewis is that he makes you sure, whatever you believe, that religion accepted or rejected means something extremely serious, demanding the entire energy of the mind.

—Review of *Mere Christianity* in *Harper's Magazine*

Chapter 4, "Good Infection," explains the coeternal relationship among the three persons of the Trinity. The "good infection" refers to being indwelt by God through the Holy Spirit, working to make us over in the image or likeness of Jesus Christ, the Son.

Chapter 5, "The Obstinate Toy Soldiers," compares human persons with tin soldiers in order to illustrate how God brings us to life or, as Jack puts it, from life in the sense of *Bios*, biological or created life, to life in the sense of *Zoe*, or uncreated, spiritual life.

Book Four: Beyond Personality II

Though Jack was asked to do more lectures for the BBC after the current series ended, he declined, saying he thought he'd said all he knew about Christian apologetics. Chapter 6 discusses two notes he received questioning points in Chapter 5. One asks why, if God wanted sons instead of toy soldiers, did he not beget many sons rather than making many "toy soldiers" who had to be born again to come into real life. Jack answers that the human beings exercised their free will to estrange themselves from son-ship with God and that he gave them free will to make them creatures worth loving rather than automatons. The second note addresses the problem of considering humanity as "one big organism" as opposed to considering individuals as having separate identities, needs, dignity, and worth in God's redemptive plan.

QUESTION

What does C. S. Lewis say is the logical necessity of God's existence in three persons?

The fact that God is love presupposes that he must have eternal objects of, and recipients of, his love. And inasmuch as only God is eternal, he must be essentially a diversity in unity.

Chapter 7, "Let's Pretend," is about "what all this theology means" and what it requires us to do. The purpose of thinking of God as our Father is to enable us to pretend that we are Christ and doing so enables us to become more like him in order to live in his kingdom.

Chapter 8, "Is Christianity Hard or Easy?" says the life is hard if we try to do it in our natural selves but easy if we realize it is only possible when we "give it all to him," surrendering our wills to his. Thinking of the Christian life as living up to all the church expects and offers as programs is hard, but that's not the Christian life. The life is obedience, surrender.

Chapter 9, "Counting the Cost," reminds readers that Christ warned people who would be his followers to count the cost first. "If you let me, I will make you perfect," Jack says of Jesus, "but you must be ready for the 'spiritual growing pains' that entails.'"

Chapter 10, "Nice People or New Men," discusses why, if Christians are being perfected, they often come across as less nice than non-Christians one meets. Jack finds the difference in the journey. Every person is at a different point in the journey to perfection and each is more perfect in some aspects than others.

Chapter 11, "The New Men," the last of Jack's broadcast lectures, describes the transformation that turns old creatures into new ones, from the nature of the "old man" to the nature of Christ.

The Preface

The preface to the 1952 edition, the last section to be written and thus treated last here, sets out the argument that gives *Mere Christianity* its wide appeal among Christians of all denominational leanings. Jack says he writes strictly as a layman and lacks the professional expertise to discuss the particulars that divide Roman Catholics from Anglicans, Methodists from Presbyterians, and all from Congregationalists.

Shared Faith

The five groupings he specified among the several hundred varieties of Western Christians (not to mention Eastern Christians like Greek Orthodox, Assyrian Christians, and Copts) represent the main denominations in England at his time, though some of these went by other names like Reformed and Baptist.

THEY SAID . . .

"In 1973...I visited the home of a friend who read to me from *Mere Christianity*. In that book, I encountered a formidable intellect and a logical argument that I found utterly persuasive. That night in the driveway of my friend's home I called out to God in a flood of tears and surrendered my life to Christ."

—Charles Colson, former chief counsel to President Richard Nixon

And although many would attribute to Jack the origin of the idea of "mere Christianity," he attributes it to Anglican divine Richard Baxter, 1615–1691, who wrote in *Church-history of the Government of Bishops* (1680):

I am a CHRISTIAN, a MEER CHRISTIAN, of no other Religion; and the Church that I am of is the Christian Church, and hath been visible where ever the Christian Religion and Church hath been visible: But must you know what Sect or Party I am of? I am against all Sects and dividing Parties: But if any will call Meer Christians by the name of a Party, because they take up with Meer Christianity, Creed, and Scripture, and will not be of any dividing or contentious Sect, I am of that Party which is so against Parties: If the Name CHRISTIAN be not enough, call me a CATHOLICK CHRISTIAN; not as that word signifieth an hereticating majority of Bishops, but as it signifieth one that hath no Religion, but that which by Christ and the Apostles was left to the Catholick Church, or the Body of Jesus Christ on Earth.

Baxter's point that he represents not religion but what Christ and the apostles taught as Christianity seems aligned with the oft-heard evangelical claim that their Good News does not present a religion but a person and a life-changing encounter. In the same vein, Jack in his preface specifies that even though he often personally sides with one or the other side on controversial lesser doctrines, discussing those preferences is not appropriate to his current course, which is to reach the whole of England (and through the decades since, the world) through the basics. "Our divisions should never be discussed except in the presence of those who have already come to believe," he adds.

Chapter 10

Into the Fantasy World

Anyone following Lewis's life story will not be surprised that he added writing stories for children to his life's work. His own childhood was full of stories both in the active and passive senses (both writing his own children's stories and reading or having other people's stories read to him). What is more surprising than Jack going in the direction of writing for children is that initially he meant to do only one Narnia tale but was persuaded to make it a series by his publisher, Geoffrey Bles, to make it more marketable. And Lewis scholar Doris T. Myers believes that Jack wrote for children for the purpose of countering the influence on them of English language textbooks, which Jack considered capable of destroying character and appreciation for beauty.

Prebaptizing Imagination

"I am aiming at a sort of prebaptism of the child's imagination," Jack told George Sayer in explaining his goal in writing *The Chronicles of Narnia*. But just as there was no need for Jack to get into a fantasy world in order to write children's fantasy stories (that world having always been part of his makeup), Jack did not painstakingly outline his stories and figure out where a moral would be appropriate or where an oblique reference from the Gospel might work.

Bird Watching

"C. S. Lewis was a genius," former psychiatry professor Thomas S. Szasz has said, and nothing better affirms this assessment than Jack's writing methodology. First, he wrote in longhand and Warnie then typed the manuscripts, a process that today sounds almost impossibly tedious.

But just as surprising as his mechanical methods was Jack's approach to composing a story. Rather than having a whole story, or even a chapter, in mind, Jack told an audience of writers that he began with a "picture in his head" and added additional pictures to that until he had enough to string together to have a story.

The first picture he had that became part of the early narrative in *The Lion, the Witch, and the Wardrobe* came to him when he was just fifteen or sixteen (1914). The thought of using it in a children's story came to him in 1939, and it was nearly ten years later before he began to develop it in 1948. It was a faun in a snowy forest holding an umbrella and carrying packages.

He was well into writing the first Narnia tale before Aslan, the central figure in *The Chronicles of Narnia*, "came bounding in" as yet another mind picture that, once he knew its purpose, made finishing not only the first book but the whole series a mat-

> "With me the process is much more like bird-watching than like either talking or building. I see pictures...Keep quiet and watch and they will begin joining themselves up. If you were very lucky...a whole group might join themselves so...you had a complete story without doing anything yourself."
>
> —*Lecture to Library Association*

ter of course. Jack said he had been dreaming about lions for a while before he realized the connection with his story.

Discouraging Reactions

After finishing the first Narnia novel at the end of 1948, Jack read it to Tolkien, who immediately disliked it for mixing mythical animal figures, classical fairies, and Father Christmas and other modern fantasy figures like witches and goblins. But other friends, including his pupil Roger Green whose *The Wood That Time Forgot* had influenced Jack's story, praised it and encouraged him to publish it. Geoffrey Bles was not enthusiastic and cautioned that its publication might hurt Jack's professional reputation but agreed to bring it out if Jack would enlarge it into a series.

Genre Fiction and Literature

Doris T. Myers describes a strange tension in the English-language literary world of the time, with Jack (understandably, as the best known professor of English of his generation at the most highly regarded university) at its center. Though Myers does not reduce it this far, it seems to have pitted a modernist approach against a traditionalist one; a new humanism (liberalism) against classical and Christian humanism, and even so-called literary short stories and books against bestsellers.

Though clearly one of the champions of the Christian humanist and traditional approach in literature, Jack was also determined to use and redeem genre fiction (bestsellers) through his science fiction and children's writing. In an essay, "On Science Fiction," first presented at Cambridge University as a lecture in 1955, Jack defends science fiction as a type of "fantastic or mythopoeic literature in general" because the stories are about "the impossible—or things so immensely improbable that they have, imaginatively, the same status as the impossible."

Myers says that the battle that Jack joined in writing *The Abolition of Man* to counter the bad influence of King and Ketley in *The Control of Language* and the modern devaluation of language in general was carried forward as one of the driving themes of *The Chronicles of Narnia*, especially in *The Silver Chair* and *The Horse and His Boy*. "The language of analysis," she proposes in *C. S. Lewis in Context*, causes "serious weaknesses of character that must be corrected."

Two concrete examples of writing that Jack thought undermine literary value and "the meaning of meaning" were realistic stories about relationships and lines like T. S. Eliot's "a patient etherized upon a table" to describe a sunset in "The Love Song of J. Alfred Prufrock." In a letter, Jack referred to an Arthur C. Clarke science fiction novel as inestimably better than the then-popular realistic novels on relationships, but it was the new realism that critics were embracing and praising while tending to dismiss all science fiction as lowbrow or subliterary.

The Faerie Queene

Myers cites the influence of E. Nesbit's *Five Children and It* as the original source of a wardrobe becoming an entryway for children into another world, and George Sayer cites Roger Green's *The Wood That Time Forgot* as influencing Jack's use of the woods in Narnia. But by far the most closely followed influence throughout *The Chronicles of Narnia*, Myers says, is Spenser's *The Faerie Queene*, one of the two most enduring works (along with *Paradise Lost*) of epic poetry in English literature.

THEY SAID . . .

"The two lobes of our brain, left for the logical and linear and right for the romantic and imaginative, were both thoroughly developed in Lewis, so that he was as strong in fantasy and fiction as he was in analysis and argument. There is always a didactic dimension to his spiritual-life writing…always a visionary dimension to his apologetics."
—J. I. Packer

Though Jack did not plan *The Chronicles of Narnia* as a unit, they are parallel to Spenser's epic in many points. Both Spenser's and Jack's works "are like living a Christian life" in which children in early years know only Christmas and Easter as Christian, then have to decide whether to personally accept Christianity, later developing a sense of community in shared vision of life, and maturing into full participation in the faith, followed by old age and death.

Virtues in The Chronicles of Narnia

Myers sees both *The Faerie Queene* and *The Chronicles of Narnia* as being organized by the six virtues: holiness, temperance, chastity, friendship, justice, and courtesy. ("As might be expected in children's books," she writes, "courage and obedience are emphasized more than chastity.") The six books of *The Faerie Queene*, she says, are organized as three groups representing two virtues each, which she sees paralleled in *The Chronicles of Narnia* with the first group of three books representing holiness and temperance (rejection of greed for money or power), the next two books representing the moral use of language, and the final volumes demonstrating God's providence.

The Seven Deadly Sins in Narnia

Don W. King, Ph.D., professor of English at Montreat College in North Carolina and editor of *Christian Scholar's Review*, has written an article, "Narnia and the Seven Deadly Sins," which asserts that "Lewis apparently emphasized one particular deadly sin in each of the seven *Chronicles of Narnia*." The list of deadly sins propounded by St. Gregory the Great (A.D. 540–605) and widely cited in medieval literature is made up of pride, greed, luxury (lust), envy, gluttony, anger, and sloth. Professor King says "William Langland's *Piers Plowman*, Dante's *Divine Comedy*, Chaucer's "The Parson's Tale," and Spenser's *The Faerie Queene* all devote serious attention to these sins" and that they also appear in Jack's *The Allegory of Love*.

Central Sins

King says that though many sins are treated in *The Chronicles of Narnia*, "it is my contention that [Lewis] may either consciously or subconsciously have emphasized one of the seven deadly sins in each one of the seven Narnian books." In *The Lion, the Witch, and the Wardrobe*, he sees the dominant deadly sin as gluttony, as Edmund Pevensie betrays his siblings to the White Witch Jadis in order to stuff his mouth with the witch's offered Turkish delight, a traditional Christmas treat in England.

In *Prince Caspian, Return to Narnia*, Professor King sees luxury (lust) as the deadly sin that is central to the story line. King Miraz, the Prince's uncle, insatiably lusts after "power, wealth, and position," which undermines the entire kingdom and forces Caspian to struggle to attain his rightful office.

Greed and Sloth

Greed is the central deadly sin in book three, *The Voyage of the Dawn Treader*, where Eustace Clarence Scrubb, "being entirely egocentric and totally selfish, is greedy beyond bounds," which eventually leads him to the den of a dying dragon where he falls in a deep comalike sleep and awakens to find that he himself has been turned into a dragon.

Sloth is the deadliest sin central to *The Silver Chair*, where Jill Poole fails to keep Aslan's commands because of waning enthusiasm. The story, the professor says, is an application of the teaching of Deuteronomy 6:6–8, in which God tells Moses to teach his words "to your sons and talk of them when you sit in your house and when you walk by the way and when you lie down and when you rise up."

THEY SAID . . .

In 1947, a *Time* cover story hailed Lewis as "one of the most influential spokesmen for Christianity in the English-speaking world." Now, fifty-eight years later (and forty-two years after his death, in 1963), he could arguably be called the hottest theologian of 2005.

—David Van Biema, *Time* magazine, November 7, 2005
(HarperSanFrancisco sold 843,000 Lewis books that year)

In *The Horse and His Boy* the deadliest sin, pride, characterizes three central characters—Bree, a talking horse; Aravis, a Calormene princess; and Prince Rabadash, Jack's most extreme example of pride. Eventually, the

Prince is eternally destroyed by letting his pride cause him to reject Aslan's offers of reconciliation.

Anger is the deadliest sin featured in the sixth Narnian tale, *The Magician's Nephew*. Throughout the story Jack interplays the "anger" against the "madness" of Uncle Andrew, who created the magic ring that first transported English mortals into the newly breathed-into-life world of Narnia.

Finally, in *The Last Battle*, envy is the deadly sin that proves the undoing of the ape Shift who covets both Aslan's power and the love he inspires. He tries to foist off a donkey wearing a lion's skin as Aslan, a ploy that works on the most vulnerable Narnians. Shift even manages to shift around the identities of Aslan and the evil god of the Calormen, Tash. All of this treachery eventually utterly destroys Narnia with the last battle being an image of Armageddon followed by the entrance of the saved into "real Narnia," or heaven.

THEY SAID . . .

"Because I lacked the kind of biblical knowledge that comes with a Christian upbringing I had completely missed what was perhaps Lewis's foremost purpose with the fantastic books about the land of Narnia. In spite of that (or perhaps because of) I had loved the books."

—Otto Dandenell, student, University of Uppsala, Sweden

Catholic Views of Narnia

Though evangelical Christians are probably the most enthusiastic supporters of *The Chronicles of Narnia* and its author, and conservatives among Anglicans claim Jack as their own, Roman Catholic authors and apostolates are also strong supporters through a variety of Web sites and books about C. S. Lewis and *The Chronicles of Narnia*. Though biographers feel that J. R. R. Tolkien, the Catholic friend who made great efforts to bring Jack from atheism to theism and to Christianity, was greatly disappointed that Jack never joined the Catholic Church, their friendship continued.

Early Supporters

Two of the earliest and most enthusiastic Catholic supporters of Jack and Narnia were his physician Robert ("Humphrey") Havard and Havard's daughter Mary Clare, to whom Jack dedicated *The Lion, the Witch, and the Wardrobe*. Dr. Havard liked it when he heard it in the Inklings meetings, and his daughter was especially enthusiastic when she read it.

Another early Catholic supporter was Jack's former student at Oxford who eventually became an overseas Catholic missionary, Dom Bede Griffiths. In the article cited earlier from *We Remember C. S. Lewis*, Griffiths says, "To my mind the Narnia stories reveal Lewis's personal religion more profoundly than any of his more theological works. He wrote those other works more from his head, but the Narnia stories came from his heart. He just allowed himself to express his inmost feelings with complete spontaneity. The figure of Aslan in the Narnia stories tells us more of how Lewis understood the nature of God than anything else he wrote. It has all the hidden power and majesty and awesomeness which Lewis associated with God, but also all the glory and the tenderness and even the humor which he believed belonged to him, so that children could run up to him and throw their arms round him and kiss him. There is nothing of 'dark imagination' or fear of devils and hell in this. It is 'mere Christianity.'"

FACT

The film *The Chronicles of Narnia: The Lion, the Witch, and the Wardrobe*, produced by Walden Media and distributed by Walt Disney Pictures, was directed by Andrew Adamson and took in $748 million worldwide. The sequel, *The Chronicles of Narnia: Prince Caspian*, is expected to open on May 16, 2008. Walden Media has rights to produce all seven Narnia novels.

Later Support

The Most Reverend Charles J. Chaput, archbishop of the Catholic diocese of Denver, was among many Catholic supporters of Narnia when the 2005 film was nearing its release. Writing in the Archdiocesan Denver

Catholic Register, October 26, 2005, he said, "One of the greatest Christian apologists of the 20th century, Lewis is remembered for classics like *Mere Christianity, The Abolition of Man, Surprised by Joy, The Screwtape Letters, The Problem of Pain,* and *The Great Divorce.* But maybe his best work was his storytelling for young people.

"In writing his seven-book *Chronicles of Narnia,* Lewis created a fantastic saga of dwarves, witches, trolls and centaurs…Lewis' Great Lion—Aslan— is unmistakably a figure of Jesus Christ. As for Aslan's father, the Emperor Across the Sea: Well, it doesn't take a lot of effort to infer Who that might be.

QUESTION
What did Lewis believe children's stories had to have to make them last?
Adult appeal. "A children's story which is enjoyed only by children is a bad children's story," he wrote in *Of Other Worlds.* "The good ones last."

"Over the years, I've known dozens of people who've gone back to the Narnia tales again and again to enjoy them as adults. Even today, half a century after Lewis published the last of *The Chronicles*, they remain bestsellers. The reason is simple. *The Chronicles* remind us that beauty, truth and goodness really do exist; that what we choose in life matters; that suffering has meaning; that sacrifice for the right things makes a difference; that heaven is real; and that God, our reason for joy and hope, loves us eternally."

Paganism in The Chronicles of Narnia

In an interview by Rob Moll in *Christianity Today*, June 1, 2004, Lewis scholar Colin Duriez says, "In order to write to a post-Christian culture, Lewis used pre-Christian, pagan ideas.

"C. S. Lewis's ideas about returning to paganism before coming to Christian faith still apply today. He recognized that we live in a post-Christian world, and for him that was the most basic category when trying to understand present society. We talk about modernism and now postmodernism, but if Lewis was around I think he'd still be saying that the fact that we're post-Christian is more fundamental.

"Contemporary people have no background at all in Christian faith. They need to be brought to paganism to prepare the way."

Eastern Orthodox film writer Peter Chattaway takes up the paganism theme in a commentary in CanadianChristianity.com. "In all of his writings, Lewis was confronting a modern, skeptical, materialistic view of the world that had no room for the supernatural. Lewis believed that paganism and Christianity had more in common with each other on this point than either had with the modern, secularized world. In the essay 'Is Theism Important?' he wrote:

"When grave persons express their fear that England is relapsing into Paganism, I am tempted to reply, 'Would that she were.' For I do not think it at all likely that we shall ever see Parliament opened by the slaughtering of a garlanded white bull in the House of Lords or Cabinet Ministers leaving sandwiches in Hyde Park as an offering for the Dryads.

"If such a state of affairs came about, then the Christian apologist would have something to work on. For a Pagan, as history shows, is a man eminently convertible to Christianity. He is essentially the pre-Christian, or sub-Christian, religious man. The post-Christian man of our day differs from him as much as a divorcee differs from a virgin.

"In *The Chronicles of Narnia*, Lewis caricatures modernism, and the belief in 'progress' that accompanied it, in his description of the Scrubbs family...[where] he writes that Eustace's parents 'were very up-to-date and advanced people. They were vegetarians, non-smokers and teetotalers and wore a special kind of underclothes.'"

Chapter 11

The Lion, the Witch, and the Wardrobe

A book-by-book survey of *The Chronicles of Narnia* may serve as more than a crash course introduction to the seven volumes. Describing each story in some detail, setting the background of the whole Narnian saga, and placing the stories in the context of Jack's other writings and his philosophy of life should whet the appetites of readers who think themselves too mature or advanced in their thinking for children's fantasies. A word to the wise: those who don't like too much detail about the plots of stories they haven't read may learn more than they want in this and the six chapters that follow.

Recovering Chests

Through a note to his goddaughter Lucy Barfield in the front of *The Lion, the Witch, and the Wardrobe*, Jack addresses all readers who consider themselves too mature for books like these: "some day you will be old enough to start reading fairy tales again." Though he may have had adolescents primarily in mind (children who've grown up enough to think themselves too old for children's stories, as he thought of himself at prep school age), in a larger sense he is addressing all the "men without chests" he described in *The Abolition of Man*, all people whose hearts (spirits) have been quenched through books and teaching that define away meaning and character. One of Jack's main aims in his literary endeavors was to restore chests to those who had lost theirs.

Book Versus Movie

Though there are arguments for not even trying to compare an original book with a film based on it, since the film of *The Lion, the Witch, and the Wardrobe* has been seen by millions of people who have not yet read the book (a safe assumption to make about any popular movie based on any book), it would be a mistake to ignore the movie, especially as the film of the first of *The Chronicles of Narnia* and the work underway on movies of the rest of them have introduced the books and their author to new and larger audiences than ever before.

Movies generally follow the aphorism that a picture is worth a thousand words, although in this case the opposite, that a phrase or clause can be worth a whole scene in a movie or a few words may merit the addition of new characters, would be appropriate as well. A simple reference in the book's first paragraph to the four Pevensie children being evacuated from London "because of the air raids" is expanded in the movie to show Nazi bombers flying over England and parents crowding train station platforms to see their children off to live in the countryside. The Pevensie children's mother developed into a speaking part with admonitions to the older children to look after the younger two.

A passing mention in the book that the house they have been sent to is in the center of the country and ten miles from the nearest train station is enlarged to show the children passing via steam train through lush English farm country, being met at a station by a stern looking woman driving a horse-drawn cart, and arriving at a manor house that could have been next-door-neighbor to another family palace made famous by another English twentieth-century classic book rooted in Oxford: *Brideshead Revisited* by Evelyn Waugh.

FACT

Pevensie, the children's family name, is pronounced in the movie with the stress on the first syllable: "PEV-en-sie." Jack probably got the name from Pevensey Bay, which is on England's south coast near Eastbourne, from which he helped Mrs. Moore move to Bristol after his first year as a student at Oxford (see Chapter 4).

Matron of the House

The most noticeable differences in the movie's early scenes with those in the book involve the household's Mrs. Macready and the Professor, whose house, presumably, it is. Mrs. Macready, the woman with the horse-drawn cart, the lady of the house whose role remains unspecified, much like Mrs. Moore's may have been to the girls who came to stay at The Kilns for the same reasons in the same era, is stern in both book and movie. In the movie she warns the children not to disturb the Professor, but in the book he comes across as glad to welcome them when they arrive and offers to be available any time they need adult counsel. He somewhat resembles Jack, and we learn in a later book in the series that his name is Digory Kirke, which is similar to Jack's tutor, William Kirkpatrick.

The book later on describes the house as a historic one often visited by tourists who want to be shown through it, a service Mrs. Macready provides, and at those times the children are asked to make themselves scarce. (Jack hints that the house's history could lend itself to another series of books, but alas that half-promise was never fulfilled.) The tourism subtext is replaced in the movie by Mrs. Macready's mentioning that the house is full of the

THE EVERYTHING GUIDE TO C. S. LEWIS & NARNIA

Professor's valuable artifacts that they should not disturb. (A nice touch, added in the movie, is that the first such artifact shown is a bust of Dante Alighieri, the Renaissance Italian poet whose writing Jack considered among the best in European history.)

Big Lea?

The book portrays the house in terms familiar to readers of Jack's autobiographical *Surprised by Joy* as describing his parents' custom-built house, Little Lea, where long corridors led into many rooms to be explored. In the book, Peter, the eldest of the four children, exclaims on their good luck at being in such surroundings with such an amenable host as the Professor, but in the movie their early feelings seem more like intimidation by the setting and the rules about living there.

In the book, a game of hide-and-seek leads Lucy into the wardrobe in the spare room and on to Narnia, for her second time and Edmund for his first, but in the movie hide-and-seek is behind the youngest child's first entrance into the closet and Narnia. In the book, Jack repeats—often enough to become comical—that any child knows better than to close the door of a wardrobe from inside it, but the movie leaves viewers wondering whether Lucy will be able to get out when (and if) she returns to the wardrobe from Narnia.

Lucy

After her first visit to Narnia, Lucy finds her siblings understandably suspicious of her reports (especially when to them her absence was no more than a minute). And when she tries to prove that the wardrobe opens into a mysterious woods where it's always winter when their visit at the manor house has begun in summer, she is fooled. All that's in the back of the wardrobe is a solid wall that has hooks like any wardrobe.

Jack leaves the question open as to why the wardrobe is a magic entrance into Narnia in some cases but not others, but it seems that it doesn't work when someone wants it to but does work when someone is trying to hide or escape others who are looking for them.

Lucy's first visit to Narnia begins with seeing a lamppost (which appears to be there just to indicate the way back out of Narnia) and then the faun Tumnus carrying an umbrella and packages that Jack first pictured in 1914. The umbrella keeps off snow (the faun is bare from the waist up, after all), which falls constantly in Narnia where it's always winter but never Christmas. But the purpose of the packages is never revealed.

THEY SAID . . .

"Lucy can be said to symbolize the virtues of humankind, whether manifested as "childhood innocence" or in more mature forms depicted in the later stories. In many instances, especially [when] she follows Aslan even though her siblings are unable to see him and believe Lucy is lying about seeing him, she seems to represent faith."

—Unsigned review in Wikipedia

Jack has fun with his young readers by having Tumnus misunderstand Lucy as being from the city of War Drobe in the land of Spare Oom. He invites her to his cave and makes her tea with several kinds of toasts and cake. After she gets drowsy in front of the raging fire in his cave, he admits he intends to kidnap her (that word is used in the movie but not the book). Not turning her in to the secret police could get him into big trouble, Tumnus explains, but obviously his heart is not in harming Lucy and she has no trouble talking him out of abducting her.

From Lucy's first visit it is apparent that the land beyond the lamppost is inhabited by at least two kinds of creatures: some who serve the evil queen-witch and some who long for her hundred-year reign of winter to end and Aslan to be returned to his rightful place (and, one suspects, also some who waver between those two positions). By returning Lucy to the lamppost so she can find her way back into the wardrobe, Tumnus is risking arrest and being turned into a statue for the queen's palace, but he does it anyway.

Lucy is crushed by her siblings' refusal to believe her report about the wardrobe and Narnia, and they—Peter and Susan, at least—in turn are concerned about Lucy's sudden change in character. She had always been truthful and reliable before they left London, but they fear she may now be showing signs of trauma.

Edmund

Neither the movie nor the book specifies the ages of the children, though Lucy appears to be about eight and the book says Edmund, who tries to act much older, is only a year older. The older siblings Susan and Peter appear to be about fourteen and fifteen respectively.

Lucy is the story's true innocent, ready to forgive even before her adversaries apologize for wronging her. Edmund, perhaps typifying the middle child, is her opposite. After her first report about visiting Narnia he refuses to stop teasing her about it and calling it a lie. But when he secretly follows her there on her second visit, he becomes increasingly treacherous or, to use Jack's word, "spiteful."

When Edmund follows Lucy into the wardrobe and stumbles into Narnia, though she was only a few seconds ahead of him, in Narnian time that was enough for her to make her way all the way to Tumnus's cave before Edmund realized she had been telling the truth and that he, too, is in Narnia. So his calling after her is not heard, though Edmund thinks she's hearing but sulking and refusing to reply.

While he looks around the woods for signs of Lucy, he is approached by a sledge (which in Pauline Baynes's illustration looks like a sleigh) drawn by two Shetland-pony-size reindeer (in the movie there are more than two) driven by a three-foot-tall dwarf for the tallest woman Edmund has ever seen, who claims to be the Queen of Narnia. By plying Edmund with a magically produced steaming hot drink of something he'd never had before and Turkish delight (jelly candies covered with powdered sugar), his favorite treat, she is able to get him to tell her about Lucy's earlier visit to Narnia, her meeting Tumnus, and his older sister and brother who haven't been there yet.

Though Don W. King's description of Edmund's gluttony for Turkish delight being his undoing is on the mark (see Chapter 10), it failed to mention that the Queen's Turkish delight was addictive: "this was enchanted Turkish Delight…anyone who had once tasted it would want more and more of it."

But Edmund's responsibility for his gluttony, despite his addiction, fits the moral code Jack means to impart.

The Queen uses Edmund's Turkish delight habit to cajole him to promise to bring all three of his siblings to see her the next time he comes to Narnia, and not mention to them that he has already met her. As she leaves, Lucy comes out of another part of the woods and finds Edmund, delighted that he has seen proof of Narnia for himself. But when they return out of the wardrobe back into the manor house, Edmund claims to Susan and Peter that he had been pretending with Lucy about her "made-up" land beyond the wardrobe.

> A statement Jack makes in *Mere Christianity* seems to perfectly describe Edmund at this time, "getting nastier every minute": "when a man is getting better, he understands more and more clearly the evil that is still left in him" and "when a man is getting worse, he understands his own badness less and less." See Chapter 9.

Peter and Susan

Lucy's distress over Edmund's setting her up so dismays Peter and Susan that they ask the Professor if he thinks she's gone mad. Just seeing Lucy, he replies, was enough to know she was not mad. And after hearing them out, he asks whether Edmund or Lucy would normally be more trustworthy, to which both reply, "Lucy." Then logically, he tells them, she is probably telling the truth.

FACT

Gene Edward Veith, in his book *The Soul of the Lion, the Witch, and the Wardrobe*, compares two elements of Lewis's novel with overlaps in the Harry Potter novels by J. K. Rowling: Lewis's witch is a villain; Rowling's witches are heroes. Lewis's children escape from public schools; Rowling's children escape to school.

When they press him for how Lucy can be telling the truth when they have seen that the wardrobe is just an ordinary piece of furniture, the Professor tells them, maybe "we might all try minding our own business." Several times during their talk, the Professor mutters, "What are they teaching them in their schools?" This supports Doris T. Myers's contention that one aim of *The Chronicles of Narnia* is counteracting what Jack considered undesirable curriculum changes in England's schools that emphasized realism at the expense of imagination and spirituality.

All into Narnia, at Last

A few days later, to avoid one of Macready's tour groups, all four children slip into the wardrobe and, for the first time, Peter and Susan find themselves in the woods between worlds, and Narnia, with their younger sister and brother. Noticing the cold, and reasoning that technically Narnia is just an extension of the wardrobe, they borrow fur coats from the wardrobe, which, being too large, look more like robes on them. As they begin walking in the woods, Edmund, forgetting himself, mentions that they ought to find and make note of the lamppost as a landmark for getting back to the wardrobe. Knowing now for certain that Edmund had earlier lied and, even worse, accused Lucy of lying about his previous visit to Narnia, Peter is furious with his younger brother, which reinforces Edmund's determination to keep his previous promise to deliver them to the Queen.

Lucy Leads

After apologizing to Lucy for having disbelieved her, Peter and Susan ask her to be their leader in Narnia. She takes them to Tumnus's cave, which they find ransacked and also find a notice of his arrest for treason. Though Susan is inclined to return home, Lucy pleads that Tumnus deserves their help as she was instrumental in his arrest, to which Peter gallantly agrees.

Not knowing where to start, they see a robin seeming to urge them in a certain direction. Lucy intuitively knows they should follow the robin but Edmund has the opposite reaction, asking how they can know it is not going to lead them into danger. The robin leads them to a talking beaver, who takes them to his home where Mrs. Beaver prepares a dinner of fish and potatoes with marmalade roll for desert and tea.

During the dinner and tea, Mr. and Mrs. Beaver tell them about Aslan and the prophecies that when four children of Adam and Eve occupy the thrones in Narnia's original royal castle, Cair Paravel, the witch Queen Jadis will rule Narnia no longer. Peter exclaims that he wants to meet Aslan, which Mr. Beaver assures him he will.

Suddenly they notice that Edmund has disappeared. He has apparently sneaked off to meet with Jadis (the White Witch or "the Queen") and tell them where to find them all. They must flee toward Aslan immediately, Mr. Beaver says, warning that Jadis will anticipate their attempt to reach Aslan at the Stone Table and intercept and destroy them on the way.

Father Christmas and Jadis

A major discrepancy between the film and written versions occurs in their flight toward Aslan. In the movie they race against the thawing of the ice-covered river on which they are running and are being chased, they believe, by the Queen in her sledge. But in the novel they hide in a cave, a beaver hiding place, to rest on their journey, and it was there, after some hours of sleeping, not while on the run, that Father Christmas (a.k.a. Santa Claus), whom they first feared to be Jadis, meets them with good news.

His appearance, after having been kept out of Narnia by the witch for years, is proof that "Aslan is on the move" and the witch-queen's spell is being broken. Jack says that despite the feelings of joy and love that children in our world feel toward Father Christmas, on actually seeing him in Narnia, these children feel "solemn and still," more like religious adoration than familial love.

QUESTION

What is basically similar between _The Lion, the Witch, and the Wardrobe_ and Jack's first space novel, _Out of the Silent Planet_?

Both involve worlds parallel to the Earth that are being challenged by Satan in other forms. Human Earthlings—believers—are used to bring about the salvation of both worlds.

Father Christmas gave Mr. and Mrs. Beaver gifts related to their home life, but he gave the children magic tools to use in the coming battle, telling Susan and Lucy they are not to fight, being girls, but may need their gifts to defend themselves and summon help. And after magically providing a luscious tea service and saluting them with, "Merry Christmas! Long live the true King!" Father Christmas, his reindeer, and sleigh are off.

No More Turkish Delight

Meanwhile, Edmund has told all he knows about Aslan, the Beavers, and his brother and sisters and is being entertained by witch-queen Jadis, who provides dry bread and water to keep his strength up rather than the promised enchanted Turkish delight. She orders her secret service (in the form of wolves) to hurry and kill anyone they find at the Beavers's house and try to intercept the fugitives en route to the Stone Table, telling them they "know what they have to do" if they succeed.

Jadis takes off in fresh snow (which providentially covers the tracks of the Beavers, Peter, Susan, and Lucy) with Edmund seated in the sledge next to her without even a coat against the cold and snow, his shirt soon soaked through to his skin. They come across a family of squirrels, two satyrs, a dwarf, and a dog-fox enjoying what appears to be plum pudding with a sprig of holly and a festive beverage. Jadis demands to know what they are eating, to which the dog-fox says it was given to them. Demanding to know by whom, she is told it was Father Christmas, to which Jadis explodes: "He can't have been here! How dare you!"

When Jadis raises her wand to turn the Christmas partiers to stone, Edmund pleads, "Oh, don't, don't, please don't." But she not only does, she whacks Edmund on the face, telling him that's what happens to people who ask favors for "spies and traitors." "And Edmund," Jack tells his readers, "for the first time in this story felt sorry for someone besides himself." As the sledge begins moving again, Edmund notices that the snow is turning to slush. Not only is Aslan's return bringing a warming trend to Narnia, a similar change is occurring in Edmund's chest.

Aslan

After the snow turns to slush and the slush turns to mud and wet grass, the reindeer are no longer able to pull the sledge. Jadis orders the reindeer returned to her palace and says she and Edmund will continue to the Stone Table on foot, a delay that makes it easy for the Beavers, Peter, Susan, and Lucy to reach the Stone Table and, beyond it, Aslan at his pavilion and feast, well ahead of when Jadis and Edmund do. After they meet Aslan, Peter confesses without prodding that Edmund's betrayal was partly his fault and Lucy pleads with Aslan to do what he can to save Edmund from the witch. Aslan replies, "All shall be done, but it may be harder than you think."

FACT

Early in the story, Tumnus the faun hints that Jadis might be human, but later Mr. Beaver says she is descended from Lilith, a "night creature" (mentioned in the Old Testament, Isaiah 34:14) and descended, on the other side, from "the giants." Aslan, on the other hand, is "the son of the Emperor-over-the-Sea" (an image of God the Father).

While Aslan is telling Peter about the thrones he and his brother and sisters are to occupy in Cair Paravel, the head of Jadis's secret service, the leader of the wolf pack, comes after Susan and chases her up a tree, where she hangs onto a limb for dear life. Susan blows the horn she was given from Father Christmas, which causes Aslan to tell Peter she is calling and in danger. Though Aslan's followers want to run to Susan's rescue, Aslan tells them to let Peter do it, to win "his spurs." Peter reaches the tree just in time to pierce the wolf through the heart with the sword Father Christmas gave him, before the wolf could reach Susan. Aslan makes Peter a knight for his bravery.

Old Magic

Jadis tells the dwarf accompanying her and Edmund that without four human occupants for the thrones at Cair Paravel, the prophecies cannot be fulfilled, and Edmund, the fourth coregent, is in her possession. They discuss dispatching Edmund before they even finish their journey to Aslan, but the Stone Table is the right place to do it, Jadis claims.

Aslan's followers rescue Edmund and the Lion tells Peter, Susan, and Lucy there's no need to discuss his failings; they are past, and Edmund is contrite and taken with Aslan. When Jadis gets near Aslan's pavilion, she requests and Aslan grants her safe passage through his lines to him, where she argues that according to the sacred writing on the Stone Table itself and the "Deep Magic" under which Narnia was created, "You know that every traitor [referring to Edmund] belongs to me as my lawful prey and that for every treachery I have a right to a kill."

Aslan orders the area cleared so he can talk to the witch alone, after which he announces, somberly, that his negotiations have succeeded in getting her to renounce her claim on Edmund's blood. But while Aslan seems troubled, the witch seems gleeful as they part.

Aslan's Sacrifice

That night Lucy and Susan cannot sleep, so they get up to see Aslan leaving the camp, dejected. They run to him and he allows them to ride on him up the hill. He orders them to hide as the witch and her subjects are coming, and they watch as Aslan allows his enemies to muzzle him, bind him, and tie him on the Stone Table. Jadis comes forward to slay him with her enchanted knife, gloating that now she will have both his and Edmund's blood and Narnia will be hers forever.

After the death of Aslan, Jadis and her horde revel for a while but eventually disperse in the deepest hours of the night. Lucy and Susan now creep out to see the lifeless Aslan close up for a last time. They remove his muzzle and try to loosen his bindings but are unable to untie them. As the darkness begins to give way to the first morning rays, the girls notice hundreds of field mice coming and chewing on Aslan's bindings until they have loosed them all.

An Older Law

Exhausted, hungry, and cold as full daylight arrives, the girls are walking around the perimeter of the hilltop to warm up when they hear a loud sound like thunder behind them. Looking back, the Stone Table has broken in two and Aslan's body is gone. When they discuss how and why, they hear a voice—Aslan's voice—coming from behind and they run to meet him, both afraid and joyful to see him alive. He explains that although the witch's knowledge of magic forced him to die, she was ignorant of an even older law of Narnia: "that when a willing victim who had committed no treachery was killed in a traitor's stead, the Table would crack and death itself would start working backward."

After dancing and playing for a while, Aslan carries the girls on his back, virtually flying to the witch's palace, where he breathes life back into all the stone statues Jadis had created through her magic wand, including the faun Tumnus. Thus swelling the ranks of his faithful subjects, they make their way back to the battlefield where Jadis and Peter are engaged in a life and death struggle. But Aslan personally pounces on Jadis, sealing her fate and freeing Narnia from her forever. Once the battle is concluded, Aslan takes the four prophesied daughters and sons of Adam and Eve to Cair Paravel to begin their reign, which lasts for many years of peace and harmony. But one day, while the four coregents are on a hunt in the far-off woods for the White Stag, just after spotting it and beginning chase, they come across a vaguely familiar lamppost that tweaks their curiosity. . . .

Chapter 12

Prince Caspian: The Return to Narnia

One of Jack's most controversial statements, especially among Protestants leaning toward the fundamentalist side, was in reaction to those who feared England was heading back into paganism. To that, all he had to say was, "Good." Paganism, he was convinced, was a stepping stone toward Christianity. Protestants complained that Catholicism had allowed itself to absorb facets of the existing religions (usually pagan) wherever it took root, making it less than pure Christianity. This was clearly visible in Jack's native Ireland, where superstitions and legends carried over from the Druid (pagan) religion before Saint Patrick are still kept alive with much enthusiasm. Narnia, in its second volume, is a world very much like Ireland before and during Saint Patrick's time—a place where magic was believed in and taken seriously.

Pulled Back

The second book of *The Chronicles*, in the sequence that Jack wrote them and they were published, is *Prince Caspian, the Return to Narnia*. Though Jack later wrote to a young correspondent that another order might be more logical (like the Star Wars movies, the novels have "prequels" after some sequels), Walden Media and Walt Disney Pictures are producing them for theatrical release in the original book publishing sequence, perhaps settling that dispute once and for all.

Give or Take a Millennium

Set just an Earth year after the first installment, *Prince Caspian* begins by the "pulling" of the four Pevensie children back to Narnia. They were standing on a railway station platform in a country town, awaiting trains they would transfer to in order to reach their respective boarding schools, Susan and Lucy on one train and Peter and Edmund on another. Though not specified, presumably the war and the Nazi bombing of England have ended, the children are no longer with the Professor at his Manor House, and the magic wardrobe isn't needed to take them back. Instead, feeling themselves being yanked, they all react as startled, grab each others' hands, and in a second they find themselves in what seems at first an unfamiliar "woody place" next to a seaside beach.

After enjoying the sandy beach and exploring a bit, they discover they are on an island separated from the mainland by a narrow strait or river. They find a fresh-water creek that has potable drinking water upstream, where they eat the sandwiches their mother had sent for their trips to school. They find an ancient apple orchard overgrown by weeds and brush alongside the ruins of a large stone edifice. The apples are ripe enough to eat and plentiful, but as the day wears on they get hungry for more substantial food.

Déjà Vu

Exploring the ruins, and especially after Susan finds a gold chess piece of the type they once played with against "fauns and good giants, and the mer-people," Peter realizes and shows the others that this ruin is what once was Cair Paravel. By the looks of the ruined castle, it must be hundreds of years, maybe even a millennium, later in Narnia than when they reigned there, but the well is still in the right location, and the treasure room under the throne room may still be there. The river that once formed a peninsula on which Cair Paravel stood had some time earlier flooded through part of the peninsula, turning it into an island.

FACT

Frank McCourt's biographical novel, *Angela's Ashes*, describes an Ireland, still a generation later than Jack's time, where ruined castles and other historic sites were open for anyone, including children and adolescents like Frank and his brother Malachy, to play in. Though the McCourts's castles were in and around Limerick, there were also some in the Lewis boys' Belfast area.

In this, too, Narnia resembles Ireland, where the ruins of castles dating from Norman times and earlier, stone monasteries and abbeys dating from the early centuries of Irish Christianity, and even prehistoric Druidic mounds and dolmens (resembling Aslan's Stone Table) dot the landscape from one coast to the other.

As the children recall more bits and pieces from their decades as kings and queens in Narnia, they even remember when they planted the apple orchard. And Lucy remembers that if this is Cair Paravel, there should be a door at the end of the dais, leading into the treasure room. Sure enough, when they dig through the ivy growing over it, there's a wooden door, which, though still locked, easily gave way when attacked. And, sure enough, the underground room was full of jewels, armor, and even the gifts Father Christmas had given Susan (her bow and arrows were there, though her enchanted horn was missing), Lucy, and Peter as recorded in *The Lion, the Witch, and the Wardrobe*. They agreed that they had to claim these again immediately. The horn, Susan eventually remembered, had been with them when they had been hunting the White Stag and, encountering the lamppost, had returned to their childhood and England, leaving the horn behind.

Trumpkin's Tale

After building a campfire, the children slept on the ground that had once been the floor of the great hall of Cair Paravel. Next morning, while looking for a way to get to the mainland, they saw a couple of soldiers in a boat in the river separating them from the mainland about to throw overboard something in a bundle that seemed to be alive and struggling for its life. Susan shot arrows at the soldiers, hitting and knocking one overboard and causing the other to jump off the boat and run, as did the one who fell off the boat, for land and find hiding places in the woods. Peter and Susan, the better swimmers of the four, quickly swam to recover the boat and its still-struggling bundle, which turned out to contain a Dwarf.

Haunted Woods

Before even introducing himself, the Dwarf exclaims that "whatever they say, you don't *feel* like ghosts." When the children ask him to explain, he replies that everyone is told that the woods at this end of Narnia are haunted by ghosts, so most "new Narnians" avoid this area. This explains why the soldiers ran away, Susan and Edmund surmise. Told that all they can offer for breakfast is apples, the Dwarf points out that there is fishing tackle in the boat, which they row out to open water to find "an excellent catch of pavenders," a rainbow-colored fish the children remembered eating when they lived at Cair Paravel.

After breakfast, Peter asks the Dwarf to tell them his story first, and the next four chapters of *Prince Caspian* is the background of the prince. The boy Caspian, or Caspian the Tenth, the King of Narnia, is being cheated out of his birthright by his uncle, Miraz, who came into power when Caspian's father, Caspian the Ninth, died when Caspian was in his infancy. First calling himself the rightful heir's "protector," Miraz had subsequently consolidated his power. Now that he and his wife have an infant son of their own, they plot to get rid of Caspian.

Caspian's dearest friend after his parents' deaths was his nurse (reminiscent of Jack's beloved childhood nurse, Lizzie Endicott), who told him stories of Old Narnia, including the White Witch's defeat by High King Peter and his siblings, and of talking beasts (which are no longer found in "new

Narnia"), led by Aslan. But the lad made the mistake of mentioning Old Narnia to his uncle Miraz, who flew into a rage, denied that there was any truth in these tales, and sent Caspian's nurse away without even allowing goodbyes.

Doctor Cornelius

Soon Miraz replaced the nurse with a tutor, Doctor Cornelius, whom Caspian expected to loathe but found instead the tutor to be "the sort of person it is almost impossible not to like." And after learning in history lessons of Caspian's fascination with Old Narnia, Doctor Cornelius also confides in the boy that the Old Narnian tales are true and that Caspian's own ancestors, of the human race of Telmarines, have ruled Narnia for only nine generations. The tutor also is the one who plots Caspian's escape from Miraz's palace. A "half-Dwarf," Cornelius also is an astronomer and a magician.

Explaining that the birth of a boy heir to Miraz and his Queen Prunaprismia almost certainly means Miraz will plot to kill Caspian, the rightful heir to the throne, Cornelius awakens him in the middle of the night and supplies him enough food and drink to get at least as far as the dreaded woods at the east of the kingdom and

"Once you're out of Narnia, you have no idea how Narnian time is going. Why shouldn't hundreds of years have gone past in Narnia while only one year [has] in England?…And now we're going back to Narnia just as if we were…Ancient Britons or someone coming back to modern England."

to try to reach the southern border into the kingdom of Archenland. After dropping on one knee and kissing Caspian's hand to impress upon him the reality of his royal birthright, as a parting gift Cornelius puts in Caspian's hands the horn of Susan, one of the queens of Old Narnia, which she left behind at the hunt for the White Stag at the end of Narnia's golden age. The horn is believed to have power to summon the aid of High King Peter and possibly that of Aslan himself.

Caspian's Flight

Escaping on his trusty horse Destrier as fireworks were going off over the castle to hail the birth of a new heir to the Narnian throne, Caspian rode through the night to the woods and on, all night and all the next day, until in the thick woods of the southern hill country he and his horse were overtaken by a lightning storm. Dodging limbs on the galloping spooked horse, Caspian was eventually caught on the forehead by one of the limbs, which knocked him off his horse and out of consciousness.

FACT

Two major elements of *Prince Caspian* are imitated in books Jack wrote for adults. Doctor Cornelius, Caspian's tutor, is like the tutor of Psyche, the princess in *Till We Have Faces*. And the return of the kings from Narnia's Golden Age to save it is like the return of Merlin the Magician to modern England in *That Hideous Strength*.

When he regains consciousness, Caspian hears the voices of three "rescuers" arguing over whether to kill him or help him regain his health. One of the voices belongs to the badger Trufflehunter, the strongest advocate for letting Caspian live. In the opposite corner is Nikabrik, a Dwarf whose attitude is that no human beings should be allowed to live. In the middle is Trumpkin, the moderate, also a Dwarf. Trumpkin, as it turns out, is the narrator of the story of Caspian being told to Peter, Susan, Edmund, and Lucy.

To Nikabrik's protest that if released Caspian will betray all the Old Narnians to the Telmarines, Trumpkin argues that "it isn't the creature's fault that it bashed its head against a tree outside our hole. And I don't think it looks like a traitor."

Aslan's How

After persuading his rescuers (except the intractable Nikabrik) that he was the legitimate heir to his father's throne, Caspian was taken by Trufflehunter and Trumpkin on a tour of the Old Narnians. Jack obviously enjoyed describing the talking beasts, which include bulgy bears obsessed with sleeping and eating; centaurs, led by Glenstorm, who is a prophet and a star gazer; a squirrel, Pattertwig, who, like all squirrels chatters (but in human language) constantly; and a mouse, Reepicheep, who is fearless and one of the most widely loved creatures in *The Chronicles of Narnia*.

Also brought to meet the new king of the Old Narnians are talking hares, hedgehogs, Black Dwarfs (in addition to the Red Dwarfs like Trumpkin and Nikabrik), owls, ravens, satyrs, and a giant, Wimbleweather. Nikabrik accuses Caspian of having hunted beasts, which Caspian admits, but the talking beasts come to his defense, saying the smaller, dumb beasts of the New Narnia are in a different category from those who populated Aslan's Narnia.

THEY SAID . . .

Some reviewers consider apostasy (falling from faith) a major subtheme of *Prince Caspian*. They compare Miraz's claim to Narnia's throne to the antichrist's claims to lead the church, prophesied by Jesus. Though Aslan's How was built as a temple to faith in him, all but a few, like Doctor Cornelius, have forgotten it and most doubt the existence of Aslan.

The talking beasts welcome Caspian readily, pledging their fealty, and Glenstorm asks when they will launch their attack on Miraz. Caspian had been thinking he might just live in hiding among the Old Narnians in the "haunted" forests, but his new counselors, especially the centaur who has seen signs in the heavens presaging Caspian's ascendancy to the throne and the restoration of Old Narnia, persuade him that pushing his claims is the best course for all concerned. A feast to celebrate Caspian's arrival in their world is recast by adding a war council to it.

Doctor Cornelius Arrives

One of the hares in their group, Camillo, announces that he senses a human intruder may be coming near, and a scouting party led by Trufflehunter, another badger, and three Dwarfs quickly apprehends Doctor Cornelius. Caspian's beloved tutor reports that the return of the prince's horse, Destrier, to Miraz's palace alerted the pretender-king that Caspian had taken flight. On learning this, Cornelius set out to find Caspian ahead of Miraz's search party and to warn him that Miraz's army was sure to find him, intent on destroying him.

After some discussion, the Old Narnians, led by Caspian and following Cornelius's counsel to fly from the Dancing Lawn immediately, where the enemies could easily surround them, head farther into the Great Forest to Aslan's How. Aslan's How, Cornelius tells them, is a huge mound deep in the Great Forest, built over a place that once had a magical stone (which may still be in the center of the How), honeycombed by tunnels that can serve as a perfect Old Narnian headquarters.

But Miraz's forces are not far behind, and seeing them from a distance disheartens Caspian and his followers, seeing that the enemies are so numerous and well equipped. Caspian plans a surprise attack at dawn, centered on the strength of their giant, Wimbleweather, but they fail to take into account the lack of cleverness typical of giants, resulting in the attack causing casualties on their side and putting them in an even more unfavorable position against the New Narnians.

Back at the How, plotting their next strategy later that day, Trufflehunter proposes that if there's ever a time to use the Horn, "the time has now come." Caspian's other counselors concur, so they plan to send emissaries to Lantern Waste and the former site of Cair Paravel, assuming that whoever responds to the sound of the Horn will arrive at either one of those historic sites or Aslan's How itself. Pattertwig the Squirrel is dispatched to the farther site, Lantern Waste, and Trumpkin, though a disbeliever in magic in general and the Horn in particular, volunteers to go to Cair Paravel.

Aslan on the Move

So it was that Trumpkin met Peter, Susan, Edmund, and Lucy near Cair Paravel the morning after their arrival. After telling the children his story, he says he will start back to Aslan's How to let them know no one came in response to the blowing of the Horn. "But we've come," Lucy objects, to which Trumpkin, always the skeptic, replies (in so many words), "no offense, dear little friends, but I don't think they were expecting little kids." Edmund jumps up to take issue, "*Little* from you is a bit too much!"

So Peter proposes that Trumpkin let Edmund spar against him with swords. In the duel, Edmund knows a trick Trumpkin doesn't and bests him. Next, Susan challenges him to an archery contest and she, even more than Edmund, proves greater skill than Trumpkin.

Little Things Matter

Finally persuaded that someone did answer the Horn's summons, Trumpkin agrees to accompany the former kings and queens of Narnia to Aslan's How, which they remember and know the way to from their many years of reigning there. "Need we go by the same way that Our Dear Little Friend came?" Edmund jibes Trumpkin, using his words back to him. Trumpkin responds that there will be no more talk of "little…if you love me." To which Edmund rejoins, "May I say our D.L.F.?" Susan attempts to stop Edmund but Trumpkin says it's alright, after which the children called him D.L.F. "till they'd almost forgotten what it meant."

The party tries to make their way to Aslan's How mostly by boat but find that the river has changed so much it is no longer navigable for far inland. So they take through the woods, looking for the best way to find a crossing over the river and the cliffs on the other side, soon reaching an impassible point. While they argue which way to go, Lucy glimpses Aslan through the trees, seeming to direct her in the way opposite Peter and Trumpkin wanted to take. But no one else sees Aslan and thinks Lucy imagined it. Putting her proposed route to a vote, only Edmund, saying he owes her from having not believed her original stories about finding Narnia through the wardrobe, sides with her. After hiking most of another day they encounter enemies firing arrows at them and must retreat the way they came. Peter later acknowledges Lucy as a hero for not saying "told you so."

That night Lucy awakes, thinking she has heard the voice she loves best in the whole world, and sees the trees begin to come to life and dance around and Aslan summoning her. He asks her why she didn't obey what she knew to be his will earlier to which she first protests but realizes she could, and should, have done despite her fear of leaving Peter and the others. Then she asks the Lion if it would have come out alright if she had followed him without the others. He replies, "To know what *would* have happened, child? No. Nobody is ever told that." But anyone can know what will happen, he says, by taking action, and he directs her to rouse the others from their sleep and tell them to follow her, as she follows him, immediately. And this time it doesn't matter whether the others believe her or not.

FACT

Lucy's faith, and Aslan's testing of her faith, during their odyssey has been cited by many students of *The Chronicles of Narnia* as the major theme of *Prince Caspian*. Jesus taught in the Sermon on the Mount that following him would cost disciples friendships and family members. Aslan tells Lucy she must risk the same loss to follow him.

Mission Accomplished

The lesson in faith that Aslan was teaching Lucy would apply to all in their party and the larger assembly at Aslan's How during the coming days. The others finally agree to follow her in the middle of the night just because they can't let her go on alone, but when she follows Aslan onto a switchback path down the face of a bluff above the river, they all fear she will fall into the gorge. But step by step they realize the path is both real and safe, and therefore someone must be leading Lucy because, from the top, she could have seen it only if someone who knew the path led her to it.

By the time they reach the bottom of the gorge and Aslan bends to drink from the rushing water, Edmund begins to see him. Peter also gets a glimpse before he bounds on to the other side and starts back up. By reaching the top, Susan, too, begins to see him and apologizes to Lucy. Within sight of the How, Aslan turns and speaks to them all, breathing on Susan to allay her fears and "almost" roaring at Trumpkin, who had never seen or believed in lions before. He picked him up in his jaws like a cat with a kitten and threw him up in the air, catching him in his "huge velveted paws."

Dancing Without, Enemies Within

Sending the boys and Trumpkin into the How to deal with whatever needed tending there, as dawn broke outside Aslan sang the woods to life and let the tree people dance. Meanwhile, inside the How troop morale is being tested as Nikabrik complains that "the Dwarfs bore the brunt of the attack and one in five of them fell" when Miraz's army struck.

Nikabrik also echoes Trumpkin's lament, but more bitterly, that "no one came" in response to the summons of Susan's Horn and suggests that Aslan is dead. He has invited two personal guests into the How, who introduce themselves as a hag (a female demon) and a wer-wolf, and Nikabrik invokes the White Witch of old as a source of power superior to Aslan's. As the wer-wolf started to change form into a beast and violence broke out between Nikabrik and his guests and those loyal to Caspian, High King Peter, Edmund, and Trumpkin came in, the head of the hag was slashed off her shoulders by Trumpkin's sword, and the light was knocked over, plunging the room into darkness. When lights were lit again, the hag, the wer-wolf, and Nikabrik all lay dead.

Once the enemies within had been taken care of, facing those encamped outside the woods was made easier, doubly so with the support of the kings from the past and with Aslan nearby. Thinking that Aslan's style was to leave the details for his followers to work out themselves, Peter, seeing the Old Narnians outnumbered, decided to challenge Miraz to a one-on-one swordfight.

Treachery

Miraz's top lieutenants, Lords Glozelle and Sopespian, considered their king a usurper and plotted to use reverse psychology to goad him into accepting Peter's challenge so that at the right instant they could dispatch Miraz and advance their own ambitions. After the swordfight went back and forth with hits on both side and both fighters reeling, Miraz tripped face first. Peter helped him back to his feet, but Glozelle and Sopespian seized the moment to stab their king in the back while yelling "Treachery! Treachery!" and that the Narnians had done it, causing the entire Telmarine army to rise and start attacking.

But at that moment, Aslan mobilized the tree people, having them plunge "through the ranks of Peter's army, and then on, in pursuit of the Telmarines." The Telmarines considered the sight apocalyptic, the end of the world, and took flight only to be confronted by an even more frightening specter, the appearance of Aslan himself, whom most of them had always believed was just a myth.

Celebrations and Restorations

After the enemy was routed, the celebration began in earnest but was soon interrupted by eleven mice carrying a twelfth, Reepicheep, on a litter, barely still breathing. Seeing his many wounds, Aslan said, "Now, Lucy." She tended each of his wounds with a drop from her diamond bottle, restoring him to health, except his tail, which was still missing. When he noticed it and apologized for looking so out of countenance, Aslan smiled and said "it becomes you very well, Small One."

Arguing that his tail was his honor and glory, Aslan asked "whether you do not think too much about your honor." And when the other mice thought Reepicheep might not be going to get his tail restored, they all drew their swords to cut off their own, in solidarity. To this, Aslan relented and said, "Not for the sake of your dignity, Reepicheep, but for the love that is between you and your people, and still more for the kindness your people showed me long ago when you ate away the cords that bound me on the Stone Table (and it was then, though you have long forgotten it, that you began to be *Talking Mice*), you shall have your tail again."

Caspian was knighted and crowned by Aslan as king of Narnia and of all the talking beasts. Then he offered the imprisoned Telmarines a way out of Narnia, back to their own country, which, he said, was originally an island on Earth. For this he ordered a doorway built at the end of the glade and invited those who wanted to return to earth to pass through it.

Having been told that Peter and Susan were now too old to return to Narnia again, Peter suddenly declared that it was time for the four English school children to leave as well. And after gathering up the things they needed to continue their train ride to their schools, they did.

Chapter 13

The Voyage of the Dawn Treader

Jack is well known for protesting that, other than *The Pilgrim's Regress*, his novels are not primarily allegorical in the classical sense that everything in them points to something beyond its surface fictional meaning. But some say *The Voyage of the Dawn Treader* can be called a loose allegory for the journey Christians make through the "islands" of life. The "dawn" can be likened to the beginning of a new life, a biblical metaphor for coming into faith in God. Every Christian is on a pilgrimage, a voyage, treading the path to salvation by walking with and following Jesus against temptations and pitfalls. It also entails getting up when stumbling and being humbled when elevated. "Dawn treader" is an analogy for the progressing pilgrim.

Eustace Clarence Scrubb

One of the most memorable and humorous lines in *The Chronicles of Narnia* is the opening sentence of *The Voyage of the Dawn Treader*: "There was a boy called Eustace Clarence Scrubb, and he almost deserved it." At home he was referred to as Eustace Clarence and at school as Scrubb, Jack says, but among friends he wasn't referred to at all, because he had no friends. Though some reviewers refer to the Scrubb family as prudish ("they were vegetarians, nonsmokers, and teetotalers"), in the context of Jack's quest to counter the trends in contemporary education and literature, the point is more that they are moderns who follow whatever is in vogue. For example, the boy calls his parents Harold and Alberta rather than Mom and Dad.

Nonkissing Cousins

Eustace, as the book calls him after the first couple of pages, had never read any of the "proper" books about adventures, magic, good and bad, and right and wrong, as his cousins the Pevensies had. He preferred reading about current events, politics, legal rights, statistics, and botany.

Though Eustace didn't much like Lucy and Edmund and they didn't feel much in common with him, they were forced to spend the summer with the Scrubbs because their father was lecturing in America. Their mother and Susan had accompanied their father because mother "hadn't had a real holiday for ten years" and Susan "would get far more out of the trip" than Edmund and Lucy. And Peter was being coached for an important examination by Professor Kirke (whose house they lived in during the first book in *The Chronicles of Narnia*).

Eustace had heard his cousins talk of their earlier adventures in Narnia but considered the talk made-up stories not worth any attention. Totally self-centered, he didn't like anything that didn't revolve around him. When Edmund and Lucy admired a painting of a ship hidden in a back room of the Scrubbs home—for the time being, Lucy's room—because Alberta didn't like it but couldn't get rid of it because it had been a wedding gift, Eustace called it "a rotten picture." But it reminded Lucy and Edmund of their seafaring days in Narnia and it made them nostalgic for their old times.

Shipped Out

While Eustace was describing the picture as looking like the ship was coming directly at him, the picture seemed to come to life, the ship appearing to come off the wall, and an instant later the three children found themselves on the deck of that ship, bound for somewhere southeast of the Narnian mainland.

King Caspian, now in the fourth year of his reign, is taking the specially built small vessel to visit the Narnian islands and explore the sea and islands beyond those previously mapped. His specific mission is to find the seven lords who had been banished by his uncle Miraz in his childhood for their loyalty to his father, a promise he made to Aslan in *Prince Caspian*. He was also somewhat curious about finding out more about the mysterious ocean from across which Aslan is said to come.

Edmund and Lucy are delighted to have been invited to join Caspian and his crew, but Eustace, true to character, threatens to sue for being kidnapped and, after being taken to sea against his wishes, for being mistreated in just about every experience he encounters from seasickness to having to sleep in a bunk.

THEY SAID . . .

"The Voyage of the Dawn Treader continues the theme of just rulership established in *Prince Caspian,* with especial emphasis on moderation… in the handling of money and power. The first major episode…contrasts the bureaucratic justice of our modern world with the justice of the king under the law."

—Doris T. Myers, *C. S. Lewis in Context*

Among other inconveniences befalling Eustace is having to make the acquaintance of Reepicheep, the beloved talking mouse and the only Narnian other than Caspian that Edmund and Lucy know from their previous visit. The book's description of the small ship and its crew and their tasks, the use of nautical terms, the effects of varied weather conditions at sea, and other details seem worthy of the best children's books about adventures at sea, like Robert Louis Stevenson's *Treasure Island* and Daniel Defoe's *Robinson Crusoe*.

The first island they encounter is a small one not far off the Narnian coast, which Lucy and Edmund remember as being uninhabited and used primarily to graze livestock. The day is so beautiful and the green grass, blue sky, and white clouds are so inviting that Lucy proposes they have the ship's captain drop herself, Edmund, Eustace, Caspian, and Reepicheep off to walk across it and be picked up on the other side.

But after they pass the hilltop in the center of the little island they encounter pirates in the valley below who take the four youngsters and the talking mouse captive, making it clear they plan to sell them into slavery. Though Caspian is the king of this island and several larger ones beyond it, he does not want the pirates to know his identity, assuming that knowledge would not work in his favor.

Sold and Bought

When they arrive on the pirates' vessel at the small town, Narrowhaven, on the next island over, where the illegal slave trade is thriving, an older man sees their captor and his prey and offers on the spot to buy Caspian. Once his buyer and Caspian are out of the pirates' hearing, the buyer says he bought Caspian not to work him but because he thought he looked familiar. After a few questions and answers back and forth, Caspian discovers that this is Lord Bern, one of the seven men he had set sail to find.

With Lord Bern's support, Caspian takes charge, exercising his prerogatives as king. He visits the island's governor and, seeing that his administration is an inhumane bureaucratic mess, declares the post of governor dissolved and installs Lord Bern in charge of the island as its new and first duke. The King and Lord Bern assert power over the local establishment and use that power to end the slave trade and free the pirates' other quarries.

Eustace and the Dragon

After restoring order on the Lone Islands, as Narnia's nearby territories are known, and approximately three weeks after their arrival there, all the passengers of the *Dawn Treader* resume their voyage east. After some days of smooth sailing, they encounter a fierce storm that lasts so long that when it breaks Eustace writes in his diary, "the first day for ages when I have been able to write." After the storm there are many more days before they finally spot land, an island with severe canyons, waterfalls, and a steep high mountain in its center.

Once they land and start exploring for new provisions of game and possible vegetation, Eustace, wanting to escape productive work, sneaks off by himself. He climbs so high up the mountain that he gets to the clouds or fog near its top, falls asleep for an undetermined time, and after awakening starts down but isn't sure of his way because the fog is so thick.

He gets to a beach inlet that's not familiar and is horrified to discover a large creature emerging from a cave (but not having read any of the right books, Eustace doesn't know it is a dragon). But after a few minutes he realizes the smoke-exhaling winged serpent is feeble and, literally, on its last legs. After it dies and Eustace gathers up enough courage to ascertain it is now incapable of harming him, a rainstorm quickly blows in. Eustace retreats into the dragon's cave where he finds a huge mound of treasure, including a jewel-encrusted bracelet that he slides over his arm to his bicep. He plots things he could do with all this treasure, but as the rain shows no sign of abating, he eventually falls asleep, this time atop his mound of gold and jewels.

A New Nature

When he awakes this time, Eustace discovers that his true nature— beastly as it was—has emerged and he himself has turned into a dragon. "Sleeping on a dragon's hoard with greedy, dragonish thoughts in his heart, he had become a dragon himself," Jack puts it. Meanwhile, the others have been looking for him without success, and gradually Eustace the dragon begins to examine his behavior toward the others and, for the first time ever, he feels loneliness and regret.

After realizing he can fly, Eustace flies over the others and tries to communicate with them. Some of the others realize this dragon seems to pose no danger and start asking him questions he can answer through shaking his head, and so they learn the truth. Eustace also tries to write in the sand, with little success. One day the dragon flies away to be by himself, and when he returns he is Eustace the boy again, but, in Jack's words, "a different boy. He had relapses. There were still many days when he could be very tiresome. But most of those I shall not notice. The cure had begun."

FACT

Bill Blockston interprets Eustace's reformation in a study guide: "We [also] find that our efforts are in vain…We become dismayed that the scales have grown back, and realize we are doomed to a cycle of trying harder, then failing. That's why Someone else has to do the job for us."

Eustace explains that while he was away he felt that he might be going to shed his skin. But after he had torn a layer off, a new set of scales grew back almost immediately. He repeated the operation over and over again. But eventually Aslan appeared and offered to take off his skin once and for all. It would be painful, the Lion said, but it would be the only way he could see lasting change. Eustace yielded to Aslan's cure.

Relapses at Deathwater

The next leg of the voyage took the *Dawn Treader* through another rainstorm that ended at the same time Lucy spotted a sea serpent much larger than their ship coming toward them. Arrows shot at it bounced off and the huge snake wrapped itself over the *Dawn Treader*'s deck and under its hull, poised to constrict it into splinters.

The moment gave Eustace his first ever instance of bravery, as he tried to cut the snake with a sword borrowed from Caspian (but the sword, not the snake, was destroyed in the effort). Reepicheep discovered the only solution that saved the ship: using the entire strength of all aboard, they pushed the snake's body away from its intended prey, a metaphor for the need of people to work in a body to defeat their spiritual adversaries.

Alchemy

Four more days' sailing took the vessel to another island where they had to wait out another gale at anchor in the harbor before coming ashore to replenish their water supply. When they were finally able to climb upstream to a river's source for fresh water, they discovered long-lost relics of some-one from Narnia who had visited that spot (among rusty pieces of a sword, mail, and armor were Narnian coins) and who, it appeared, had perished there. Another of the seven lords, Edmund and Caspian deduced.

THEY SAID . . .

"Deathwater Island was a small, rugged island...covered by coarse grass and heather. Two streams met the ocean, one coming from a deep moun-tain pool. [T]his pool seems to have the ability to turn things to gold. This is where the Lord Restimar met his end after being turned to gold."

—Lands of Narnia Web site

Walking upstream to a small lake, they discovered what appeared to be a perfect statue of a man made of pure gold standing in the clear water of the lakeshore. But when Edmund put his spear in the water to see if he could reach the statue, he discovered that the spear immediately became so heavy he could hardly hold it. The submerged part of it, like the statue, had turned into pure gold.

Temptation

The mountain lake or pool was the fulfillment of centuries of alche-mists' dreams, a chemical bath capable of turning things into gold. But this worked not only with inferior metals like lead, which alchemists sought to convert, but anything put into this bath turned into gold. What was standing in the pool was not a statue but the actual body of one of the missing lords, Lord Restimar, turned into solid gold.

Eustace had learned his lesson about greed, but this time it was Edmund and Caspian who were tempted. "'The King who owned this island,' said

Caspian slowly…'would soon be the richest of all Kings of the world.'" And so saying he claimed the land and the lake for Narnia, naming it Goldwater Island, binding all the others to secrecy about it.

To this, Edmund replied, "Who are you talking to? I'm no subject of yours." And with this Caspian reached for his sword, but Lucy interrupted, "Stop it, both of you." And at that moment she gave a start, a jerking reaction to something she'd seen, and caused everyone to look at it too. It was the largest lion human eyes had ever seen. "They knew it was Aslan."

After a few minutes of silence, Caspian confessed that he had been making an ass of himself, and Reepicheep suggested that instead of Goldwater Island they name it Deathwater. And thus it was and ever since remains. And so leaving their discovery behind, they pulled anchor to continue toward the East.

Lucy Gets Greedy

Their next stop was an island that was as well manicured as a formal palace garden, and though no living creature met them as they walked up the tree-lined lane from their landing, that lane did lead to such a mansion. Lucy, lagging behind the others, hears a thumping sound that seemed to be getting closer, so she hides behind a tree to see what was coming. She never saw it, but as the thumping sounded like it was just in front of her, she heard voices plotting to attack the occupants of their ship, which the unseen "thumpers" see anchored in their harbor.

After they apparently pass on, Lucy warns the others of what she heard, and after much delicate negotiation they confront the invisible creatures. The thumpers report that they are caretakers of the estate, the owner of which—a powerful magician—had cast a spell that "uglified" them. And to get even, they had induced a young girl who had previously visited the mansion to use a spell recorded in the magician's book to make them invisible. But now that another little girl, Lucy, is in their midst, they want her to reverse the spells to make them visible and restore their good looks.

The invisible beings are known as Duffers, and they report not having seen the magician for some time. He may be gone or just invisible. They are too afraid to go above the first floor of the mansion and, as only a little girl can work the magic spells, they persuade and coerce Lucy to agree to go upstairs to the room housing the book of spells and reverse their invisibility and their uglification.

Spellbound

Lucy finds the book of spells, in a word, spellbinding. The pictures accompanying various spells seem to come alive and show the effects of the spells. She is especially tempted by one page that promises to turn any woman using it beautiful "beyond the lot of mortals." The pictures accompanying that spell include one of Lucy, and another shows Lucy and her sister Susan back in England but the always-more-attractive Susan now looks plain next to the surpassingly beautiful Lucy.

> ## THEY SAID . . .
> The Slip-Up Archive points out that in the first of three chapters about the invisible creatures their leader tells the Narnians that as they are invisible so are their weapons. But the second sentence of the next chapter reads, "It was very funny to see the plates and dishes coming to the table and nothing carrying them."

Though Lucy has been resisting the urge to say other spells she found tempting, she doesn't hesitate to say about this one, "I *will* say the spell." But when she looks at the opening words of the spell to start reading, in front of them she sees the "face of a lion, of The Lion, Aslan himself, staring into hers." She had seen the "growling" expression on Aslan's face before and, becoming "horribly afraid," she immediately turned the page.

Another page allows her to see a couple of girls, one of whom she had considered a best friend, discussing Lucy and hearing that friend berate her. Finally, she sees the page with a spell promising to make visible again things that have been made invisible. When she reads it, the first thing she sees, not in a picture but in life this time, is Aslan. He explains that he appeared because of the spell she read, because he would not disobey his own rules.

In other words, he is always with her, usually invisible, but when his "magic formula" is invoked, even he, its owner, will appear.

Aslan in Charge

Aslan tells Lucy that she erred in listening in on her friend's conversation and assures Lucy that the friend does in fact love her but had been too "cowed" to stand up for her in the face of the other girl's putdowns. And again he reminded Lucy that it is never the privilege of anyone to know how things would have turned out if some other course had been followed. Aslan introduces her to the magician, Coriakin, a wizard (reminiscent of Merlin as presented in Jack's *That Hideous Strength*) who is a friend of Aslan and who had been rendered invisible by the Duffers' interference and made to reappear when Lucy used the visibility spell.

Aslan's Protection

After convincing the Duffers that they look better as monopods than they previously did as dwarfs, and that their single huge feet are more fun because they enable them to spring almost as on pogo sticks for long distances and to use them (bottoms up) on hot, sunny days to shade them and as pontoons enabling them to skim over bodies of water, they decide not to change back. And the voyagers go back on the ocean and resume traveling east.

Dark Island

Their next great adventure was encountering a large black mist hanging over an island so dark and thick that they never did see the land, but just before their ship struck it they heard a voice calling for help. They pulled aboard a man who turned out to be one of the seven missing lords and who told them the island was the place where all dreams were made to come true.

When some of the sailors call out "hurrah, what I've always wanted," he assures them these are not daydreams but their real, sleeping dreams, where every nightmare becomes reality. Seeing the man's inconsolable fear, they begin trying to get away. And when it seems they're making no progress, Lucy says what appears to be the first actual prayer, or invocation of Aslan's help recorded in *The Chronicles of Narnia*. Aslan appears to her to assure her he will help, but they still have to work as hard as everyone aboard can to row the *Dawn Treader* back out of the black vortex and into light.

FACT

As *Prince Caspian* shares themes and ideas also used in *Until We Have Faces* and *That Hideous Strength*, *The Voyage of the Dawn Treader* shares elements of Jack's adult allegory, *The Pilgrim's Regress* (islands representing tests and crises) and his novel *The Great Divorce* (getting a preview of heaven).

After Aslan's assurance, the voyagers find the blackness of the dark mist turning gray, and shortly after the *Dawn Treader* shoots out into full daylight under blue skies. The Lord Rhoop, whom they had rescued, asks them never to ask him about the terrors he'd seen in the Dark Island. Seeing the effects they'd had on him, none of them are tempted to do so.

Going Toward the Light

Throughout all the final two great adventures while traveling toward Aslan's country, the light becomes brighter, the sun bigger and bigger, and everything appears easier to see at greater distances. Yet the light, even looking toward the sun itself, doesn't seem to hurt the voyagers' eyes. As they sail on southeasterly, the water becomes calmer and the temperatures warmer, and the night skies are filled with never-before-seen constellations.

On the last island they visit, they find a mysterious edifice, which by Jack's description (but without using the name) sounds reminiscent of Stonehenge: "a wide oblong space flagged with smooth stones and surrounded by grey pillars but unroofed." Inside they find a banquet table and chairs with a meal laid out "as had never been seen" even in High King Peter's reign at Cair Paravel.

QUESTION

Why does Aslan (or his author, Jack) put an age limit on visitors to Narnia from Earth?

A commercial answer might be because he wanted to appeal to children as his main audience. But the plausible logical reason is that only innocents—children below the age of accountability—are allowed in, lest adult visitors add Earth's diseases to Narnia's own.

But as the voyagers are about to help themselves to the sumptuous feast, they notice at the end of the table three men in a deep sleep who, by the growth of their beards and hair, appear to have been there that way for years. Fearing the same enchantment might fall on any who eat of the feast, they hold their appetites in check.

A Mystery Woman

But Reephicheep, always seeking adventure, persuades the visitors from Earth and Caspian to spend the night at the table to see what will happen. In the middle of the night they awake to see a woman carrying a candle come to the table from a room hidden in a hillside.

"Travelers who have come from afar to Aslan's table," she says, "why do you not eat?" When they reply that they fear the food had enchanted the three men at the table's end, the lady says the three men never tasted the food, but in a quarrel one of them took up the knife of stone lying on the table—the knife that the witch, Jadis, had used to kill Aslan—which was something not right for him to touch. So they were put under a spell that could be broken only by someone who had traveled all the way to Aslan's country and returned.

A Wizard

They meet the woman's father, Ramandu, who, like Coriakin the magician on the island of voices, describes himself as a "retired star" (as in a celestial body) who can teach Caspian how to dissolve the enchantment binding the sleepers. He tells them they must sail to the end of the world, or as close as it's possible to get to it, and there leave behind one of their members.

Though the prospect of being left off at the end of the world may seem daunting, the closer to the end the voyagers get, the more enticing it is. Lucy and Reepicheep play peek-a-boo with merpeople (mermaids and mermen) who ride sea horses under the water beneath the *Dawn Treader*. The water becomes so clear and pure looking that Reepicheep jumps in on a whim to see if it is sweet (as opposed to salty) and finds that it is. The voyagers start drinking it and find that with it they have no desire for food; it supplies all the nutrients they need.

The End of the World

They encounter a sea full of lilies that are whiter than snow and seem to go on forever. They speculate on whether the world is round or flat, and when they get as far as the sea allows, they see Aslan's country beyond what seems to be a curtain of water, or a waterfall that goes up instead of down. Caspian himself decides to stay behind in Aslan's country, but everyone else—even Reepicheep who is always up for adventure—objects, reminding him of his responsibility to the kingdom he has won and his promise to the woman at Aslan's Table to see her on his return.

When the water becomes so shallow that the pilgrims can walk in it, they get out and walk along the wall of water until they see something at the point that the sky seems to meet the land and realize it is a dazzlingly white lamb. "Come and have breakfast," it says. They eat fish (reminiscent of the breakfast Jesus gave his disciples after the resurrection). As the Lamb speaks, he turns into Aslan and tells the children from Earth they must go to his country by their own world, not Narnia. And when they realize the time has come to leave Narnia again, Lucy asks how soon they may return. Aslan says never; they are now too old. Lucy cries, saying they'll never see Aslan again, but he tells them they must learn to recognize him in their world, by the name he is known there. With a kiss of his tongue on their foreheads, they are returned to Cambridge at the Scrubbs' back room.

Reepicheep stays with Aslan and Caspian returns to Ramandu's island and marries his daughter. Everyone back in England is impressed by the changes in Eustace, thinking how he has improved, except his mother Alberta, who thinks "he'd become commonplace and tiresome and it must have been the influence of the Pevensie children."

Chapter 14

The Silver Chair

The opening scene of *The Silver Chair* presents a born-again Eustace Scrubb. Still at Experiment House School, Eustace, no longer a self-absorbed prig, comes to the aid of a damsel in distress. He finds Jill Pole, the damsel, crying behind the gymnasium and tries to console her. And in the second paragraph on his way to explaining Jill's distress, Jack gives a straightforward commentary on the educational trends he opposed. The school, he says, is "what used to be called a 'mixed' school; some said it was not nearly so mixed as the minds of the people who ran it. These people had the idea that boys and girls should be allowed to do what they liked. And unfortunately what ten or fifteen of the biggest boys and girls liked best was bullying the others."

The Lost Prince

Horrible things went on at Experiment House that would have been nipped in the bud in most schools, but here they were treated as psychological cases to be studied rather than behavior lapses to be punished. Nervous about her vulnerability, rather than being grateful for Eustace's support, Jill accuses him of being the same sort of boy as the bullies. But he hasn't been like that this year—has he?—he replies. She admits he's seemed somewhat changed, which gets him to talking about his adventures in Narnia. When Jill asks if they can go there now, Scrubb (as she calls him; "Christian names" are not used at Experiment House) says the way in is by magic.

She asks if they should draw a circle on the ground and start incantations, to which Eustace says, "I don't think he'd like them." Who? Jill asks. Aslan, he replied. How then do we get there? Jill asks. Eustace tells her to face east and repeat after him, "Aslan, Aslan, Aslan."

THEY SAID . . .

The third sentence of *The Silver Chair* promises, "This is not going to be a school story." But it is…Casual similes suggest that education is the central theme. Trumpkin the Dwarf is compared to "some crusty teacher, whom everyone is a little afraid of and everyone makes fun of and nobody really dislikes."

—Doris T. Myers

Before they finish, Jill and Eustace hear voices of some of her bully accosters getting close, so they sneak into the laurel behind the gym and up a bank where there's a wall with a door, which is usually locked. But in desperation, they try it anyway and it opens into another world.

Called

Ironically, considering how close the passengers in the *Dawn Treader* came and yet how far it still was at the climax of *The Voyage of the Dawn*

Treader, Eustace and Jill walk through the door into, not Narnia, but Aslan's country, just a few feet from the edge of a cliff. Eustace warns caution while Jill boldly steps to the very edge, only then realizing that this is not just a cliff. It is as high above the rest of the world as an airliner would be, far above massive cloud formations which, in turn, are far above the plains, hills, and valleys below them.

Panicking, Jill grabs for Eustace's arm to get back from the edge, and in the confusion Eustace plummets off the cliff, screaming. Immediately a lion—Aslan—appears at Jill's side and, crouching over the cliff, starts blowing. His breath is an airstream that lifts Scrubb and sends him flying, on to Narnia. After he is safely in the other world, Aslan explains to Jill her responsibility for their arrival in Aslan's country going off-kilter, then lectures her about four signs she must remember to look for when she arrives in Narnia. His speech about her remembering the signs is reminiscent of God's speech to Moses when he gave Israel the Law and stressed that it be committed to the people's hearts and taught diligently to the generations to follow (Exodus 13:8).

Aslan has called her and Scrubb to his country, he explains, to which Jill objects that he must be thinking of someone else, because no one called them but, in fact, they were calling him. "'You would not have called to me unless I had been calling to you,' said the Lion." This is Jack's variation on the theological doctrine of grace. Faith is what believers bring to God, but that happens only after he has first given them faith to believe.

The first sign Jill is to remember is that when Eustace arrives in Narnia, the first person he will see will be a dear friend he knew from his previous visit, Aslan says. Scrubb is to immediately go up to that friend and tell him he has come to assist the friend in his quest. The friend, as the story unfolds, is King Caspian X, now seventy years older than when Eustace last saw him, just embarking on a sea voyage in search of his long-lost son and only heir, who has been missing for ten years.

Aslan tells Jill their mission is to help find the missing Prince Rilian. After Aslan blows Jill on to Narnia after Eustace, Jill fails to get the word to Scrubb in time for him to realize that this old king he saw departing from Cair Paravel was his dear friend Caspian, grown old in what, in Scrubb's world, was only a year. Caspian's ship has sailed. So they must find other possibilities to fulfill the remaining three signs.

Hooty Owls

Another hint that this story is in a way "a school story," Doris Myers says in *C. S. Lewis in Context*, is that, "Instead of beavers and badgers, the children first meet an owl, the bird of Athena and a symbol of rationality." The first creature Scrubb and Jill meet as Caspian's ship pulls away from the quay is a white talking owl, Glimfeather, much larger than any Jill has ever seen before. He asks the children to introduce themselves and informs them they are at Cair Paravel in Narnia.

FACT

Though *The Silver Chair* was published fourth in the series, it was written after the fifth-published title, *The Horse and His Boy*. Thus *The Silver Chair* refers to its successor as "the grand old tale of Prince Cor and Aravis and the horse Bree," which a blind poet tells as entertainment after the feast following King Caspian's bon voyage.

Glimfeather invites Scrubb and Jill to a late-night "Parliament of Owls" and flies them on his back, one at a time, to the meeting place, a ruined tower some distance from Cair Paravel (suggesting it may have been the same tower of Caspian's Uncle Miraz's castle from two books earlier where Caspian was taught by Doctor Cornelius about Old Narnia and a plot against him).

Rilian's Revenge

The purpose of the parliament is to tell Jill and Scrubb the story of Prince Rilian's disappearance and to get the distilled wisdom of Glimfeather's fellow owls about the strategy the youngsters should use in their quest to recover him. When he was a young knight, they relate, Prince Rilian and his mother, the queen, had traveled with many members of the court to the north country to celebrate the May. When the queen became sleepy, a bed was prepared for her on the lawn to nap while Rilian played games a short way off. A great serpent "shining, and as green as poison" slithered out of the bushes and stung the queen on her hand. Hearing her cries, Rilian ran and saw the "worm" retreating into the bushes but was unable to follow it into the underbrush. Ten minutes later the queen died.

Thus the prince dedicated himself to avenging his mother's death by trying to find and kill the serpent. But after one of his ventures to the north he returned to say he had found something more fascinating than his search for the snake: a lovely woman dressed in green. The next time he went north, he never returned, and many who tried to find him perished in their quests. It was because of the many fatal failed attempts that King Caspian had declared that no one else should go looking for Rilian, but that he, in his latter stage of life, would go. The owls conclude that the best guide for Scrubb and Jill's quest for Rilian is a marsh-wiggle, Puddleglum, who lives in Narnia's great marshland.

Marsh-wiggles and Giants

Though most creatures in *The Chronicles of Narnia* are either ones common in traditional myths, like fauns, centaurs, giants, and dwarfs, or common wildlife like owls, mice, and beavers, marsh-wiggles apparently are an original creation of Jack's. They are about the size of adult human beings but have bodies resembling those of frogs, with elongated legs and arms. They wear steeple-shaped hats and live in wigwams. Puddleglum, the only marsh-wiggle actually introduced in the book, is loyal to Aslan and Narnia and tends to look at everything with a worst-case attitude. But he is courageous and clever and considers himself lacking sobriety and seriousness.

The owls deposit Scrubb and Jill with Puddleglum late in their first night in Narnia, so they fall asleep without much time for making acquaintances. When they arise the next day Puddleglum is fishing and catches eels that he prepares for breakfast and for taking along in their journey to the ruined city of the giants. His pessimistic mindset shows in saying he probably will not catch enough eels to make a meal and that the children are not likely to find eel pleasant to eat, both of which turn out to be untrue.

Despite his reservations that the weather will become too wintry for them to get far, Puddleglum leads Scrubb and Pole out of the marsh to the north where, he has heard, lie the ruins of an ancient giants' city. All of the previous search parties that went to find Rilian started at the fountain in the park where the queen was killed, he tells them, but that's not the way to the ruined city, if there is a ruined city.

That's going to be found by going through Ettinsmoor. And Ettinsmoor, he adds, pointing toward the distant mountains, cliffs, and waterfalls, is due north. (North, says Lewis specialist Myers, in both Lewis's books and Spenser's *The Faerie Queene*, is the crux between knowledge and moral character, over against South, where feelings and emotions rule.)

FACT

Though the first three books in *The Chronicles of Narnia* educate the feelings of young readers, Doris Myers suggests, *The Silver Chair* is about education as a process. It opposes the trend Jack found in schools of manipulating language to teach new ideologies rather than teaching virtue. Teaching content over character is still at the center of debates about education's purpose.

In the wild waste lands of the north, the heads of giants, who live in a canyon, stick above the canyon rim looking like boulders. But stealthy progress on their way enables Puddleglum's party to elude the giants who, as was illustrated in *Prince Caspian*, tend to be somewhat rock-headed.

Among the Gentle Giants

At the end of the moor, even more to the north, the travelers see a different kind of country separated from them by a gorge. But while discussing how to get there, Scrubb discovers a huge single-arch bridge that spans the gorge "from cliff-top to cliff-top." Jill speculates that it might be a giants' bridge, but the always pessimistic Puddleglum suggests it is a sorcerer's work.

As they come down the bridge they see what appears to be a giants' road leading into the lands beyond, with two human-sized people on horses approaching them. They are "a knight in complete armor with his visor down" riding a black horse and a lady on a white horse so beautiful "that you wanted to kiss its nose and give it a lump of sugar at once." And the lady, in a green dress described as "dazzling," is even lovelier, and her voice sounds as sweet as birdsong.

Roadside Assistance

Though Puddleglum is wary, Scrubb and Jill are taken by her charm and beauty. Jill tells her they are looking for the ruined city. When she asks why, Puddleglum interjects that they would rather not share their business with an unknown stranger. She commends his wisdom and relates that though she has often heard of the "City Ruinous," she doesn't know how to find it or anyone else who may.

But she does know, she says, another city up the road, Harfang, that is home to "gentle giants" who will offer them good food, hot baths, and warm beds, and where she advises them to winter, as snow has started blowing down. To get the giants to invite them to stay, "tell them," she says, "that she of the Green Kirtle salutes them by you, and has sent them two fair Southern children for the Autumn Feast." (A *kirtle* is a dress with a bodice reinforced with boning. The style, reminiscent of medieval gowns, is popular for bridesmaids.)

> In this section Jack uses real structures that would have been known by English school children for comparisons. The arch of the bridge, he says, "was as high above the cliff-tops as the dome of St. Paul's [Cathedral] is above the street." And the individual stones of the bridge were as big "as those at Stonehenge."

Harfang

After her departure, the youngsters remain delighted by the lady, but Puddleglum continues to doubt her trustworthiness and wonders about the knight, who seemed to have been no more than a suit of armor sitting in silence the whole time. The marsh-wiggle even opposes their going on to Harfang, which both Jill and Scrubb are eager to do, especially in light of the onset of winter weather. Jack says that despite Jill's and Scrubb's frequent bickering with each other, this issue became the closest they came to an outright quarrel, so Puddleglum acceded to their wishes.

They still have a long way to travel across what seemed terraced hills or ledges and a long plain to Harfang. At one point, Jill falls into a trench and, not seriously hurt, wonders if the trench may be an alternate path to Harfang, as being below the surface the weather is less bitter. But the trench seemed to have several turns, followed in each case by dead ends, so they continued on the surface to the giants' castle.

They rush on through blowing snow, fearing they may not be allowed into Harfang, but find they are welcomed just as warmly as the Green Lady has predicted. The porter of the castle even gives Puddleglum drinks from a dark bottle that put the marsh-wiggle into a less glum frame of mind and gave him a headache next morning.

A Dream of Signs

Their message that the Green Lady has sent the giants "two fair Southern children for the Autumn Feast" is received with knowing smiles between the king and queen of the giants, which makes Jill feel uneasy and makes the king lick his lips. That night, in her room the size of a church, Jill dreams of Aslan asking her to recite the signs, which she has forgotten. She sees the words UNDER ME outside her window but doesn't understand their meaning.

The snow turns to rain in the night, and next morning the sun is shining. Scrubb and Puddleglum are brought to Jill's room "to play," and when they see that her window has a window seat enabling them to see outside, they all climb up and look down at the world beyond the castle. From here everything they had crossed the day before has an entirely different perspective.

The terraces, or ledges, they had climbed are walls, and for miles around they can see what are unmistakably the ruins of an old city. It had been under their feet the whole day before without their realizing it. And even more startling, they can clearly see the words UNDER ME carved in trenches in the walls of the ruined city. The trench Jill had fallen into was the letter E in "ME." The words are the third of the four signs, but what do they mean? Puddleglum says they must signify that they should look for the prince under the ruins of that city.

They resolve to find a way to leave the castle without being pursued and caught, and in the meantime they are fed cold venison that Puddleglum discovers, by overhearing giants' conversation, is from a talking stag, the eating of which he considers a sin so serious that it will likely bring a curse down upon them. And while looking in the kitchen for clues that may enable them to escape, Jill discovers that the cook has been looking in a cookbook with a recipe for preparing children.

Underland

The giants' weak minds work to the travelers' advantage. When most members of the royal court are out on a hunt, they wait for the remaining staff members to take afternoon naps so they can sneak through the scullery and outside. Though the hunters return from the woods before the rescue team is able to hide in the ruins, they outrun the giants fast enough to drop down a ledge and, finding a hole into the ground there, crawl through and quickly fill the hole behind them with rocks.

An Underground Slide

Once underground, the fugitives have to feel their way in total darkness through a tunnel maze that may get them completely and permanently lost. But just as they begin wondering if being entrées at the giants' autumn feast might be better than being lost and perhaps torn to pieces by dragons deep underground, they start sliding down a long slope that seems endless, deeper and deeper into the earth. At the end, though they expected worse, they are covered with bruises but otherwise whole.

After they sit in the darkness for a long time, immobilized by their bruises and fatigue, they hear a voice saying "What make you here, creatures of the Overworld?" The voice identifies himself as the Warden of the Marches of Underland, adding that he is accompanied by an army of a hundred Earthmen. Earthmen are analogous to earthworms, it seems, as they live under the dirt; they have no correspondence to men of planet Earth. "Earthmen" and "gnomes" are used to describe them throughout the novel's Underland (also often called Underworld) section. A pale green light presently comes on, showing the travelers that the warden's claim was true.

They Meet the Black Knight

The gnomes say they are going to take the travelers to the Queen of the Underland and march them through miles of underground caverns and tunnels, sometimes crawling through claustrophobia-inducing entrances and at other times walking in cathedral-sized underground rooms. When they arrive at the queen's quarters and find her to be out and abroad, the warden says he'll have to put them in prison until her return, but he is interrupted by a man's voice coming from an apartment atop an adjacent staircase. He commands that the warden bring his prisoners up to him, which the warden reluctantly does. The man says he has seen the three Overworlders before, near the bridge on the border of Ettinsmoor when he rode by his lady's side.

"'Oh…you were the black Knight who never spoke?' exclaimed Jill." As they converse, Jill reveals their quest to find Rilian of Narnia, neither of which the Knight can remember ever hearing of. And when she tells him about the sign of UNDER ME, he laughs and recites the full ancient inscription from which those two words had come. This discourages both Jill and Scrubb, who think the Knight must be right; the words on the ruined city wall were no sign after all. But Puddleglum, against his type, reassures them, saying, "There are no accidents. Our guide is Aslan." Aslan, he continues, knew the origin of those words and it was he who told them they would be a sign to them.

After they have dinner, the Knight says he cannot remember any time before his life with the queen, and adds that each evening he comes under an enchantment that makes him violent, so he has to be bound by restraints in a silver chair until the enchantment wears off. When the queen's men who do the restraining approach, he asks his visitors to go into the next room until his restraints are fast and his restrainers leave, so they can then come out and witness his enchantment.

Disenchanted

The Knight warns them that when he is enchanted he may plead for his release, but he makes them swear they will not release him. This they do, and when the enchantment begins, the Knight starts protesting that *now* he is in his right mind and that he has been held captive down here under the ground for years. He says that what they heard earlier was a lie and that what he is saying now is the truth, which confuses the Overworlders. After pleading for a long time, the Knight says, "Once and for all...I adjure you to set me free. By all fears and all loves, by the bright skies of Overland, by the great Lion, by Aslan himself, I charge you..."

QUESTION
Why was Puddleglum cast as ever the skeptical pessimist?
Logically, his layer of skepticism enabled him to doubt, and thus resist, the enchantment of the witch longer than anyone else. His courage to stomp out the fire on which her magic incense was burning was the first step toward saving the prince and his would-be rescuers.

The fourth and final sign that Aslan gave Jill was that the prince would be identified by his calling out in the name of Aslan. Having "muffed" the first two signs and unsure whether they read the third one correctly, the three are stumped, but only for a moment. Quickly they cut the restraints on the Knight, who is indeed Rilian, and the first thing he does once released is cut the silver chair in two, ending the witch-queen's enchantment that has held him underground for more than ten years.

The Queen of Underland Returns

No sooner is Rilian's enchantment ended than the witch-queen appears. She immediately starts spinning a spell to not only re-enchant Rilian but to enchant his would-be rescuers too. She throws some incense on the fire and speaks in a way that seems to hypnotize everyone, convincing them all that there is no such place as Narnia or the Overland and no such person as Aslan.

All except for Puddleglum are quickly repeating after her, but the marsh-wiggle asserts that they have all seen the world above ground and they all know Aslan. And his resistance works to begin resistance in Rilian and Scrubb, who says that Puddleglum is the only one of them who has said anything true in the past few minutes. Emboldened by the effect his stand has caused, Puddleglum dares to walk over to the open fire and stomp it out to end the enchantment created by the witch's incense.

The pain in his burned foot clears Puddleglum's mind, a piece of which he proceeds to give the witch. The ensuing speech is the defining moment and climax in *The Silver Chair*, concluding with the assertion that he and the other three are ready to leave Underland forever.

At this declaration that brings "huzzahs" from the others, the witch turns herself into the serpent that had killed Rilian's mother and wraps herself around his body. But the prince grabs the serpent by the throat with one hand and pulls and swings his sword at her throat. Scrubb and Puddleglum also draw weapons and wield them against the serpent until they manage to cut off its head.

Escape to Narnia and Home

With the witch dead, some of her enchantments are undone. But there are still adventures to come as the Underland is being flooded and a volcano is coming to life, the Earthmen are all organizing as though preparing for war, and the prince and his rescuers have to find their way to the surface.

FACT
The use of the words UNDER ME as a major sign, and the use of Puddleglum's speech of great persuasive power to face down the witch's alternative description of reality, should be seen as clues to Jack's underlying theme in *The Silver Chair*: opposing the misuse and reinvention of language in philosophy and education.

But it turns out that the catastrophes striking Underland at the witch's death, like Puddleglum's intentionally burning his foot, embolden the gnomes to take arms to fight for their freedom from her, as she had enchanted them all. And when they learn that Prince Rilian and his friends were her executioners, they offer to assist them in escaping to the Over-world, even though they cannot imagine anyone wanting to live under bare skies.

Caspian's Death

Rilian and his rescuers emerge into Narnia just as a winter festival is underway under the first full moon after the first snowfall. When they get to Cair Paravel, King Caspian's ship is also returning, but when they meet it, it is only in time to see King Caspian bless Rilian as his successor and breathe his last. During the public grief, Aslan appears to Jill and Scrubb, and instead of blowing them back to his country, he blows away Narnia itself as though it is smoke or vapor. Back atop the cliff where Scrubb and Jill entered Narnia, Caspian appears as a young man again, an indication of Jack's leaning toward the opinion that, in heaven, all will be restored to their youthful or their ideal age.

Caspian asks for a glimpse of the world that Scrubb and Jill come from, so Aslan grants him five minutes there. Rather than reopening the door through the wall at Experiment House, he blows a large portion of the wall down. Students and staff of the school panic and the head (who is a woman, Jack interjects) calls the police to report a terrorist or fascist gang attack. Jill and Scrubb slip into the school unnoticed and get into their school clothes. When the police arrive, Aslan has put the wall back to normal, there are no attackers to be found, and the head is later removed from her job (pro-moted, actually, to an inspector over other school heads). After her replace-ment gets rid of ten or so of the worst bullies and reforms the curriculum and behavior codes, sanity finally reigns at Experiment House.

Chapter 15

The Horse and His Boy

In the first three books of *The Chronicles of Narnia,* children entered Narnia by accident and instantaneous magic. In the fourth, Eustace and Jill prayed to enter Narnia in the name of Aslan and their wish was granted. But in *The Horse and His Boy,* a pair of older children want to go to Narnia so much they risk their lives to journey for weeks before reaching it. Some have compared Shasta, the boy of the title of *The Horse and His Boy,* to Moses in the Old Testament, as he was rescued from the water in infancy and became a nation's leader. Christin Ditchfield, in *A Family Guide to Narnia: Biblical Truths in C. S. Lewis's the Chronicles of Narnia,* compares the book to the Old Testament's book of Esther, because neither Shasta nor Esther are aware of God's (Aslan's) intervention throughout their adventures, though all that happens is his doing.

Longing to Be Up North

Shasta is a boy who lives with a poor fisherman, Arsheesh, on the coast of Calormen, south of Archenland on its northern border and of Narnia farther north. Though Shasta calls Arsheesh father, the man deals with him harshly, works him slavishly on the tasks involved in the fishing enterprise, and reproves his curiosity about the distant north with its mountains and forests. (This longing suggests Jack's own "Northernness" in his Irish childhood.)

FACT

Set in Narnia's golden age under High King Peter, King Edmund, and Queens Susan and Lucy, *The Horse and His Boy* is the only book in the series in which children are not brought into Narnia from England. Though written before *The Silver Chair*, it was published afterward to keep the three books dealing with King Caspian together.

One evening a Tarkaan, a nobleman of Calormen, rides up on a magnificent warhorse and demands hospitality in Arsheesh's hut. Eavesdropping at a crack in the hut's wall, Shasta overhears the Tarkaan offering to buy him from Arsheesh and learns that Arsheesh is not his father but found him as an infant in a small boat that came ashore nearby.

Talking Horse

When the two men start bickering over Shasta's price, the boy steals off to the stable to consider his options, speaking out loud to himself. When he wonders how life might be with the Tarkaan, the horse speaks up to say it will be worse than death. Shasta is startled because he had never met or heard of a talking animal, so the horse introduces himself as Bree and explains that he is a talking horse from Narnia who has been kidnapped into Calormene slavery.

Though he never talks to Calormene lest they show him off like a freak, Bree likes Shasta's idea of escaping to the north and proposes they do so together, as Bree has long been waiting for such an opportunity. Though Shasta has never ridden, Bree promises to teach him. After confirming that Arsheesh and the Tarkaan are sound asleep, Shasta and Bree make tracks in one direction along a creek and then follow the creek bed in another to misdirect anyone likely to start looking for them the next morning.

Lion

Though they cross the countryside adjacent to the coast to avoid passing other people on the highways for as long as they can, Bree tells Shasta they will have to turn north and go through Tashbaan, the capital city, as it is the one place they can cross the great river and continue north toward Archenland and Narnia. After several weeks on the run, Bree senses that they are being followed and ascertains that another horse, apparently a superior breed probably ridden by a Tarkaan, is nearby.

When Bree stops, the other horse stops, and while he waits a fog rolls in. Then a lion roars nearby, causing Bree to light out full speed, with the other horse and rider also taking flight. Bree stops after crossing a river, thinking he has eluded his pursuers, but again the lion roars and both Bree and the other horse gallop off, this time almost colliding with each other.

When they all finally seem to have eluded the lion, they stop and Bree and Shasta discover that the Tarkaan is actually a Tarkeena, a girl. And the horses recognize each other as Narnian talking horses and establish that they are both attempting to escape, with their young riders, to the north. Both horses think the four of them traveling together will be safer than separately and, despite the girl's objections, they prevail.

Tashbaan

Before resuming their journey, they rest and Bree and Shasta urge the Tarkeena, Aravis, to tell her story. Her stepmother and her father had promised her in marriage to an up-and-coming Tarkaan, Ahoshta. This man is much older than Aravis and had risen from a lowly birth to a position of favor with the Tisroc, the sultan, and is in line to become the Grand Vizier. (A *vizier* is an advisor to the sultan.)

Aravis loathed Ahoshta and was prepared to end her life to avoid the marriage by falling on her dagger, but her horse, Hwin, spoke up to dissuade her. Startled, she put down the dagger but quickly thought she had imagined that her mare had spoken. But when she took up the dagger again, Hwin put her head between the knife and Aravis's breast and began extolling the virtues of Narnia. Like Bree, Hwin was eager to escape a life of slavery to the Calormene. So she and her owner, similarly, plotted to escape to the north.

THEY SAID . . .

"Whereas both *The Magician's Nephew* and *The Lion, the Witch, and the Wardrobe* were children's fables with a fairly simple narrative structure, *The Horse and His Boy* is a full-blown adventure novel, aimed squarely at readers who were children when *Wardrobe* was first published, but [are] teens with more sophisticated tastes now."

—Review by T. M. Wagner on SF Reviews.net

Escape

Aravis concocted a story about going into the woods to spend three nights sacrificing to Zardeenah, Lady of Maidens, which she said was proper as she would soon be marrying. She then confided in her most trusted member of the household staff and had him write "a certain letter" for her. And she drugged the wine of the maid who accompanied her to the woods with things that would make her sleep so she could make her escape and get a long head start before being missed.

The letter her household servant provided was written as though by Ahoshta, saying that he had been en route to the Tarkaan's house to see his betrothed when he met her and her maid in the woods, and being so taken by her beauty, thought he should marry her immediately, which he did, and took her back to his palace to live with him.

When Aravis finishes her story, Shasta questions its validity, saying she is just a girl, about his age, too young to marry. But Bree accuses Shasta of showing ignorance, as all daughters of Tarkaan families marry that young. Shasta is embarrassed and as they started traveling on the next day, he thinks it had been more pleasant with just himself and Bree.

City Gate

After traveling many more nights they come, at last, to the gate of Calormen's great city. They plan their strategy for getting through the city without arousing suspicion, agreeing to disguise the horses as pack horses and themselves as poor peasant children (which Shasta already is) and lead rather than ride the horses. They also agree to meet, if they become separated, at the tombs across the northern branch of the river surrounding the city.

They sleep in a wooded hilltop with thousands of lights of the city below them their last night before going in. And at dawn the next day horns sound to announce the opening of the city gates. A throng queues up on the bridge over to the gate, and throngs crowd all the streets throughout their painstakingly slow progress up its often steep lanes.

Giving Way

As they wind their way to the summit in the city's center, where the Tisroc's palace and other government buildings are, they are interrupted often in their inch-at-a-time progress by loud voices demanding, "Way, way, way." The crowd has to stop moving to make room for the arrival of Tarkaans, diplomats, and other dignitaries being carried on litters by slaves at the height of the heads of most of the people.

And Shasta's progress is interrupted again when, near the Tisroc's palace, the sound comes again: "Way! Way! Way!...Way for the White Barbarian King, the guest of the Tisroc (may he live forever)! Way for the Narnian lords."

Captured

Shasta is trying to push Bree out of the way when a woman accuses him of shoving her and pushes him toward the advancing dignitaries who, unlike all their predecessors, are on foot. The one calling "way" is Calormene, and all the others are fair-haired.

At this moment the leader of the Narnians notices Shasta and excitedly shouts, "There he is! There's our runaway!" Shasta is grabbed by his shoulder, smacked to indicate he is in disgrace, and shaken. The fair-haired men all grab him and he has no chance to break free.

Corin and Lasaraleen

The white barbarian Narnian king is Edmund, on his way to join his sister, Queen Susan, at the Tisroc's guest palace. Susan has been invited to visit, with her entourage, because the Tisroc's son, Rabadash, has fallen for her and wants to ask her to marry him. Susan and Edmund are now adults, and Tumnus the faun (from *The Lion, the Witch, and the Wardrobe*) is with them, now serving as an advisor to Narnia's kings and queens.

Shasta realizes that he has been mistaken for Corin, the prince of Archenland, Narnia's neighboring kingdom and ally. The boy prince had come to Calormen with Queen Susan and had run away and been gone since the previous day. Though Shasta knows he could object to his captors that he is the son of the poor fisherman Arsheesh, under the circumstances his stronger impulse is to say nothing that might get people looking into him and his background, so he keeps silent.

FACT
There's obvious correspondence between *The Horse and His Boy* and Mark Twain's 1882 novel, *The Prince and the Pauper*, though in Twain's book the boys look alike but don't turn out to be twins. Besides both books having boys as a prince and a pauper who change roles, each boy is more comfortable or inclined to the other's lifestyle.

Shasta learns from conversations he overhears in the guest palace that Susan has no intention of marrying Rabadash but fears she may be kidnapped if she makes this known to him. Looking for a means to leave before that scenario plays out, Tumnus devises a plan for the Narnians to invite the Tisroc and his party to a banquet on the Narnian yacht, at anchor in the river.

Means of Escape

Though Calormen is the superior power in every other way, Narnia has superior naval skills and vessels. They will pretend to be preparing the ship for the great banquet two nights hence, and the night before that they will slip out into the sea and back to Cair Paravel.

Eventually Shasta is left alone, and after he gets to sleep a loud noise wakens him. It is Corin, his lookalike prince, trying to sneak back into his room through the open window. After Corin explains that he had sneaked off to settle a score with a boy he'd heard insulting Queen Susan, Shasta persuades him to let him sneak out the way Corin came in.

Shasta fears that Aravis and the horses will be ready to leave without him, but when he gets to the tombs, none of the others are there. Frightened by the prospect of spending the night alone in a strange place allegedly inhabited by ghouls, he is comforted by a large cat that appears and curls up next to him.

Aravis's Adventure

Shortly after Shasta's capture by the Narnians, Aravis, still standing on the crowded street with the horses, is recognized by an old friend, the Tarkheena Lasaraleen, riding in a curtained litter. Like Aravis, Lasaraleen was also betrothed to an old Tarkaan, but unlike Aravis she considered it the opportunity of a lifetime.

When she insists that Aravis explain her appearance here as a poor slave girl, Aravis joins her on the litter so no one will hear their talk and closes the curtain to be taken with Lasaraleen to her palace apartment. Lasaraleen orders one of her servants to bring the horses and, after Aravis discloses their plan to meet Shasta, has them sent on to the tombs.

Another Plot Uncovered

Reluctantly, Lasaraleen agrees to help Aravis escape through a water gate leading to boats on the river directly from the Tisroc's palace. In order to get to it, they go into a corridor where they find the Tisroc is approaching. They hide in a room off the corridor only to find the Tisroc and his entourage entering to use it.

The girls dive behind a sofa and have to be deathly still while the Tisroc, Ahoshta, and Prince Rabadash discuss what to do in the wake of the Narnians' deception and flight back home to avoid Rabadash's plans for Queen Susan. Rabadash argues that he should take an army of two hundred to Archenland, conquer it, and then move on to Narnia to take Cair Paravel.

Finally, Aravis escapes the Tisroc's palace, finds a boat, and crosses the river and makes her way to the tombs. After revealing the plot she overheard with Lasaraleen in the Tisroc's secret room, she and Shasta, Bree, and Hwin start immediately on the long journey across the great desert between Tashbaan and the border of Archenland, desperate to arrive before Rabadash and his army.

War with Rabadash

Following a route that Shasta had been told about by talking ravens, eventually they arrive in a narrow canyon that leads to a spring that becomes a stream that turns into a river in a valley and takes them into Archenland. After swimming in the river, Bree becomes lethargic, but soon they are terrified by the roar of a lion forcing them to run at full speed. The lion reaches Hwin and Aravis and seems about to kill Aravis. As Bree gallops even faster, Shasta jumps off Bree and turns to confront the lion to save Aravis, whose back is already seriously scratched. Unarmed, all Shasta can do is shout at the lion to leave them alone. And the lion stops, turns, and goes.

When they get across the border, they find a hermit (a spiritual clairvoyant or monk) who can see visions of other places in a pool in the garden of his hut or cell. He is expecting them and tells them Rabadash has not yet reached Archenland and advises Shasta to continue, running on foot, to warn King Lune his castle will soon be attacked.

After examining Aravis's wounds, the Hermit declares she has ten sore but not dangerous scratches, to which she replies, "I say! I *have* had luck." His reply to this confirms the Hermit as a a holy man: "Daughter, I have now lived a hundred and nine winters in this world and have never yet met any such thing as Luck." This profession of faith is Narnia's version of the Christian belief in providence, that everything happens for a purpose under God's will (1 Thessalonians 5:18, Romans 8:28). It is elaborated twice later in the story.

The focus then follows Shasta's flight to meet King Lune. He meets the king with a hunting party and the king, like King Edmund in Tashbaan, mistakes Shasta for Corin, but Shasta explains the mix-up while rushing to convey his warning of Rabadash's invasion. The king supplies a horse for Shasta to ride with them back to the castle, but it is a slow horse and not a talking one. Shasta has never used reins and spurs, so he quickly falls behind the king and his men and soon gets lost in a dense fog.

Unwelcome Visitor

Hardly able to see even the horse's head in front of him, he hears a thunder of hooves from behind and guesses that it is Rabadash's army. He gets off the trail to let them pass and confirms by their voices that they are indeed the enemy force. Then he lets his horse lead him on an alternate route, still shrouded in fog and on which, after a while, he can hear the breathing of another traveler in his ear, though he sees nothing. After not being able to endure the suspense any longer, he whispers, "Who are you?"

Shasta had just recited how unfortunate he had been to have been left to a cruel fisherman as a baby, to be left behind when the Narnians sailed safely from Tashbaan, to risk his life alone while Aravis and the horses stayed back with the Hermit, and now to have a horse too slow to keep up.

"I do not call you unfortunate," the rider hidden in the fog says. To which the boy asks, "what about all the lions" that chased him. "There was only one lion," the other's voice replies. "How do you know?" Shasta asks, and hears in reply, "I was the lion." Aslan asks him to unburden his woes to him.

When Shasta asks why he had wounded Aravis, the Lion replies, "Child, I am telling you your story, not hers. I tell no one any story but his own." And he tells Shasta that he had been in the boat when he landed in front of Arsheesh's hut years earlier and had been with him at every crisis since: he had been the cat that kept him company at the tombs, and he had given the horses the adrenalin to run faster when they thought they could run no longer.

After Aslan leaves him, Shasta wonders if it could have been real. But then he sees that Aslan left a huge paw print next to the trail and that it is filling with perfectly clear fresh water, which Shasta drinks and uses to wash.

After his "baptism," Shasta feels faint with hunger and is fed by dwarfs who find him shortly after he crosses the border from Archenland into Narnia. He tells them of the need to alert Cair Paravel about Rabadash's invasion, and they send the message on through a series of talking animals. Soon afterward, the Narnian cavalry led by King Edmund and including Corin (who had gone with them back to Cair Paravel), Queen Lucy (Queen Susan considered warfare inappropriate for queens), and all kinds of talking animals and creatures, ranging from leopards to centaurs, arrive to take up the battle. He and Corin have a warm reunion and Corin urges Shasta to join him in fighting Rabadash's forces. King Edmund gets wind of this plan and orders them not to fight because war is not a game for boys. Corin and Shasta fall to the back of the lines but still keep their weapons ready to use.

Shasta has no knowledge of warfare and is knocked off his horse, expecting to be trampled. By the time he gets his bearings, he discovers that the Narnians have prevailed and that the only Calormene left are now prisoners of Kings Lune and Edmund.

Bree's Conceit

At the Hermit's hut, Aravis, Bree, and Hwin are apprised by the Hermit's magic pool that the Calormene have been defeated and that Shasta has not been seriously wounded. The next day, Hwin says she and Bree should continue on to Narnia, but Bree is in a funk. Hwin guesses accurately that he is too vain about his tail having been cut short as part of their disguise to get through Tashbaan without being considered suspicious. And to this Hwin reminds him that they don't even know how talking horses wear their tails in Narnia.

Then Aravis asks Bree why he sometimes swears "by the Lion," and he replies it's a common expression in Narnia, where everyone believes that the Lion defeated the White Witch and liberated all the talking animals and installed High King Peter, King Edmund, and Queens Susan and Lucy at Cair Paravel. But lions had been such threats on their journey from Calormen, Aravis recalls. Was Narnia's deliverer really a lion? Of course not, Bree replies, adding that the expression probably means only that the witch killer had been strong as a lion. As Bree talks, Aslan appears behind him, seen only by Aravis and Hwin, and, at Bree's reply, tickles his ear.

FACT

The Horse and His Boy, published in 1954, was dedicated to David and Douglas Gresham, who visited Jack at The Kilns from America with their mother in 1953, at ages nine and eight, respectively. Jack wrote that the boys (who later became his stepsons) were a handful and hard to keep up with, but he enjoyed their company.

When Hwin tells Aslan he is so beautiful that she would rather be eaten by him than be fed by anyone else, Aslan blesses Hwin with a lion kiss on her forehead, saying he knew she "would not be long in coming to me. Joy shall be yours." Then he tells "poor, proud, frightened Horse" Bree, to come close, touch him, and smell him to see that "I am a true Beast."

When Bree admits that he's been a fool, Aslan assures him that it's better to learn that early rather than late. Then Aslan calls Aravis to him and says his paws are velveted this time, to which she asks, "This time?" and he replies that it was he who scratched her earlier. When she asks why, he says the scratches were equal to the lashes Aravis's servant, whom she drugged in the forest so she could escape her father, had received for failing to keep track of Aravis. "You needed to know how it felt," he explains. When Aravis asks if her servant will receive any more punishment for what she has caused her to do, again Aslan says he tells no one anyone else's story.

Later that day, Shasta, now called Prince Cor, arrives at the Hermit's hut to invite Aravis, on behalf of King Lune, to join them as a permanent resident at the king's castle, which has lacked a royal lady's leadership since the death of the late queen.

First-Born

From the time he had met Shasta at the hunt, King Lune had concluded that he could only be his first-born son, Corin's brother Cor, who arrived from the womb twenty minutes earlier than Corin and therefore is by law the rightful heir to the throne of Archenland when King Lune passes on. Though Cor objects that Corin was more deserving, Corin counterprotests that he much prefers being a prince to a king, as princes have more fun.

QUESTION

What mythical archetypes influenced Shasta (Cor) and Corin?
Mythical twins with divine or royal connections can be traced to the Vedic (Hindu) tradition, Old German myths, and both Greek and Roman mythology. The Romans Castor and Pollux (based on the Greek Kastor and Polydeuces) are closest to Cor and Corin. Pollux is a horseman and Castor is a renowned boxer.

While growing up, despite their identical looks and their closeness, Cor and Corin had as many fights as any brothers, the storyteller relates. And after they grow up, Cor and Aravis marry in order to make it more convenient to keep their friendly arguments going on. Corin becomes famous as a boxer. And Bree and Hwin, who learn that only during war battles do talking horses carry riders in Narnia, settle in the northern kingdom and both marry, but not each other.

Rabadash the Ridiculous

In the short war with Rabadash and his two hundred men, Rabadash had tried to jump from a battering ram being used to break open the castle gates onto King Edmund. But his mail shirt got caught on a hook in the castle wall and there he hung when the battle ended. He demanded that he either be killed or freed to fight anyone willing to take him on, and though Edmund recommended killing him forthwith, King Lune preferred showing mercy. Throughout the deliberations to determine his fate, Rabadash continued hurling curses and threats, until Aslan himself appeared.

When he would not respect and speak politely to Aslan, the Lion turned Rabadash into a donkey and told him that at an appointed time he could be turned back into Prince Rabadash at the Temple of Tash, the god of Calormen. If he ever went ten miles farther than that temple, he would be permanently turned back into an ass.

Having received his most deplored punishment, being ridiculed by all who knew him, Rabadash was silenced at last. Though he eventually became the Tisroc in Calormen, he never went to war because he didn't want to let any of his noblemen advance their careers by leading military ventures that he could not, being confined to greater Tashbaan. And behind his back, he was always known as "Rabadash the Ridiculous."

Chapter 16

The Magician's Nephew

The Magician's Nephew is a prequel that reveals background facts about earlier books in *The Chronicles of Narnia*. In the narrative sequence, it is the first book, though it was the sixth published. It explains why the wardrobe in Professor Kirke's spare room was magical and how the Professor came to own the wardrobe and why he didn't doubt Lucy when she claimed she had entered Narnia through it. It explains how the lamppost came to be in the woods that seemed to be between the wardrobe and Narnia. It even shows Aslan singing Narnia's world into existence, and it reveals how Jadis the White Witch came to Narnia after having destroyed other worlds.

Digory Kirke

Though Professor Kirke may have been named for Jack's esteemed tutor William T. Kirkpatrick, strong clues in *The Magician's Nephew* suggest that his character is drawn more from Jack's own life than Kirkpatrick's. The author begins by saying this story is set in the time in which your grandparents were children, which, in 1955 when the book was written and Jack was fifty-seven, would have been the early twentieth century, not the last quarter of the nineteenth when Kirkpatrick was a child. The author calls the era the time when the famous detective "still lived at Baker Street," the "still" indicating it was the latter time of the Sherlock Holmes stories, which ran from 1887 to 1914.

But if this story is set around 1908 and as its protagonist, Digory—Professor Kirke as a child—is fearing the imminent death of his mother, that coincides exactly with Jack's tragic loss of his mother at age nine. He also mentions that the schools were not as pleasant then but the food was better. The story takes place in a summer when Digory and his mother could not take their usual trips to the seashore, which is what Jack and Warnie did a number of summers before their mother's death.

> ## FACT
> The fact that a sister and a brother of the parents of central characters in two of the Narnia books are portrayed negatively parallels Jack's feelings toward some of his parent's brothers and sisters. In *The Voyage of the Dawn Treader* Eustace's parents (especially his mother Alberta), Lucy Pevensie's uncle and aunt, are strange modernists, and in *The Magician's Nephew* Uncle Andrew's pursuit of magic is villainous.

Though Digory is the protagonist—the "nephew" of *The Magician's Nephew*—the first character introduced is Polly Plummer, a London girl who lives in a row house and is surprised to see the head of a grubby little boy about her age popping over the fence between her backyard and the neighbor's, where she had never seen another child before. When she teases him about his grubbiness, a result of crying and rubbing his face with dirty hands, he objects that she might cry, too, if her father were away in India and he and his mother, who was sick and might be dying, had to live with an aunt and an uncle who was mad.

Madness

Uncle Andrew must have appeared strange enough to his neighbors that Polly asks if he is truly mad. Digory replies that Uncle Andrew is always trying to engage him in discussions that his Aunt Letty (Andrew's sister, not his wife) thought were inappropriate for the young boy and tried to stop. Uncle Andrew is usually holed up in his study in the attic and is sometimes heard speaking loudly or crying out from that retreat.

Polly tells Digory that she has discovered an entry into the crawlspace between the roof and the attic and that it extends the whole length of the row of houses, like a pretend cave or tunnel. Since one of the houses has long been vacant, they might make their way across the joists and drop down into that house and see what it's like inside. Though probably haunted (why else would it have been vacant so long?), doing so in broad daylight might be more adventurous than dangerous.

Hostages

So they climb to the top of her family's house to the entry to the crawlspace, using candles for light, and try to estimate the distance from one house to the next. But when they come through the door in the ceiling they enter a furnished room that has strange items, suggesting a laboratory, and with a fire in the fireplace. After Digory suggests they go back up the way they came because they must have made a mistake, someone suddenly stands up from the oversized chair in front of the fire.

Having miscalculated their distance, they have come down in Uncle Andrew's study, where he seems more happy than startled to see them and quickly reaches for the door to lock it. When they started moving back to the ceiling trapdoor, he blocks their way and begins to tell them about experiments he has been doing. When they persist about leaving, he agrees to let them go but asks Polly if she'd like to have one of the shining—almost glowing—rings she noticed on his table. She accepts one of the yellow ones and, on touching it, Polly immediately vanishes.

Rings, Woods, and New Worlds

Uncle Andrew explains that by touching the yellow ring, Polly has been transported to another world. He has already sent a guinea pig out of the world, but he couldn't tell it how to get back so it could tell him what it was like, so he didn't have complete results from that experiment.

He says the rings had been created with powder that he had been bequeathed by his fairy godmother, adding that he may have been the last man ever to actually have a fairy godmother. The dust had come to her from the lost continent Atlantis and before that it had come there from another world. He had learned that it could not be touched directly, but by using instruments he had tried various ways to make the dust work, finally turning it into rings.

FACT

Considering the name correspondence between the real Kirkpatrick and the fictional Kirke, it's not much of a jump to assume that the fictional Andrew Ketterley, villain in *The Magician's Nephew*, is named after Martin Ketley, coauthor of a book directly attacked by Jack in *The Abolition of Man* and indirectly in *That Hideous Strength* and throughout *The Chronicles of Narnia*.

Though Uncle Andrew doesn't know where or what the other worlds are that the rings might take one to, or whether the rings designated to return their users actually work, he proposes that Digory use the remaining yellow ring to follow Polly. After finding her, they must use the green rings to get them back to London.

A Boy's Honor

With virtually no hesitation, Digory agrees that this is what he will have to do. After having the remaining rings put in his pockets by his uncle (using tongs to avoid touching them), he touches the yellow ring and feels himself being propelled as though through space (reminiscent of Ransom in *Out of the Silent Planet*) and eventually rising up through water. Though frightening, the underwater sensation quickly ends with his emergence from a small shallow pool in a parklike setting of woods with many similar small pools scattered about.

The place is so "quiet and sleepy" that he slips into an almost trancelike state. He sees a girl lying on the grass, and when he approaches she recognizes him but isn't sure from where. He says he has the same feeling about her. But when they see another living creature and realize that it's a guinea pig with a ring around its middle, it shakes them out of their lethargy and they realize who they are, where they came from, and what they must try to do to get back.

Digory's Discovery

After considering their options, the young friends decide to try to return through the pool from which they emerged. When they jump in, holding hands, nothing happens. Then they realize they failed to use the green rings, but Digory gets a flash of inspiration.

What if, he proposes, this is a world between all other worlds, and jumping into another pool would take them to another world? He wants to try it immediately, but Polly says they must first make sure it's possible to get back home. So they decide to touch the green rings until they see Uncle Andrew's study getting close, then they will switch rings to return to the woods and try another pool.

This works, and after marking the pool leading back home and realizing that the green rings are always used to leave the woods, they get into another pool that leads them into a world that is bathed in red light and seems empty of all other life. They are in cavernous decaying buildings consisting of a series of huge halls, one entering into the next. Once they are almost convinced the place is an unending maze of more of the same, they come into one hall where sit hundreds of images of people that seem to have been frozen in time.

Charn and Its Evil Queen

Polly and Digory realize there's a progression of expressions on the faces in the people represented by the statues (or people who've been turned into statues), going from pleasant and happy-looking at the beginning to more serious to unhappy and, eventually, to miserable. And finally they are looking at the likeness of the largest and, Digory thinks, most beautiful woman he has ever seen, though Polly isn't impressed by her beauty.

QUESTION

What elements in this book overlap ones in works by fellow Inkling J. R. R. Tolkien?

The magic rings in this book compare with the enchanted ring in Tolkien's *Lord of the Rings*. And Aslan sings a new world into being, similar to a "singing into creation" in Tolkien's *Silmarillion*. The authors were reading each others works in progress at the time.

Around the same time, Digory discovers a pillar with a golden bell and a hammer on it. An inscription on the pillar, which seems indecipherable at first but becomes clearer as they scrutinize it, seems to say that striking the bell can put anyone doing so in danger, but failing to do so will drive anyone not striking it mad over wondering what might have happened.

Sticking Points

This became one of many sticking points over which Digory and Polly disagreed. Polly points out that not knowing what might have happened means nothing, but, as usual, Digory prevailed. He struck the golden bell, causing it to produce a sweet note. The note continued to build, sounding louder and louder until the building in which they were standing started to shake and the roof started falling in.

When the rumbling, shaking, and collapsing ended, the children thought they were safe and that the crisis was over. But then they heard a noise of movement in the far corner of the hall and found that the beautiful woman was rising from her stone chair, looking even larger than when she'd been sitting frozen.

Awakening the Witch

The woman wasn't nearly as beautiful once she began speaking and ordering the children around, identifying herself as Jadis, the queen of the former empire of Charn, in the ruins of which they now stood. She epitomized imperiousness and, even more than Uncle Andrew, showed no interest in the needs or wants of anyone other than herself. She had been forced to destroy Charn and everything living in it by using "the deplorable word" in order to foil the scheme of her sister to take over. The enchantments in "the deplorable word," which she refused to utter again, included turning all of Charn's previous rulers into statues, including herself, but enabled her to be wakened if someone should strike the bell.

She questioned the children and found the world they were from was relatively new in contrast to Charn, which was already old before she had destroyed its last vestiges of life. Hearing of Uncle Andrew's magical rings, she assumes he must be the ruler of their world. She orders them to take her there, and though they try to escape her, when they touch the rings she has hold of Polly's hair and they all find that the rings have a magnetism that pulls anything touching anyone using one of them along with the user.

Power Drain

Back in the woods between the worlds, they find that Jadis's powers are even more drained than their energy had been when they first got there. They are even stronger than her when they try to force her away from holding Polly by the hair. They jump into the pool leading back home, but when Jadis cries out for mercy Digory is moved enough to hesitate, and that hesitation is just enough for her to clutch his ear as he touches the ring.

Uncle Andrew, not surprisingly, is even more taken by Jadis's beauty and her presence when she materializes with the children in his study. She epitomizes everything he has dreamed of for most of his life, spent in magic experiments in the quest of power or at least a persona. But she, not surprisingly, seeing that he is not even of royal blood and not impressed with his long family line, considers him beneath even contempt and declares herself the Empress of the World.

Digory fears that the presence of Jadis in the house will terrorize his mother and perhaps cause her death. So after Jadis leaves the study and Polly says she'll take the crawlspace tunnel back home, Digory pleads with her to come back quickly and try to help him get Jadis out of their world. Some apologies would be in order first, Polly replies, reminding him of all the instances, such as striking the bell and hesitating at Jadis's appeal for mercy, when she had tried to warn him and which warnings he had ignored to their peril. Realizing his failings, the goodhearted boy quickly admits them and apologizes, in return for which Polly promises to return if and when her parents let her out of the house.

Out of This World

After the witch orders Andrew to get a chariot so she can go and get the jewels appropriate to her role as queen, Andrew rushes to get dressed in his finest clothes—complete with Eton collar, frock coat, and top hat—murmuring that Jadis is "one dem fine woman." Actually hoping to woo Jadis, Andrew, the author remarks, is proving that at times like these adults often behave just as foolishly as children do.

Andrew finds his sister Letty mending a mattress and he tries to coax her to give him money for the cab he needs for Jadis, telling Letty he has to entertain an important guest. When Jadis storms into the room, Letty responds to her brash speech and bare arms by calling her a shameless hussy. When Jadis's attempt to put a spell on Letty fails, she picks Letty up and throws her across the room, where she lands on the mattress. Digory goes to Letty's aid as Andrew and Jadis leave the house, walking off in search of a cab.

After Letty regains her equilibrium, she sends a servant out to find a police officer to tell him a wild woman is at large. After lunch, Digory sits next to a front window to plot how to get Jadis out of England and watch for her return. While he waits, he hears a neighbor come to the door to present some grapes to Letty for his mother and hears Letty say she fears it will take a visit to the land of youth to cure her sister. This starts Digory thinking that, with the rings and his access to the wood between the worlds, it might be possible for him to find a land of youth that he could take his mother to.

Chaos Breaks Out

Suddenly a hansom cab driven by Jadis, standing on its roof like a charioteer, flies around the corner, almost hitting the lamppost outside the window where Digory is sitting, and crashes, falling in pieces. It is followed by another hansom cab occupied by a jeweler and police officers, the jeweler shouting that Jadis has robbed his store. The horse is terrified by Jadis, and the cabby and Uncle Andrew emerge from the cab's rubble to try to tell their stories. As neighbors pour out of doorways to watch and take sides, Digory runs out, hoping to grab Jadis by the heel and use the yellow ring to leave the world. Police officers try to take hold of Jadis, but she breaks a steel bar off the lamppost and swings it to knock the policemen to the ground. Polly also runs out of her house, and Digory shouts to her to hold on and, when he gives the signal, touch her yellow ring.

> "Children have one kind of silliness, as you know, and grown-ups have another kind."..."There was a long, dull story of a grown-up kind behind these words. All you need to know." Jack's use of such direct address, showing understanding of his young audience, is a key to his enduring popularity.

Drawn Apart

A moment later Digory, Polly, Andrew, Jadis, the cabby, and the horse all emerge in the wood between worlds. Jadis still has the steel bar in her hand, but she is powerless there. But almost as soon as he surveys the scene, Digory touches his green ring, causing them all to leave again, this time arriving in a land in total darkness. Jadis says that she has come to her doom, but the cabby says it might just be the next work site for the London Tube, and he suggests they sing a hymn, selecting the one he knew best, about giving thanks for the harvest being brought in.

The children join him, and before they end singing they hear another voice singing what the children and the cabby think is the most beautiful thing they've ever heard. Jadis and Andrew think the singing is horrid. When the cabby and children stop singing, the unknown singer continued alone, but after a time other voices started in perfect harmony, in correlation with the appearance in the sky of stars, one after another, until the sky was full of thousands of stars and the singing continued from thousands of voices.

FACT

Pythagoras, the ancient Greek mathematician and astronomer, proposed that each of the stars and planets emits its own song, a concept thoroughly developed in Dante's *Divine Comedy*.

A World's Beginning

Eventually the blackness turned grey and pinks and reds of sunrise penetrated the darkness. As the stars' songs faded, day broke and the travelers saw that the singer, now singing alone again, was a lion—The Lion, Aslan—and as he continued the bare earth gave birth to grasses and other plants, trees, and every type of vegetation until the world for as far as they could see was like a fully mature garden. Bumps appeared in the newly created sod and from them animals of various species and sizes emerged until everything from moles to elephants were gathering around the Lion.

Seeing the Lion, Andrew said he wished he had his gun along. As Aslan approached the human visitors and the horse that came with them, Jadis threw the steel bar from the lamppost, hitting Aslan squarely in the middle of his forehead, but he continued, ignoring them as though he had felt nothing. With this, Jadis fled to hide in the woods.

Andrew Is Planted

After Aslan finished creating the many species of animals, he kissed two of each species and told them to gather around him, dismissing the others to scatter, which they did. The chosen animals were given the gift of speech. But though the children and the cabby can understand Aslan's speech and that of the animals he blesses, to Uncle Andrew Aslan seems to be simply growling or roaring and the other species are just making the noises they are known for. After Aslan finished with the talking animals, they turned and some of them noticed Andrew standing apart from everyone else (Digory, Polly, and the cabby and his horse having drawn closer as Digory had decided to ask the Lion for help for his mother).

THEY SAID . . .

"In *The Abolition of Man* Lewis calls magic the twin of science, especially applied science, and contrasts the knowledge of magic and science with the wisdom of the past. It is not surprising, then, that in *The Magician's Nephew* the evil characters, Jadis and Uncle Andrew, are both magicians and that the good adults, Frank [the cabby] and Helen [the cabby's wife], are simple rural folks."

—Doris Myers

Terrified, Andrew falls down in a dead faint. After the animals discuss what he is, they decide to plant him, feet down, in the ground in the belief that he is probably a tree. While they are moving him, trying to decide which end is the roots and which the branches, coins fall out of his pockets into the dirt.

King Cabby

Aslan also makes the cabby's horse, Strawberry, a talking horse. Telling the cabby that he has known him for a long time, Aslan asks if he would accept appointment as the first king of Narnia. The cabby says he is an uneducated man, but Aslan says that's not important. Then the cabby says that he would not like to leave his wife alone in London, never knowing what happened to him, at which Aslan directly calls her into Narnia and offers them both the thrones of Narnia.

The questions Aslan puts to the cabby and his wife in the following paragraphs may be the most complete summary in Jack's writings about the correct role of government or rulers and their interaction with their people. He asks if they can raise food from the earth, rule kindly and fairly, not treat the talking animals as slaves like the dumb creatures, raise their children in the same knowledge, not play favorites when judging among disputants, and lead his forces if war should become necessary and be the last in case of retreat.

Flying Horse

Digory asked Aslan to give him something to cure his mother, but first the Lion required Digory to own up to his failings that resulted in the entrance of evil, in the person of Jadis, into the new world. Digory understood and confessed his shortcomings, so Aslan gave him an assignment to win his pardon. Digory was to go to an apple tree across the world outside Narnia's borders, get an apple, and return it so he could plant it. Its presence in Narnia would keep Jadis from returning to wreak her evil for centuries to come, Aslan said.

Digory agreed, despite fears about his mother's condition, but said fulfilling the assignment would take him a long time. Aslan said he would have help and offered Strawberry wings if he would take Digory and Polly to the distant walled garden containing the special apple tree.

Happily After

Getting the apple entailed some adventure for the three, including an appearance at the walled garden by Jadis, who tried to entice Digory to eat one of the apples for his own immortality, or at least to take an extra one to take back to his mother. But remembering his promise to Aslan, he resisted and got back to Aslan with the single apple he'd been sent for.

FACT
Some speculate that "the deplorable word" Jadis uttered to destroy
Charn was not a literal word but a technology, perhaps a nuclear bomb.
But in the context of Jack's opposition to language reform, the deplor-
able word may be seen as the opposite of the Word, as in "In the begin-
ning was the Word" (John 1:1).

Aslan (making an exception to his earlier rule against not telling what
would have happened) told Digory that if he or his mother had eaten one
of the apples from the garden tree, it would have given them immortality,
as doing so had already done to Jadis. But her having eaten it was the very
reason she would not come into Narnia because she so despised this kind
of apple, and he and his mother would have come to hate immortality
after their generation had passed. The tree growing up in Narnia from the
apple Digory procured produced fruit the very next day, and as a reward
Aslan gave one of the apples to Digory for his mother, saying that an apple
from this tree would not give her immortality but would cure her current
illness. He told Digory and Polly to bury the magic rings once they got
back to London.

Meanwhile, the steel bar from the lamppost grew into a lamppost that
had a lamp that was always lit and that welcomed Lucy to Narnia in *The Lion,
the Witch, and the Wardrobe*. And the coins that fell out of Uncle Andrew's
pockets grew up into trees bearing silver and gold.

End and Beginning

Aslan had been instructing the cabby, Frank, and his wife, Helen, on
their duties as king and queen while the travelers were away. Now as all
gathered around, Aslan crowned them. The author says one of their sons
succeeded them as Narnia's second king and another became the first king
of Archenland, and that both sons married tree nymphs. Aslan told them no
rings were necessary when he was with them, so he instantaneously transported Digory, Polly, and Andrew back to London, where no time at all had

seemed to have passed since their leaving. But Jadis, the cabby, and his horse had mysteriously disappeared.

After eating the apple, Mrs. Kirke's healing began and eventually she was restored to full health. Some time later, Digory's father inherited a fortune from an uncle who died, so he returned from India to stay and they all moved into the manor house that Digory later inherited from his father and owned when the Pevensie children (who knew him as the Professor) had lived in it at the time of *The Lion, the Witch, and the Wardrobe.*

Immediately after their return from Narnia, Uncle Andrew ran to his bedroom to hide and Digory and Polly went to Andrew's attic study to recover all the rings and bury them, alongside the core of the apple Digory had given his mother to cure her. Though it didn't grow up overnight as its parent tree had in Narnia, the tree from that apple thrived and its fruit, though not magical, was superior to other apples available in their world. Years later, a storm blew over the apple tree and Digory had its wood finished and turned into a wardrobe that he moved to the spare room when he inherited his parents' country estate.

Chapter 17

The Last Battle

As the *The Magician's Nephew* is Narnia's creation story (comparable to the first chapters of Genesis), the seventh book published, *The Last Battle*, is the story of its apocalypse (comparable to the book of Revelation). Though the author ends *The Magician's Nephew* by saying there could come a day when something comparable to the witch's deplorable word that destroyed Charn destroys our world, he describes in this final book how a similar destruction comes to Narnia. Similar to the New Testament prophecies about the end of the world following the rise of an antichrist and assorted false messiahs, sometimes coming as wolves dressed up like sheep, in *The Last Battle* the end is brought about through the belief in an anti-Aslan, a false divinity who is a donkey clothed in a lion's skin.

Apostle of Apostasy

Though all the encounters with Aslan up till now have been one-to-one meetings and "faith" has been a very personal (rather than an organized or corporate) matter, at the beginning of *The Last Battle* the reader meets a first preacher of Aslan who holds nighttime public meetings to impart the latest teachings received from The Lion. This preacher, a talking ape named Shift, calls for cutting down the woods at Lantern Waste and putting Narnia's talking beasts to work.

FACT

Though reviewers of the early books in *The Chronicles of Narnia* were lukewarm, the books' reception among young readers was enthusiastic and their sales became brisk quickly as word of mouth spread. In 1956, when *The Last Battle* was published, it was chosen to receive the United Kingdom's Carnegie Medal for Children's Literature, comparable to the Newberry Medal in the United States.

Faith in Aslan was so weak among the Narnian population at this time that many were not sure he existed, but Shift the Ape was able to talk many of them into selling themselves into slavery to the Calormene by parading a false Aslan in front of them. The Ape promised the people that Aslan's new programs would "make Narnia a country worth living in." He promised that roads, big cities, schools, prisons, whips, offices, and other signs of progress were just around the corner. But a grumpy bear in his audience said they didn't want progress but preferred their freedom. Shift called the bear and all those who thought like him stupid and concluded, "True freedom means doing what I tell you."

Shifting Priorities

The public meetings were held in the darkness of night to keep the people from having a close look at the poor imitation of Aslan, portrayed by a feckless donkey named Puzzle, who went along with Shift's deceptions because Shift was his only friend and Puzzle was unsure Shift was a false prophet. The Narnians gathered on a hillside below a stable where Puzzle the anti-Aslan was quartered and where Shift the Ape expounded his ever-evolving word with a Calormene consultant at his side.

Though at first it seems that Shift is a small-time conniver trying to promote his own interests, later in the story his treachery against Narnia as a collaborator with their traditional enemies, the Calormene, is fully revealed. By successfully manipulating the donkey Puzzle to carry out his unreasonable requests and serve as virtually his slave, Shift gains the confidence he needs to mislead the Narnian population. Many of them are willing to follow his anti-Aslan, his phony lion, rather than the true Lion, into serving the program of their enemies rather than defending their own land and its principles.

Good News and Bad

The pseudo-Aslan whispers in the ear of Shift (Shift claims) the changes in his plans for Narnia and its people. Among the most egregious of these are cutting down spirit-inhabited trees for export to Calormen and using talking animals for manual labor, such as talking horses being used as draft horses.

The king of Narnia at this time was a young man named Tirian, no more than twenty-five years old, whose closest friend, confidant, and counselor was Jewel, a unicorn. They had been discussing the "wonderful news" of rumors that Aslan was again on the move in Narnia and recounting a series of incidences of the rumor reaching them by varied sources when a centaur named Roonwit, a student of the stars, arrived at their hunting lodge not far from Lantern Waste.

Disaster Foretold

Roonwit told them that the rumors of Aslan's appearances must be lies. There had not only been no indication in the stars of his visiting Narnia, but the stars had recently been forecasting disastrous events just ahead for the kingdom. And on the heels of this revelation to the king and his counsel arrives a disembodied voice, that of a dryad from one of the Lantern Waste trees. The trees inhabited by naiads and dryads have been considered untouchable in the past, as cutting one of them down causes the death of one of the tree spirits. "Great trees are falling, falling, falling," the dryad tells Tirian, Jewel, and Roonwit, and almost immediately she is silenced as her own tree some distance away is hewn down.

Tirian immediately called for action to end this villainy by going upriver to Lantern Waste to intervene. He took Jewel with him and sent Roonwit back south to Cair Paravel to rally as many fighters as he could in case force might be required to put down insurrection or incursion.

When Tirian and Jewel arrived at the site of the logging at Lantern Waste, they were horrified to see the sacred trees being cut down and dragged by horses to the river, where they were loaded on rafts and sent on south to Calormen. But when they saw that the horses pulling the logs were not the Calormene's own but talking, presumably free, Narnian horses, Tirian and Jewel became enraged and in an instant Tirian swung his sword and beheaded one of the two Calormene beating a talking horse. Jewel gored the other one through the heart with his horn.

The Rebellion

Calormene workers nearby noticed Jewel and Tirian (but did not know their identities), and they started toward them to see what the two had done to their coworkers. Jewel told Tirian to get on his back and they started fleeing. But after a little time to reflect, Tirian told Jewel to stop and, after dismounting, faced him and said, "We have done a dreadful deed."

Jewel argued that they had been provoked, but the king replied that killing without first confronting the abusive workers was murder. They turned themselves in to the Calormene and asked to be taken to Aslan, so the Calormene took them to Shift the Ape. Shift was in the midst of an afternoon public presentation of the latest word from Aslan, so Tirian and Jewel got to witness a sampling of what had been going on to undermine the people's faith in Aslan.

When a cat, Ginger, in the crowd asked where Tash, the Calormene god, fit into Shift's new teachings, Shift replied that Tash is just another name for Aslan and added that from now on they will call him Tashlan. Silent until now, Tirian was outraged by this, shouting, "Ape, you lie." And before he could finish his defense of Aslan against this defamation, two Calormene attacked him and Shift ordered that Tirian be tied to a tree, saying that he, "or I mean Aslan," will do justice to him later. Jewel was taken behind the stable and tied there while Tirian was led to the bottom of the hill and bound to the nearest tree in standing position.

The King in Bondage

From the bottom of the hill, Tirian was able to see and hear Shift holding forth before his ever-more-captive audience, like a cult leader imposing his will on a mesmerized congregation. After the gathering broke up and darkness fell, Tirian got thirsty and hungry with nothing to sustain him. Three mice, a rabbit, and two moles came to offer their support, knowing he was their king, but nonetheless they had been taken in by Shift to believe that the donkey in a lion's skin was Aslan and Shift was his prophet. They worked together to give Tirian wine and cheese and clean up the blood on his face.

THEY SAID . . .

"Don't let anyone deceive you in any way, for that day will not come until the rebellion occurs and the man of lawlessness is revealed, the man doomed to destruction. He will oppose and will exalt himself over everything that is…worshiped, so that he sets himself up…proclaiming himself to be God."

—2 Thessalonians 2:1–4

Later, Tirian noticed that a bonfire had been lit and the Narnian beasts were gathering again to hear Shift in the hopes that Aslan would appear to them again. He could see the donkey in the yellow lion skin but the action was too far away for him to know what it really was, and Tirian had never seen Aslan. And for a moment he had desperate doubts.

Tirian's Vision

Tirian's desperation turned him to contemplation. In his pain and humiliation he closed his eyes and rehearsed the accounts he'd learned from his lessons on Narnia's history of Aslan's previous interactions with the land and its rulers. Rilian, his own great-grandfather's great-grandfather, had been rescued by children called to Narnia by Aslan to go to the ruined city of the giants and, far below it, to uncover and destroy a plot against the crown prince and return him to his people.

> ## THEY SAID . . .
> Lewis researchers find the two final books of *The Chronicles of Narnia*, *The Magician's Nephew* and *The Last Battle*, are the favorites among adult readers. *The Lion, the Witch, and the Wardrobe* is the favorite of children. In the final book, the child protagonists are not introduced until the fifth chapter, so children may not be as captivated by it from its beginning.

Caspian the Seafarer, Rilian's father, eight generations earlier than Tirian, had also been saved by children called by Aslan from a plot by a devious uncle to kill him and take away his birthright. High King Peter, Queen Susan, King Edmund, and Queen Lucy had been called into Narnia by Aslan to end a hundred-year rule of the tyrannical witch queen Jadis. The Aslan in these stories from Narnia's history could not be the skinny and whispering beast with some sort of yellow coat that Tirian could dimly see at the top of the hill.

Tirian wished that someone could be brought to Narnia now to intervene in his darkest hour, and he cried out, like Eustace had instructed Jill Pole to do earlier, "Aslan! Aslan! Aslan! Come and help us now!" He said he was not asking for himself but for the deliverance of Narnia alone. Then Tirian seemed to go into a dream state where he saw himself in a room with seven people, who seemed able to see him but couldn't hear his words. The eldest of the group told him to speak if he was, as they sensed, a messenger from Narnia, because they were the seven friends of Narnia.

His dream or vision faded, and Tirian came out of it, moist with the dew of morning and cold in addition to his other miseries of being forced to stand all through the night. But a moment later a boy and a girl appeared in front him out of nowhere and introduced themselves as Eustace Scrubb and Jill Pole. Before the boy could even react to his jolt at finding himself in another world, Jill was saying, "Untie him; we can talk later."

The same children who had rescued Rilian had been brought to help him, and once that was established Tirian lost no time directing what they had to do to escape from his captors. They dashed into the adjacent woods to rocky ground where they would leave no tracks, so they could go on from there to plan their strategy to stand against Shift the Ape and the Calormene.

They first put on disguises and darkened their skin with juice so they could pass as Calormene if spotted as they sneaked into Shift's compound to find and rescue Jewel. They then decided they would ride to meet Roonwit and return with the enforcements he was sent to Cair Paravel to rally.

While Tirian and Eustace found and freed Jewel, Jill stole away and surprised her comrades by reappearing with a donkey, none other than the pseudo-Aslan himself, Puzzle. Tirian immediately moved to kill Puzzle, but Jill intervened, saying that the donkey was guileless and had been Shift's dupe.

Dwarfs for Dwarfs

Before heading out to Cair Paravel, Tirian took a detour to try to persuade the dwarfs who had spoken up against Shift to come over to his side, thinking that by showing them the donkey and the yellow lion's skin he had been wearing to pass as Aslan would change their minds. But the dwarfs had decided that the phony Aslan presented by Shift was no more reprehensible than the alleged real Aslan, whom they hadn't seen in their generation. They said they didn't need anyone to lead them or represent them. "The Dwarfs are for the Dwarfs," they declared.

The dwarfs started off in another direction, to Tirian's dismay. But a little later one dwarf, named Poggin, caught up with Tirian's party to offer his loyalty and support to the king. Tirian led his remnant of followers to a fortified tower to compare information provided by Jewel, who had been listening as best he could during his incarceration, and Poggin, who had followed the rise of Shift and his anti-Aslan. And there they planned their strategy for saving Narnia.

The Real Powers

Poggin told them that Ginger the Cat and Rishda Tarkaan had told Narnians that Tirian was no longer with them because while tied up to the tree he had cursed Aslan and had been swallowed up by him. He also reported hearing Ginger the Cat and Rishda speaking as though they were the real powers behind Shift and that their goal was to make Narnia a Calormene province. And Ginger confirmed Rishda's suspicion about his faithlessness and that of many Narnians by saying "there's no such person as either" Aslan or Tash. To this, Rishda replied in words Jack may have often heard in the halls of Oxford, applied to Christianity, and words that he may even have used some years earlier: "all who are enlightened know that."

No sooner had they made this assessment of Narnia's spiritual health than they saw an apparition flying over, appearing like a huge, ghostly vulture emitting the smell of a dead body. They concluded that because Shift had invoked a demon, Tash was on his way to join them but not to be manipulated by them.

Disastrous News

Tirian, Eustace, Jill, Jewel, and Poggin discussed whether they should first go to Shift and confront him in front of his audience with their evidence of the false Aslan or meet Roonwit and his army on their way. They chose to meet their reinforcements and began moving toward Cair Paravel. As they went on, their spirits felt buoyed by having made their decision and feeling it was a workable plan. Jill talked about the glories of Narnia and her desire to see it continue forever, but Jewel replied that all kingdoms must eventually end.

Presently, they were met by an eagle, named Farsight, who said he bore bad news. He reported that from the air he had witnessed Cair Paravel being taken by the Calormene army and Roonwit himself being killed in the attack. The centaur had not had time to organize an army, so no help would be on the way. Narnia had already fallen.

Narnia No More

Though there seemed no way to fight on or hope for turning things around, Tirian and his companions decided to confront Shift, the embodiment of evil in their view, with the evidence that he had created an anti-Aslan and deceived his countrymen. Believing this course to be the right thing to do despite knowing it would probably prove fatal, they made their way back to Lantern Waste. Tirian tried to talk Eustace and Jill into returning to their own world as their fate here seemed apparent.

Both refused to consider Tirian's proposal, believing that Aslan had brought them to him for a purpose and had not left it to them to determine when their mission was done. Furthermore, they had no control over their return; their experience and the testimony of the other five friends of Narnia gave them no reason to think that just wanting to return would make that happen. Eustace, in particular, knew that not wanting to be in Narnia had never changed his reality when he'd been there before.

Discussing Death

Eustace and Jill discussed what would happen if they died in Narnia. Would they also be dead in their world? Eustace said he would rather put his fate in Narnia than in British Railways. When Jill found this a strange thing to say, Eustace explained that at the moment they were jerked into Narnia while sitting in a railway coach, he had immediately supposed the train had crashed.

THEY SAID . . .

[Should children] read books that have such frightening content[?] C. S. Lewis tackled this issue head-on and offered some good advice…:
"Since it is so likely that they will meet cruel enemies, let them at least have heard of brave knights and heroic courage. Otherwise you are making their destiny not brighter but darker."

—Michael Flaherty, President, Walden Media

The others were discussing whether it would be better to confront Shift and the Calormene and face almost certain death, or rather go into hiding as the Narnians who were faithful to Aslan had done before when cruel Queen Jadis ruled and when Miraz had ruled. This time, they concluded, was a time for taking a stand against disbelief and deception.

The Stable

Tirian also suggested that Jill and Eustace go toward Archenland to wait there for Aslan's orders, but after they considered this all concluded that if Narnia had fallen Archenland would not stand much longer either. When they arrived at the rear of the stable poised to make their dramatic entrance, they bid each other farewell. Tirian asked Jewel to forgive any offenses he had ever committed, to which Jewel answered he almost wished there had been something to forgive.

Before they could expose the phony Aslan by bringing Puzzle before the crowd and holding up the lion's skin, Shift the Ape began his evening talk by saying Aslan—or rather "Tashlan"—had become angered because a beast who had been in the stable just behind him had dared to dress up like Tashlan and walk out among the people as a brazen fraud. Tirian's planned exposure of the actual fraud had been undercut. Now if Puzzle was shown off he would prove not their claim but seem to support that of Shift the Ape.

While Jewel and the others removed the lion skin from Puzzle's back, Shift was continuing to tell the audience that Tashlan was so angered by this development that he had decided to make no more appearances before them. Some of the disgruntled dwarfs in the audience mocked this proposition, saying Aslan or Tashlan had never been with Shift, that what they'd been shown was just a donkey in a lion skin.

Visiting Tashlan

But Shift countered that anyone who wanted to see Tashlan could do so by going into the stable one at a time. To this, the dwarfs jeered back that if anyone dared to meet with Tashlan it would mean death by the hands of a Calormene waiting inside. Nevertheless, Ginger the Cat said he was ready to go in, but no sooner than he had passed through the door did he jump back out with a kitty scream. Asked to describe what had been there, he tried to speak but could not. He was no longer a talking cat, and this terrified the audience of mostly talking animals as they had all been taught in infancy that Aslan would revoke their gift of speech if they did evil.

Ginger's experience notwithstanding, a Calormen army officer insisted that it was his lifelong dream to meet Tash, and he would go in. Though Rishda tried to dissuade him, he couldn't be deterred, so he was allowed in. A moment later a body, apparently his, was thrown back out, but Tirian and his companions could see, being close to the front, that the face on the officer thrown outside was not that of the one who went in. But Shift and Rishda assured the audience that it was.

Last Battles

Having no more volunteers to meet Tashlan, Shift said he would start ordering members of the audience to enter the stable, singling out a boar as the first. The boar had no desire to be sacrificed to whatever was in the stable and began resisting the Calormene soldiers who tried to drag him to the door. At this, Tirian decided to make his stand. He gave the word to his companions to take up their arms, and they began fighting on the boar's behalf. Tirian quickly pushed Shift into the stable as the next victim of his own treachery. Then the dogs who were in the audience ran together to offer Tirian their support, followed by the small animals (who had ministered to Tirian when he was bound to the tree) who also joined them, and the battle was joined.

In a few minutes, Rishda ordered those loyal to him to retreat in order to reconnoiter. The battle was won. But the next—the last battle of the last king of Narnia—was about to begin. The Calormene army was arriving from its conquest of Cair Paravel, and this time the Calormene were unstoppable. Rishda ordered the slaying of the animals with Tirian and rounding up all the "two-legged" members on his side to throw them to Tash (a fact he no longer tried to hide) behind the stable door.

On to Real Narnia

When he was forced through the stable door, Tirian was surprised to find it was not dark but bright and beautiful on the other side. Soon he saw seven kings and queens of Narnia coming to greet him. After a minute he realized that the youngest queen was Jill, who had been fighting at his side just moments earlier, dressed much differently than she now was. And next to her was Eustace. All the famous children who had been brought to save Narnia by Aslan over its history were together, all looking at their prime age. Peter invited Tirian to try the fruit on the tree next to them, and when he tasted it he realized they were in Aslan's country.

The only one not with them was Susan who, Tirian was told, had felt she'd outgrown Narnia and didn't want to participate in the friends of Narnia get-togethers. All had been brought into Narnia through the train wreck in England, some inside the train and some on the platform where it crashed.

And with them was Aslan himself. He walked over to the door that had been the door of the stable but now was the door between Narnia and Aslan's country. Standing at the door looking out, Aslan began to roar, "'Now it is time!' then louder, 'Time!'; then so loud that it could have shaken the stars, 'TIME.'" At which the door opened.

The three final chapters of *The Last Battle* describe the final destruction of Narnia and its world by Aslan, including the pulling of its stars out of the heavens, followed by the experiencing of Aslan's country, or "the real Narnia" as they came to know it, by Tirian and the friends of Narnia and all the talking animals who had been taken inside. In this section is the passage already discussed that describes the blindness of the dwarfs, who find themselves inside Aslan's country but, because of the blinders they have chosen to wear, they see it not as paradise but as a dark, smelly stable.

QUESTION
What have some taken objection to in this passage?
Some have claimed that Susan was barred from Narnian heaven for losing her faith, considering that a negative message to give to children. Lewis defenders point out that Susan's final destiny is not dealt with. She is still alive in this part of the saga and may not have finally renounced her faith.

Many believe these chapters are Jack's masterpiece, as he successfully answers those who jeer that heaven or eternal life would be boring, with nothing to do but praise God. But by finding that there is always more of the real Narnia "further up and further in," those now on the other side find it is a place of endless delight and exploration.

This is also where Jack introduces his concept of "Shadowlands," which is how the real Narnians now come to regard the Narnia, as well as the England, of their previous lives. Those were the relatively colorless and flat shadows of the real lands to come, they realize, revisiting some of Jack's themes in *The Great Divorce*. Here, everything is "bigger" and more visible, more tangible, than it was in the shadowlands they once lived in. And also, Jack concludes, it is only now that the children and the Narnians are just beginning Chapter One of the Real Story.

Chapter 18

Books Meanwhile and After

As promised in Chapter 9, the focus now turns to the other books published during the years after Jack started and brought to completion *The Chronicles of Narnia* (1939–1956). This chapter will also look at several of the best-known volumes of his later years.

That Hideous Strength

That Hideous Strength, the third of Jack's Space Trilogy science fiction novels for adult readers, continues where *Out of the Silent Planet* and *Perelandra* left off. Published in 1945, *That Hideous Strength* can be considered a fictional complement to *The Abolition of Man*. It is Jack's largest novel (slightly longer than the first two volumes together) and it takes on everything from cliques that try to run establishments like college departments to the use of science to control the world, or at least other people.

THEY SAID . . .

"All superfluous life is to be wiped out, all natural forces tamed, the common people are to be used as slaves...by the ruling caste of scientists, who even [confer] immortal life upon themselves. Man, in short, is to storm the heavens and overthrow the gods, or even to become a god himself."
—George Orwell, from a 1945 review of *That Hideous Strength*

Set on the planet Earth, Jack's third space odyssey brings back his god-fearing central character, Dr. Elwin Ransom, but without his satanic nemesis from the previous novels, Professor Edward Rolles Weston, who was killed in *Perelandra*. However, Dick Devine, Weston's companion in the previous novel, reappears here where he becomes Lord Feverstone, one of the controllers of Belbury. And having put his interplanetary travels behind him, Ransom is now the pendragon, the director of the St. Anne's-on-the-Hill Community, and is also called the Fisher-King. Both Pendragon and Fisher-King are names for a figure from Arthurian legend who is always portrayed as wounded in the legs, as Ransom is as a result of his battle with Weston in *Perelandra*.

An Un-nice Conspiracy

That Hideous Strength is strongly influenced by writings of Jack's close friend Charles Williams and relies on ideas about law and natural law propounded by another close friend, Owen Barfield. Some have observed that

Ransom, who seems to be modeled after Jack himself in the earlier novels, this time more resembles Williams, who died unexpectedly while *That Hideous Strength* was being written. Two institutions compete. One—Belbury and its National Institute for Co-ordinated Experiments (N.I.C.E.)—seeks to gain control over the human race through science, occult magic, and the control of language. The other—St. Anne's Community—is dedicated to thwarting the not so nice schemes of N.I.C.E. Both are involved in a small university, Edgestow, in a small city in central England, which Jack compares in the preface to Durham.

George Sayer claims in *Jack* that many of the members of the N.I.C.E. conspiracy are modeled after colleagues Jack knew well at Oxford, "progressives," who "rigged meetings and held traditional values in contempt." Jack says in the preface, "This is a 'tall story' about devilry, though it has behind it a serious 'point' which I have tried to make in my *Abolition of Man*."

Mark and Jane Studdock, married only six months and attached to the university by his teaching position and her work on a doctoral thesis on Donne, are cast as ordinary people caught up in a cosmic struggle between angels (the side Jane joins after finding supportive acceptance at St. Anne's) and devils (the side Mark joins by accepting a job writing articles on behalf of Belbury and N.I.C.E.).

Control of Language

Doris T. Myers says the book's title, taken from a medieval commentary on the story of the Tower of Babel in Genesis, suggests the control of language as its central issue. The Tower of Babel account is the Bible's explanation of how human language became diversified as God's punishment for human rebellion against him and attempts to seize his place of power. The same occurs in Belbury when Merlin, the Arthurian wizard wakened from his thousand-year slumber, which both the Pendragon and the heads of N.I.C.E. anticipate, "uses the power of language" to confound the N.I.C.E. conspirators.

Even Jack considered *That Hideous Strength* problematic, at one point calling it "bosh" and "rubbish," according to Myers. Writing to E. R. Eddison, Jack says that "the thought of trying to mend it, and of abandoning it, seem equally unbearable," yet it has remained the best-selling of his novels for adults. And though most reviewers considered it flawed, attempting too much on too many fronts, most also saw it as groundbreaking and better written and more worth reading than most popular novels.

The Great Divorce

Also published in 1945, *The Great Divorce* is the shortest of Jack's seven novels for adult readers and, in the opinion of many, his most profound. The title is a reversal of William Blake's title, *The Marriage of Heaven and Hell*, and represents a homage to one of his favorite works of classical literature, Dante's *Divine Comedy*. As Dante used Virgil as a guide, Jack uses his favorite author (whom he called his mentor), George Macdonald, to guide the narrator (presumably the author) in a tourbus excursion from a grim gray city to the foothills of heaven, or paradise.

Sayer relates an entry that Warnie wrote in his diary about Jack's getting the idea for the novel in 1933: "J has a new idea for a religious work, based on the opinion of some of the Fathers, that while punishment for the damned is eternal, it is intermittent: he proposes to do a sort of infernal day excursion to Paradise."

"I do not think that all who choose wrong roads perish; but their rescue consists in being put back on the right road. A wrong sum can be put right: but only by going back till you find the error and working it afresh from that point, never by simply going on."

—*From the preface*

Second Chance

As the story developed more than a decade later, it wasn't just an intermittent reprieve or field trip away from the gray city but an opportunity to stay in paradise if the tourist so chose. But the narrator is amazed to see that all but one of the tourists gets back on the bus for the return trip to hell. Some of the fathers of the church have proposed that the love and grace of God are heaven to those who want it and hell to those who don't.

And one notable father, St. Gregory of Nyssa (circa. 335–after 394), believed that it is proper for Christians to hope and pray that the love of God will win over even those most disinclined to receive it. A similar inclination to universalism came through the homiletical (preaching) writings of the

Scottish Protestant minister and novelist George Macdonald. Though Lewis doesn't agree with it, he also considers it a sign of Macdonald's great compassion and love for both God and mankind that Macdonald so ardently wanted the reconciliation of the lost to their creator.

Two Kinds of People

It is in this pursuit of reconciliation that Jack provides what many consider his most sublime theological principle: "There are only two kinds of people in the end: those who say to God, 'Thy will be done,' and those to whom God says, in the end, '*Thy* will be done.' All that are in Hell, choose it."

The Great Divorce lends several of its major theses to *The Last Battle*, the final book in *The Chronicles of Narnia*, published a decade later. Like most of the people who take the day trip from the gray city to paradise and return to their lonely self-centered lives in hell, the group of dwarfs who chose to live by the maxim "The Dwarfs are for the Dwarfs" could not see the paradise of the real Narnia even though they were in it, choosing to believe it was a foul stable, their own private hell. And as the real Narnia was so much brighter and crisper in every way than the shadowland that had been previously called Narnia, some of the day-trippers in *The Great Divorce* can't stand the "sharpness" of paradise, even finding the blades of grass painful on their feet. They realize the sharpness is caused by their own incorporeality, for they are ghosts or disembodied spirits. They are approached by residents of paradise who look familiar to them from life and encourage them to repent from the attitudes that keep them from heaven, assuring them that as they repent they will become less ghostly, more corporeal, and thus will not be tormented by a raindrop or blade of grass.

Like *The Screwtape Letters*, Jack's second novel, *The Great Divorce* was first published as a series in the church paper, *The Guardian*, in 1944 and 1945. Its original title was *Who Goes Home? or the Great Divorce*, which was changed by the publisher for its release in book form to *The Great Divorce, A Dream*. Macmillan shortened the title for the American edition to just *The Great Divorce*. By presenting its controversial ideas as a dream, Jack deflected criticisms that some have made that an opportunity for a second chance for salvation after death is not part of the orthodox tradition of the church. Another favorite Lewis quotation from the book sums up its thesis:

"If we insist on keeping Hell (or even earth) we shall not see Heaven: if we accept Heaven we shall not be able to retain even the smallest and most intimate souvenirs of Hell." The book ends in the same words as John Bunyan's *The Pilgrim's Progress*, "And I awoke, and behold, it was all a Dream," which hearkens back to Jack's first novel, *The Pilgrim's Regress*, a recasting of Bunyan's classic allegory.

Miracles

Though Jack said when he ended the final one of his talks on the BBC in 1944 that became *Mere Christianity* that he could not undertake yet another series of radio talks because his apologetics cup was empty, over the years he had heard enough arguments against accepting Christianity based on skepticism about miracles to get his apologetic juices flowing again.

THEY SAID . . .

"If I were ever to stray into the Christian camp, it would be because of Lewis's arguments as expressed in books like *Miracles*."

—Kenneth Tynan (a former student of Jack, famous for the play, *Oh, Calcutta!*)

"I read Lewis for comfort and pleasure many years ago, and a glance into the books revives my old admiration."

—John Updike

The result was *Miracles*, which in some ways is more ambitious than either *Mere Christianity* or *The Problem of Pain*. In the view of some—including George Sayer—*Miracles* is less effective than either of those earlier landmark works. It may be that the book's ambition, being more theoretical and abstract than the other two, is the reason Jack didn't consider using it for another series of radio talks, though the topic would probably have had wide public appeal.

Nature and Supernature

Before addressing the miracle accounts in the Bible, Jack lays out the framework of logical reasoning and argues that many people think that nature is all there is or that everything can be accounted for within natural processes. The idea that there is something outside nature he calls "supernaturalism." A "miracle" is defined as an occurrence of nature being invaded by "supernature" (or, at least in one case that he cites, by "subnature"). Later, he compares the miraculous turning of water into wine by Jesus at the wedding in Cana as recorded in the New Testament (John 2) with the natural process, common every year, of turning water into grape juice by grape vines. And grape juice, if not pasteurized, soon naturally turns into wine.

A Humbling

On February 2, 1948, Elizabeth Anscombe, one of philosopher Ludwig Wittgenstein's top students at Cambridge and later a major British philosopher in her own right, presented a paper at the Oxford Socratic Club (organized by Jack and where he had honed his formidable debating skills) refuting Chapter 3 of the original edition of *Miracles*, then entitled "Naturalism is Self-Refuting." Sayer reports that Jack was devastated by having his argument for proof of the existence of God undermined by Anscombe and it turned him away from apologetical writing from that time on. Anscombe, a convert and devoted follower of Catholicism, wrote that she and Humphrey Havard, Jack's close friend and physician, and Professor Jack Bennet had dinner with Jack a few weeks after the debate and didn't get the impression he felt defeated or humiliated by the debate. He did rewrite Chapter 3 of the book under the title "The Cardinal Difficulty of Naturalism." (In later editions it is "The Self-Contradiction of the Naturalist.") Anscombe thought the rewrite demonstrated Jack's honesty and the seriousness of his purpose in publishing *Miracles*.

Sayer felt the debate (which many attendees considered to be a draw) changed Jack's approach to writing for the rest of his life. It demonstrated that he had not kept up with the new schools of philosophy since the Hegelianism dominant in his own undergraduate days. And as the theme of some of his own best writings attest, being humbled is good for the soul.

Surprised by Joy

Though Jack's 1955 story of his early life, *Surprised by Joy,* has illuminated the accounts of his childhood and pre-Christian adult phases throughout this book, it has not been the focus of review here until now. Considered highly readable and enjoyable by Lewis fans and among his bestselling books year after year, it is flawed as autobiography by several omissions.

It does not mention Mrs. Moore, a major figure in his early life, and, ironically, underplays the writing he did in childhood. It also fails to address the grief he felt over the loss of his mother, but it overemphasizes his public school miseries. This topic, Sayer points out, takes up a third of the book for reasons Jack explained in a letter to Bede Griffiths in February 1956 (see sidebar).

> "I feel the whole of one's youth to be immensely important and even of immense length. The gradual reading of one's own life, seeing a pattern emerge, is a great illumination at our age. And partly, I hope, getting freed from the past as past by apprehending it as structure."
>
> —*Letter to Bede Griffiths*

In the preface, Jack describes his own purposes in writing the early life story as sharing his testimony of conversion from atheism to Christ and his lifelong experience of Joy, which had been transfigured from ill-defined "Northernness" or *sehnsucht* to spiritual union with God. But some reviewers felt it failed as a testimony or evangelizing tool.

Clearing the Decks

Sayer reports that although it wasn't published until 1955, Jack began work on the memoir in 1948 in order to rid himself of obsessions that had bothered him since his boarding school days and was so pleased with the results he saw in his creativity that he didn't care how it might be received. It was neither a tract to persuade inquirers to convert to Christianity nor a confession, though it seemed to have the therapeutic effect often associated with the latter on its author.

It's ironic, however, that Jack had written against "the personal heresy" of trying to gain insights into writers' works by looking at their life stories. *Surprised by Joy* opens the door to wanting to know more and more about his personal life, so that the fascination continues to inspire new biographies, screenplays, and essays, even to the current time. On the other hand, anyone who assumes leadership in the church, which Jack had certainly attained by this stage in his life by virtue of his writing, lectures, broadcasts, counseling thousands through correspondence, and serving on a Bible translation committee, is, arguably, expected to demonstrate some transparency and accountability. So this desire or obligation to open himself up to scrutiny was most likely a major factor in Jack's deciding to share the story of his early life. He had already encouraged Warnie to collect, organize, and edit his letters, in all likelihood aware that there would come a day when future students of his work, if not the general public, would find those looks into the family's life worth considering.

Reflections on the Psalms

Jack was encouraged by his friend, theologian Austin Farrer, to write *Reflections on the Psalms*, his only book of Bible commentary and his first religious writing since *Miracles*. Jack's own health was failing, his wife was suffering from cancer at the time (see Chapter 19), and he was going through a period of creative drought in 1957. Acknowledging no expertise in the Hebrew in which the Psalms were originally composed, he approached the Psalms as he would English poetry, a field in which he did possess considerable expertise. But some have complained that the inferences he makes about the Jewish religion through his comments on Psalms, especially those known as cursing psalms (which plead for God to pour out his wrath on Israel's enemies), display anti-Semitic leanings.

Jack's non-Christian peers at Oxford often accused him of being a fundamentalist for taking Christianity seriously and openly defending it, but some Protestant fundamentalists object to some of his comments in this book as well. As expressed on one Web page discussing it, "Lewis did believe that the Bible was the Word of God, but he also believed that we were given our minds to use them. In his *Reflections on the Psalms* Lewis says, 'At one point I had to explain how I differed on a certain point from both Catholics and Fundamentalists: I hope I shall not for this forfeit the goodwill or the prayers of either. Nor do I much fear it.' The 'certain matter' [was] the source of authority: although he regards much of the Bible as being the historical truth, he cannot regard it as a source of absolute certainty, as fundamentalists do."

Praising God

One of his most profound passages in this work is his treatment of praising God, which is the focus of most of the Psalms. Praise is part of the enjoyment of anything that is received with gratitude and joy, he says. "I think we delight to praise what we enjoy because the praise not merely expresses but completes the enjoyment; it is its appointed consummation." Praising God is nothing more than what people usually do when they discuss those things they most value in life. And the main thing received from God is God himself: "It is in the process of being worshipped that God communicates His presence to men."

> "I write as one amateur to another, talking about the difficulties I have met, or lights I have gained, with the hope that this might at any rate interest, and sometimes even help, other inexpert readers."
>
> —*Reflections on Psalms*

The most widely quoted line from the book is one he applied to some of the cursing psalms: "Of all bad men religious bad men are the worst." Carol Ann Brown, writing in the *C. S. Lewis Bulletin*, said that although his commentary on the Psalms is one of the lesser known of Jack's works, it "remains the one book on the Psalms that would satisfy the general reader in our time."

The Four Loves

One of Jack's shorter volumes, *The Four Loves* originated in 1957 in response to a request of the Episcopal Radio-TV Foundation, based in Atlanta, Georgia, to make tape-recorded programs for broadcast in the United States on any subject of his choosing. Happily married to Joy at the time (as recounted in more detail in Chapter 19), the topic most in Jack's thinking at the time was love, so he suggested he speak on five variations on the theme: liking versus love, affection, friendship, eros, and charity or the "gift love" of God.

After the radio programs were written off, Jack got permission to publish their content in book form, and *The Four Loves* was released in 1960. In the introduction, Jack discusses the Gospel of John's declaration that "God is love" and claims that "love begins to be a demon the moment he begins to be a god." In other words, there's a difference between God being love and love being God. He first considered this Gospel declaration in terms of "need love" (like that of a dependent person, like an infant, toward a parent) and "gift love" (like that of fathers providing for the needs of their families even after their passing on or, more to the point, the love expressed as God's grace by making a way for his children to know and join themselves to him).

QUESTION

What came of Jack's foray into American radio?
The sponsoring foundation was uncomfortable with the treatment of sex in his program on eros. Having cleared his topic list with foundation representatives before preparing the talk, Jack, when told of their reaction, replied, "How could eros be discussed without getting into sex?" The programs were never widely broadcast.

The second of the short book's six chapters, "Likings and Loves for the Sub-human," discusses the universal tendency to describe favorite interests as things we love, such as loving certain foods. Chapter 3 addresses affection, especially among family members and people brought together by circumstances beyond their choosing, such as military or work teammates.

Chapter 4 discusses friendship and describes those loving relationships chosen because we discover traits or, even more importantly, common interests with acquaintances. Jack says that the survival of the early church depended on it. The early disciples had to love one another in order to support and encourage one another, and the church has always existed for and by the friendship of its members.

Eros, the topic of Chapter 5, talks about the sexual love between people committed to building their lives together. And charity, as it was called in the

King James Version of the Bible but was in the Greek and more commonly in later translations referred to as *agape*, is the focus of the final chapter.

The book has been well reviewed, widely used by church groups, and highly praised. Even Pope John Paul II, who cited it in some of his sermons and lectures, told Lewis biographer and one-time secretary Walter Hooper that it was among his favorite books.

Chapter 19

Life with Joy

After a long period of declining health, Mrs. Moore died in 1951. Her death left Jack free to consider marriage, but being a man in his late fifties he did not at first think it probable. He entered into a civil marriage with Joy Gresham in 1956 as, at first, a means for her to stay in the country. But their relationship soon blossomed and became a legendary love story.

The Lifelong Bachelor Meets His Match

Jack met one of his early ardent American admirers, Joy Davidman Gresham, in 1952 when she came to England to get his advice on her failing marriage and the book she was writing about the Ten Commandments, *Smoke on the Mountain*. While she was in England her sometimes abusive husband, William Lindsay Gresham, wrote to tell her he had fallen in love with Joy's cousin, Renee, who had come to New York from Florida to stay with the young Gresham boys in Joy's absence. Bill added that he wanted a divorce, which he was granted by the State of New York in 1954.

THEY SAID . . .

"For Jack the attraction was at first undoubtedly intellectual. Joy was the only woman whom he had met…who had a brain which matched his own in suppleness, in width of interest, and in analytical grasp, and above all in humor and a sense of fun."

—Warnie (Maj. Warren Lewis), Jack's brother

As mentioned in Chapter 15, Joy returned in 1953 with the boys, David, nine, and Douglas, seven and a half, to start a new life in London. Douglas, born in 1945, is now the trustee of Jack's literary estate and a coproducer of the Walden Media Narnia movies. He describes his coming with David and their mother to visit Jack and Warnie that December in his autobiographical memoir, *Lenten Lands*. His mother "had talked so much and so often [about Jack] that in my childish mind he had taken on the aspect of a cross between Sir Galahad and Merlin the Wise," he recalls.

Changed Circumstances

After a long period of declining health climaxing in dementia and being moved to a nursing home, Mrs. Moore died in 1951. In 1954, after Jack's hopes for a professorship at Oxford were finally quashed, he accepted an offer as Chair of Medieval and Renaissance Literature at Magdalene College,

Joy Gresham Lewis in 1960. Used by permission of The Marion E. Wade Center, Wheaton College, Wheaton, IL.

Cambridge. It meant having to travel for some hours by train or being driven each week, but it freed him from the petty politics that had kept him from rising above the lecturer rank at Oxford. He gave his inaugural address at Cambridge on November 29, to an overflow crowd of enthusiastic admirers, and began work there in January 1955.

Both Mrs. Moore's death and his new job freed Jack to consider marriage. George Sayer says that Jack had shown much interest in Ruth Pitter, probably the most highly honored woman poet in England at the time, and had visited her in Buckinghamshire. George even served as his driver on several occasions. Mentioning on one such trip that he thought Ruth Pitter would be the woman he would like to marry if he were not a confirmed bachelor, George replied, "it's not too late," to which Jack said yes, it was, "I've burnt my boats," with no more elaboration.

Planning Ahead

George came to think Jack had been alluding to his commitment to enter into a civil marriage with Joy to enable her to stay in England after her visa expired. That legal commitment took place on April 23, 1956, though they continued living in separate houses and Jack told friends they had no plans to consummate the union. And Douglas confirms George's suspicion in reporting that Jack told him he had left Oxford (which Douglas considered a betrayal) for the higher salary Cambridge was offering because undertaking the support of a wife and her two sons was going to require more than Oxford provided.

When Jack asked George Sayer's opinion of his plans for a civil marriage to Joy, George warned that such an arrangement would make Jack liable for her sons' care if anything should happen to her. But Jack, who had sacrificed much of his own life for Mrs. Moore and her daughter Maureen over many years and was known to support a wide variety of needy causes, was not dissuaded by this. In fact, he was already supporting the boys in their boarding school education.

Married At Last

Though some biographies of Jack cast his decision to have the civil marriage blessed by the church as rather spur of the moment or spontaneous, Douglas believes that it had been Jack's plan from even before the civil "non-marriage" took place, from "as early as 1954." Joy and the boys moved from London to Headington Quarry, about a mile from The Kilns, in the summer of 1955, and Jack was a constant guest in their duplex during his time away from Cambridge. Douglas says Jack was also paying the rent for it.

Jack asked the Anglican bishop of Oxford to bless their marriage on the basis that Bill Gresham had married and divorced another woman before marrying Joy, thus rendering their marriage invalid by some church standards. Today, it seems likely that most American Catholic Church bishops would consider this previous marriage by Bill grounds for granting an annulment to Joy, and most Evangelicals would consider Bill's infidelity grounds for allowing Joy to remarry after Bill divorced her. But Jack's bishop refused to waive the rule.

Joy's Faith Journey

Joy was one of the top American women poets in her generation, and she had won the Yale Younger Poets award in 1938. In the competition she bested Sylvia Plath, who went on to greater fame. Joy had entered Hunter College at age fifteen and finished her master's degree at Columbia University before she turned twenty. From a Jewish home in which no religion was practiced, she became an atheist after reading H. G. Wells's *Outline of History* and a Communist in reaction to the suffering of the poor in New York during the Great Depression. But, like Jack, without pursuing religion she experienced spiritual interventions. The following sidebar describes one such instance in her words, after her husband Bill had disappeared for an extended time, leaving her alone in a remote farm in upstate New York with her small boys and no means of support.

> ## THEY SAID . . .
>
> "There was a Person with me in that room, directly present to my consciousness—a Person so real that all my previous life was by comparison a mere shadow play. And I myself was more alive than I had ever been; it was like waking from sleep. So intense a life cannot be endured long by flesh and blood..."   —Joy Gresham Lewis

An acquaintance of the Greshams, Chad Walsh, had written a groundbreaking biography of Jack in 1949 entitled *C. S. Lewis: Apostle to the Skeptics*. Reading it introduced Joy to Jack's works, after which she began to voraciously read them, and on Walsh's suggestion she started writing Jack. Both Joy and Bill, who had published a highly successful novel made into a major movie, *Nightmare Alley*, professed to become Christians, though Joy's journey of faith seemed to ascend while Bill's seemed to fall off the path into an early version of Scientology and other forms of spiritual quest. Douglas reports that Joy's first letter to Jack was warmly received as he probably saw in it a kindred spirit and intellect.

Devastating Development

A few months after the civil marriage took place, Joy developed severe pains in one hip. In October, while the boys were off at boarding school and Jack was in Cambridge, she collapsed in her Headington home and was unable to get up. As she prayed and called for help, a neighbor came to look and almost simultaneously one of Jack and Joy's close friends, Katherine Farrer, wife of theologian Austin Farrer, arrived having had an intuitive urge to visit Joy. Joy was rushed to a hospital where X-rays showed that she was suffering from bone cancer, which was found in her legs, shoulders, and chest.

Ironically, a London antiques dealer—something of a groupie—who had been sending letters to Jack proposing intimate liaisons became especially persistent that same fall, going so far as to announce to London newspapers that she and Jack were to be married. One of the tabloid papers sent a reporter to see Jack at Cambridge and got him to say that on the day of the alleged wedding he would be miles away. But rumors of his marrying were flying everywhere, so on Christmas Eve he put a notice in the London *Times* that he, of Cambridge, and Mrs. Joy Gresham, of Churchill Hospital, Oxford, had been married and asked that no mail be sent regarding it.

On the same day, Jack wrote a letter to Dorothy Sayers, the famous author of detective mysteries and less famous theological studies, telling her the marriage was intended to give Mrs. Gresham, who was dying, a home to live in through her final days and assuring Sayers that "certain problems" were not likely to transpire between the dying woman and the elderly man. Jack was fifty-eight at the time.

Laying on of Hands

The following March, after Joy had been hospitalized for months, Jack invited his former Oxford pupil, the Rev. Peter Bide, a pastor in the Chichester Diocese, to come to visit him at The Kilns and go with him to the hospital to pray for Joy's healing. While he was at the house, Jack asked him, as he had already asked other acquaintances in the clergy, if he would confer the marriage sacrament on him and Joy, saying this was her dying wish.

Though he was not authorized to perform marriages outside his own diocese and he knew the Oxford bishop had refused to bless it, Bide asked Jack to give him some time alone. In *C. S. Lewis: A Complete Guide to His Life and Works*, Walter Hooper says the pastor prayed and, taking the request "to his only one Court of Appeal, I asked myself what he would have done and somehow that finished the argument." He conducted the marriage sacrament on March 21, 1957, in Wingfield-Morris Hospital. Elder brother Warnie was the only additional witness on hand.

Brother's Blessing

Though George Sayer says most of Jack's friends didn't like Joy, Warnie had become extremely fond of Joy, referring to her as "sister." He recorded in his diary that evening Mr. Bide's charitable deed, saying that the ceremony was held after the pastor, Jack, Joy, and himself were gathered and had taken communion in her hospital room at 11 A.M. He added that Joy was to be moved to The Kilns the next week, where she would sleep in the common room on the ground floor.

Douglas, in *Lenten Lands*, records that after he first learned of his mother's illness on the boys' return from school during the Christmas holidays, while Jack, David, and he walked back to The Kilns from seeing her in the hospital, he took a detour into the local churchyard and, for the first time in his life, he prayed, asking God for a miracle for his mother. Though he told no one of it then, he said he knew God had answered his prayer; Joy would get well.

A Miracle

Even more important than the rite of marriage finally being performed was that after Mr. Bide's prayers for healing, the miracle Douglas had learned about began. Joy slowly but steadily got better, against all odds. "In fact," Sayer's biography says, "Joy lived to enjoy three years and four months of married life with Jack."

He tells of Jack praying for long periods in the days after Joy was moved to The Kilns, asking not only for her healing but that he might be able to bear some of her pain and suffering. This he was granted when, by the middle of the following summer, he was in more pain—from osteoporosis—than Joy was from her cancer.

THEY SAID . . .

"He was a very humorous man. That is what is missed in most people's impressions of Jack. If Jack was in a room, there was laughter. If he was sitting by the bedside of someone dying of cancer, there was laughter. If he was talking to his colleagues, his peers, there was laughter."

—Douglas Gresham, Joy's son

Within a month of Joy's return to the house, she was able to start taking charge of its running and get around on her own. Douglas recounts how she transformed The Kilns from a rundown, dingy cold house to a warm, well outfitted, inviting home, with thriving gardens. She tried to improve the grounds, too, and even bought and used a gun to run off vandalizing young trespassers who used The Kilns' woods for makeout and drinking parties.

Remission

Joy also took up much of the secretarial work Warnie had previously done, as Warnie escaped Jack's pain and suffering by going off alone to holiday in Ireland. There he had to be hospitalized for his recurring alcoholism. By fall and the return of his duties at Cambridge, Jack was responding to new treatments for his osteoporosis and told George Sayer that his suffering didn't matter. "All that matters is that I'm in love. At times I'm tempted to think it's a double miracle. Recovery for her, and for me the love that passed me by in youth and middle age." By November, he told a correspondent that he was pain free and was wearing a brace.

The next year, 1958, Joy was enjoying almost complete remission from her cancer, and by April, Jack's osteoporosis was so well controlled that he was able to walk a mile at a time without becoming fatigued. He asked his doctor if it was possible for a man in his condition to engage in sexual intercourse, to which the physician replied, "if you are careful and sensible." Biographer Sayer believes this was when, at last, the marriage was finally "complete and consummated."

Ireland Holiday

In the summer of 1958, Jack took Joy to his homeland, which he had long desired to do. It was the first time he flew in a plane, and that was because their doctor warned that if the sea crossing were to be rough, either of them could be seriously injured by a routine fall. Sayer claims that Jack feared flying and was terrified during takeoff but enjoyed the flight once airborne, speaking enthusiastically later of his first aerial views of clouds below and the coast of Ireland from the pre-jet airliner days. Arthur Greeves met them at Belfast airport and drove them around County Down, and they later toured County Donegal in Ireland's unspoiled northwest. After their return,

Joy took David and Douglas to the seashore town of Solva, one of the west-ernmost points in Wales, which Douglas remembers as an unspoiled true fishing village at that time.

Though Sayer calls 1958 Joy's best year, Douglas says 1959 was Joy and Jack's best year of marriage. Though Jack expressed regret in a letter to Arthur that they couldn't afford another holiday in Ireland that year, they returned to Solva with Douglas in the summer, and Jack came to love it once it cast its spell. And Douglas says Jack and Joy returned to Ireland after he went back to school.

The Return of Joy's Illness

In October 1959, Joy was feeling the return of severe pains, and new tests showed that her cancer had begun advancing and had spread to new parts of her body. Jack wrote to George Sayer in November that "The doctors say there is some hope of her being able to live without pain for a year or two." But he said he doubted it would be right to ask for another miracle after the wonderful one they had just received.

"They tell me," he went on, "that there is no example on record of anyone who was granted the same miracle twice." Ironically, Douglas writes that when he revisited the churchyard at Headington after getting the new round of bad news, he had the same feeling. Now that he was older, he couldn't tell God he could not continue without his mother, and he had already had the miracle he'd requested.

Holiday in Greece

Despite the realization that her time was now short, Joy continued to be optimistic and tried to keep going. Sayer says that during a visit with Roger and June Lancelyn Green, they had told about a wonderful trip they had been on to Greece in April 1959. Joy said she wished she could have been with them, to which they immediately suggested that they plan another trip together, over Easter 1960.

Douglas says that Jack was reluctant to risk such a trip considering Joy's condition (and his own osteoporosis), but when he asked Warnie for advice, Warnie advised making the most of whatever time they had left together.

And so they went, flying in prop planes that required three fueling stops just to get across Europe in those days. After resting the morning after their arrival, they spent eleven days touring Athens, the bay of Corinth, Mycenae, and Crete. Both Joy and Jack loved the trip, and Roger Lancelyn Green recalled in a diary he kept of it that Jack "was the life and soul of the party" at most of their dinners together.

A Matter of Character

Douglas tells a story from their trip that he said "made me realize for the first time that Jack was probably a better person than Mother was, in one way, at least." At Mycenae she had told Jack she couldn't go farther than the lion gate and he should go on while she rested. But Jack replied that he, too, was tired and he would rest with her. As they sat, another member of their tour group, "a painted, over-weight tourist lady" came up the hill and made a snide comment: "Well! You didn't get very far, did you?" Douglas continues that "Jack's iron self-control bent for a split second. 'Oh, go and have a heart attack!' he snapped."

> ## THEY SAID . . .
> "At Rhodes…they went to the Greek Orthodox cathedral for part of the Easter service…Thereafter, whenever the subject came up between us, he said that he preferred the Orthodox liturgy to either the Catholic or Protestant liturgies. He was also impressed by the Greek Orthodox priests, whose faces, he thought, looked more spiritual."
> —George Sayer, *Jack*

And the lady pressed on and did just that. Shortly afterward, Jack and Joy saw a team of medics arriving and carrying her down the hill on a stretcher. Joy thought the incident was hilarious, but Jack was embarrassed that she had related it and felt ashamed and guilty for making such a comment to another person. He asked Joy never to repeat it again.

Sayer says that Joy was "radiant" after her return from Greece, and that for some weeks, despite her failing health, their life went on in an afterglow, with Sunday afternoons and dinners at the Studley Priory, one of Jack's favorite places to go for a short outing from Oxford. But on June 20, Joy was taken back to the Acland Nursing Home with severe nausea. Warnie wrote in his diary the next day, "Joy is dying."

The Axe Falls

Douglas's memoir, published more than a quarter century later, refers to Joy's relapse as the "axe falling": "On the 21st of June [1960], the great axe of Minos of Crete swung at Mother and she became desperately ill." But a week later she was allowed to return home from the Acland Nursing Home where, though "she looked deathly ill, as indeed she was," Jack pushed her in a wheelchair as she "glowed" at seeing once more the flowers and trees and improvements on The Kilns that she had brought about.

A bit later Douglas, now fifteen, returned to the summer term at his boarding school in Wales, relieved to be free of "the general embarrassment of having a dying mother." On July 3, Sayer recounts, she had one more outing with Jack to Studley Priory and on the following day she went for a drive with her nurse. But just a week after that, Joy awoke the household a little after six in the morning, screaming in pain. The doctor arrived shortly after and gave her a shot that relieved her pain. Jack had her taken to the hospital by ambulance after noon, and he wrote in a letter afterward, "She was conscious for the short remainder of her life, and in very little pain, thanks to drugs; and died peacefully about 10:15 the same night." One of her last wishes was to have a plain coffin, and she told the chaplain "I am at peace with God."

Douglas says that when he was driven back to The Kilns from school, he entered the house to see Jack across the room next to the fireplace, looking like he had aged twenty years in the week since he'd seen him. He describes

> "Here the whole world | (stars, water, air, | And field, and forest, as they were | Reflected in a single mind) | Like cast off clothes was left behind | In ashes, yet with hopes that she, | Re-born from holy poverty, | In lenten lands, hereafter may | Resume them on her Easter Day."
>
> —*Joy's epitaph*

a scene ending in the same line, but quite unlike the one set in the attic where Douglas first sees the widowed Jack in the film *Shadowlands.* "My brittle shell smashed, and I broke. 'Oh, Jack,' I burst out, and then the tears came. Jack rushed across the room and put his arm around me. I held on to him, as we both wept."

A Grief Observed

Douglas describes *A Grief Observed,* Jack's reflections on his own reactions to losing Joy and his shortest book, but one of his most influential, as a great gift from a man barely able to cope with his own bereavement to the world of others who inevitably also face the shadow of death and its sorrows. But reviewer Anne Freemantle, presaging a frequent refrain of George Sayer's regarding Jack's books, is probably more on the mark in saying "the author has done something I had believed impossible—assuaged his own grief by conveying it."

QUESTION

Which of Jack's books were inspired by Joy?
The most obvious is *A Grief Observed,* his memoir about his grief after Joy's death. Joy also inspired Jack's final novel, *Till We Have Faces* (1956), enabling him to complete an idea he had years before. She is also credited for Jack's *Reflections on the Psalms* (1958) and *The Four Loves* (1960).

Jack originally published the memoir in 1961 under the pseudonym N. W. Clerk, and in it refers to Joy as "H." In *Lenten Lands,* Douglas describes watching Jack work on it. Sayer says Jack always learned about the new experiences and challenges in his life by writing about them, so it's not surprising that he faced this one too by writing through it. "I almost prefer the moments of agony," Jack writes, and as most writers could attest, writing that reaches readers enables, even requires, its creators to relive and re-endure the full range of emotions, including the agony of grief.

Sayer says Jack used the pen name to avoid the flood of mail the topic would have inspired if it had been in his name. The book did not sell well until, after his death, it was reissued under his name in 1964.

The Gift

One thing *A Grief Observed* should dispel once and for all is, though some still persist in believing it, that Jack and Joy's relationship was entirely platonic, a marriage never consummated. Republished in a Bantam paperback in 1973 along with a fifty-eight-page biography of Jack by Chad Walsh, *A Grief Observed* has become, along with Douglas's *Lenten Lands*, the basis of what can be called one of the great love stories of the twentieth century.

Though the feature-length film by Richard Attenborough and the script written by William Nicholson (who also wrote a stage play and a television play of the same name and subject) has many inaccuracies (like the attic scene between Jack and Douglas that didn't occur in real life), *Shadowlands* is likely to be retold repeatedly as the myth of C. S. Lewis continues through new permutations for new generations. Its title is based on a chapter in the final book of *The Chronicles of Narnia*. The film captures many highlights of an authentic love affair. Sayer says that, "Jack felt that he had achieved full maturity and manhood only through marriage...They were a most blessed and richly gifted pair."

Chapter 20

C. S. Lewis's Legacy

Douglas Gresham writes that his beloved stepfather Jack never recovered after Joy's death, and the remaining three years and four months of his life (almost exactly the same amount of time he and Joy lived as man and wife after receiving the church's sacrament of marriage) was a time of steady decline. Douglas stresses that although Jack presented a courageous face in public and with friends, at home Douglas was able to see Jack's other face, a face of despair and resignation. Sayer's biography, however, proposes that Jack had produced some impressive work (both *A Grief Observed* and *An Experiment in Criticism*) within the first year after Joy's death. Jack's final illness was a combination of kidney failure, toxemia (toxins in the blood), and a weakened heart that were by-products of an untreated enlarged prostate.

A Last Year at Cambridge

Though "obsessed" with Joy and her death, Jack, Sayer relates, functioned much as usual for the first year. He continued to meet with his Inklings friends at the Lamb and Flag or the Eagle and Child pubs and have them come to The Kilns, though he often declined to visit their homes because he didn't want to be around their wives. (A clue to why Douglas may have known a "much different" Jack after Joy's death is that the now full-grown teenager probably reminded him of Joy more than anyone else did.)

Effects of Grief

Douglas says that Jack gave Joy's belongings away quickly after she was gone, indicating that such reminders affected him deeply. But, conversely, he spoke enthusiastically about "sensing" and communing with Joy after her death, and communicating with her as if "mind to mind." Sayer says that such communion and communication enabled Jack to move from feelings of total loss to regaining a renewed and deeper relationship with Joy through the grieving process.

In fact, Jack, who throughout his life had often exhibited loneliness when left alone for long, leaned on his friends even more than usual after Joy's death, and his rhetorical style of discourse showed a noticeable softening. This was especially true, Sayer believed, in his major scholarly project at Cambridge, *An Experiment in Criticism*. This 151-page monograph addressed a problem he saw in reading—that students were more and more influenced by critical reviews of classical and important books than by the books themselves, which were less and less being read on their own terms.

Concluding that the book showed Jack at the peak of his powers, Sayer said it might have inaugurated a new phase of productivity. But that was precluded by a downturn in his health in June 1961, eleven months after Joy's death. He felt ill but put off seeing his doctor because he was looking forward to a visit from Arthur Greeves on June 21 and 22.

Grim Prognosis

After Arthur's visit, Jack's doctor, Humphrey Havard, diagnosed a seriously enlarged prostate, inserted a catheter, and recommended surgery. But the surgeon quickly determined that Jack's health was too poor to let him operate. Jack was not able to return to Cambridge that fall and seemed to decline throughout the summer and fall but showed some improvement in early 1962. The improvement seemed to continue for a year and a half, to July 1963. But he eventually gave up ever getting well enough for the surgery, without which he had no hope of long-term recovery.

A smoker since his youth, Jack declined to follow his doctor's order to quit, saying it would make him too bad-tempered. He told George Sayer it would be "better to die cheerfully with the aid of a little tobacco than to live disagreeably and remorseful without." Bravery was also reflected in his sense of humor, which Sayer maintains he valued even more in the face of death. He cites a letter written when Jack was required to get frequent blood transfusions in which he expressed "sympathy with Dracula. He must have led a miserable life."

Jack spoke of organizing his papers and talks he had given into book-length collections. Despite his poor health, his publisher at Geoffrey Bles was pushing him to complete the collection he was currently working on.

> "Literature enlarges our being by admitting us to experiences not our own. They may be beautiful, terrible, awe-inspiring, exhilarating, pathetic, comic, or merely piquant. Literature gives the entrée to them all...In reading great literature I become a thousand men and yet remain myself...I transcend myself: and am never more myself than when I do."
>
> —An Experiment in Criticism

Walter Hooper

Depending on what source you believe, Walter Hooper (born in 1931 in North Carolina) is either one of the most important contributors to Jack's continuing place in English literature or the perpetrator of the C. S. Lewis hoax, which is the title of a book by Kathryn Lindskoog (1934–2003) making the latter accusations. But both Douglas Gresham and George Sayer confirm Hooper's account of his dealings with Jack in 1963 and with his literary estate after Jack's death.

THEY SAID . . .

"Walter Hooper…was a handsome young man about fourteen years older than I, and he had a charming and gentle manner about him. He…quickly took in the strange and difficult situation that existed at The Kilns and he tried to assist in every possible way."

—Douglas Gresham, *Lenten Lands*

Sayer first heard of Hooper in a conversation with Jack at the Acland Nursing Home in July 1963, shortly after Jack regained consciousness after a coma that had begun with his first heart attack. When Jack referred to Mrs. Moore as though she were still alive and mentioned that he had hired a secretary to help him in Warnie's absence, George suspected that Jack was suffering from dementia and wondered whether Walter Hooper, as Jack called his new secretary, was any more real than Mrs. Moore was alive. But he soon learned from Jack's doctor that Hooper was real and was helping Jack answer correspondence and organize his papers.

Walter's Acceptance

Douglas recalls that in the beginning Walter's enthusiasm and constant stream of questions irritated and tired Jack, but "with Warnie away in Ireland, presumably drinking himself silly," Douglas writes, Jack offered the job of secretarial assistant to Walter. Having recently taken a teaching job at the University of Kentucky, it had not been Walter's intention to look for work with Jack, but the opportunity to provide a service Jack sorely needed may have been too great to pass by. Hooper's critics are more likely to say he was looking for ways to exploit Jack's vulnerability, but considering that he won over Douglas, George, Roger Green, Dr. Havard, and other close friends of Jack seems vindicating.

And George recalls Jack saying, "I've engaged him as my secretary. I want you to like him. I want all my friends to like him. He is a young American, very devoted and charming. He is almost too anxious to please, but no fool. Certainly no fool. I must have someone in the house when I go home."

The only people that Douglas mentions not accepting Walter at The Kilns were the Millers. Mrs. Miller was the household's cook, and after Jack's illness became more serious, Douglas believes Mr. Miller joined her as a regular at the house in an effort to find ways to profit from Jack's illness and, eventually, from his death.

Warnie's Replacement

After Jack returned from his hospital stay following his heart attack and coma, he sent Walter and Douglas to Magdalene College, Cambridge, with a lengthy list to gather up all the belongings Jack had left in his college rooms, having concluded that he would never be able to resume his post. Douglas says that he was along to help with lifting boxes of heavy books, and both he and Walter sorted handwritten papers and organized them day after day for a week. Then they rented a truck to move it all back to The Kilns.

When Walter had to return to his job in Kentucky in late August (Sayer says late September, but Douglas's memory seems to better fit the typical American academic calendar) it was with an understanding with Jack that he would close out his obligations in the United States and return at the end of the term to take up the work that Warnie, apparently in despair over Jack's grim prognosis, had put aside. He was to be Jack's permanent assistant.

Jack's Final Weeks

George Sayer visited the Lady of Lourdes Hospital in Drogheda, Ireland, where Warnie was known to stay when on "drinking vacations." Warnie was away from the facility when George arrived, and his doctor and the nuns cautioned that if Warnie learned his brother was near death it would make his drinking even worse. So George returned to England without seeing Warnie, who would be back in September, his friends at the hospital advised.

Sayer writes that Jack spent that autumn quietly at The Kilns, reading most of the time. Once he got back from Ireland, Warnie sat with Jack a lot of the time and they conversed, though he said it was painful to see Jack in his terminal condition. It seemed like a full circle, after their mostly separate lives since boyhood, to be united alone for the end.

"Again we were together in a new 'little end room,'" Warnie wrote, "shutting out from our talk the ever-present knowledge that as in the black years of Belsen, the holidays were drawing swiftly to a close and a new term fraught with unknown possibilities awaited both of us."

Morning and Evening Star

Sayer recalls taking Jack on a drive on "the London Road" on one fine autumn afternoon, stopping at the side of the road to gaze over "marvelously colored" beech trees. Jack prayed and praised God, George writes. They drove back in twilight and when Venus appeared above the horizon Jack recited Shelley's quatrain:

Thou wert my morning star among the living,
Ere thy fair light had fled;
Now, having died, thou art as Hesperus giving
New splendor to the dead.

Douglas was studying at Applegarth School in Surrey that November. He remembers a rainy and cold day on which the news came over the televisions of President John F. Kennedy's assassination. The community there, as in much of the rest of the media-connected world, was stunned. But while Douglas sat in a study building after that dark evening turned to night, he couldn't study. After a time one of the daughters of the school's headmaster came and asked him to come with her. "It's bad news, I'm afraid," she said, to which Douglas replied, "My stepfather has died, hasn't he?"

New Splendor

When Sayer wrote his biography, *Jack*, twenty-five years later, he remembered only thirteen people, including himself, at Jack's funeral at Headington Quarry Church on November 26, 1963. The others were Owen Barfield, A. C. Harwood, J. R. R. Tolkien, Colin Hardie, John Lawlor, Peter Bayley, Maureen Moore (by now she had become Lady Dunbar of Hempriggs),

David and Douglas Gresham, the Millers, and Fred Paxford. Though future developments would soon amply disprove it, had any media covered the funeral they might have concluded that Jack, as he had once prophesied, had already become a writer who was famous in his forties and forgotten by the end of his life.

Both Sayer and Douglas, whose books both came out in 1988, remembered that the day was very still, so much so that the flame of a candle set atop Jack's coffin burned steadily and did not flicker when the coffin reached the grave. Jack had been a light of their lives, Sayer concluded, a steadfast friend, and the flame "symbolized his unflagging pursuit of illumination." And Douglas adds: "The flame stood straight and still and glowed against the darkness that seemed to be all around me."

Considering that all accounts claim that more than a hundred million copies of Jack's books have been sold, he left only a modest estate. Its net value after probate, Sayer records, was £37,772. Though Sayer says this was small because Jack had been very generous in his life, giving freely to people in need, it is worth noting that a pound sterling in 1963 was worth nearly three American dollars, so the estate would have been well over $100,000. And in 1963, that would buy real estate valued, at today's prices, in the millions of dollars.

THEY SAID . . .

"He invited me to come over in the spring of 1963 from my native United States for what I hoped would be as much as a single conversation over a cup of tea…[T]he coveted tea party turned out to be…"The Observations of a Late Arrival" or "A single Summer with C.S.L."
—Walter Hooper, Introduction to C. S. Lewis's *The Weight of Glory*

Sayer says that Jack willed the bulk of his estate for David's and Douglas's education, leaving it in trust to Warnie for the rest of his life. Douglas's memoir does not discuss the inheritance directly, but he indicates that he was dependant on Warnie for spending money while he was a full-time student several years later and that Warnie provided him just ten shillings a week, which Douglas compares to one dollar. Apparently, Warnie was not in on the discussion Sayer records between Jack and Joy, who had agreed that the boys should always have enough money for school to be on par with their peers. Instead, Warnie's allotment was comparable to the penury of his own and Jack's school years.

More Than Money

But as the sales figures on Jack's books suggest, his real legacy was his writing. The trustee of that treasure, probably based on Jack's expressed intent to his attorney Owen Barfield, was Walter Hooper, the young American fan whose tea date with Jack led to a job as his secretary and all-around assistant. Having been telephoned by Douglas at the University of Kentucky as the first American to be told of Jack's death, Walter gave up his teaching position to return to The Kilns at the end of the term, as he and Jack had planned, and stayed as a permanent resident of Oxford ever since.

Online blogger Richard Drake writes of Hooper's prodigious work to keep Jack's writing in bookstores for years after his death and reports, "J. R. R. Tolkien once teased Hooper that C. S. Lewis was his only friend who was publishing far more books after his death than before."

Enduring Fame

Will C. S. Lewis's status as one of the twentieth century's most highly regarded authors be permanent or fading? So many factors pertain in the answer to that question that it's not possible to be certain, but defenders of both the affirmative and the negative enjoy making their cases. In terms of political status, it can be argued that as an advocate without peer for traditional values like loyalty, fairness, truth, and moral principle, Jack will always have whole subcultures of promoters who will remember and continue to quote and cite him as a stalwart on their side of cultural debates. Likewise, orthodox Christians of Protestant, Catholic, and Orthodox parties will find in Lewis's writings such lucid argumentation that they will never let him be forgotten.

One problem in predicting Jack's cultural relevance is how resilient Christianity and Christian apologetics may remain over the next century. Though twenty centuries seem to suggest a secure track record, the extreme falloff of references to Christianity in European culture since Jack's time suggests that even his adulation among serious Christians cannot be a sure bet on keeping his memory and influence alive.

Christianity and Relevance

Those who have openly opposed Jack in the British and American media have generally opposed him in just this category. Christianity is irrelevant to modern life, they argue, and since Jack is remembered mainly among Christians for his apologetic and metaphorical writing, his fame will wane. Somewhat in the middle is Laura Miller, an editor of *Salon* (see the sidebar) who says Jack's work is remembered mostly for its Christian content and references but that his work contains much more than that and deserves to be remembered for more.

Another gauge of an earlier scholar or writer in the secular world's pantheon of values is the person's standing among contemporary scholars. Though Jack's logical method of philosophizing was already eclipsed (at least in popular scholarship) by linguistic analysis and existentialism during his lifetime, there is hope for his academic resurrection through the fact that such philosophical movements as existentialism have risen and waned while Platonism, Aristotelian logic, and Judeo-Christian systems have enjoyed cyclical revivals through all such eclipses.

How much is Jack's work regarded in scholarship today? Works of Doris Myers, Bruce Edwards, Don King, Peter Kreeft, and Peter Schakel have been cited here as examples of postgraduate studies focusing on Lewis, and the number of unpublished graduate theses and dissertations referring to him is substantial, as a quick search under "dissertations on C. S. Lewis" in any major online search engine reveals. But *Salon*'s Laura Miller largely dismisses such work. "Lewis scholarship exists," she says, "but it's a hagiographic wasteland roamed by worshipful, third-rate Christian academics who see his work as something close to divine revelation."

Yet Miller also argues that *The Chronicles of Narnia* tower high above *The Wizard of Oz*, probably the most enduring children's myth by an American author. Lewis, she says, is "a leading literary scholar of his generation and a writer of uncommon eloquence." And she calls Jack's British children's fantasy "a far cry from the modest American talent [L. Frank Baum] who leads with a promise to dispense with all 'disagreeable incident.'"

Role Model

In his thirteen-page introduction to the collection of Jack's sermons and addresses published as *The Weight of Glory* (1980), Walter Hooper cites two examples of Jack's exemplary behavior rooted deeply in his character. In the first, Walter remembers discussing with Jack a difficult observation he had made while walking in the neighborhood of The Kilns. On his walks he would meet a ninety-seven-year-old atheist who would invariably ask about Jack's health. Walter would reply that Jack was quite ill, to which the atheist would reply, "Nothing wrong with *me*! I've got a long time yet!"

Walter told Jack he was tempted to ask the Lord, in his prayers, why he allowed this old reprobate to enjoy good health and prospects while Jack, at age sixty-four, seemed close to death.

"And what do you think our Lord would say to that?" Jack asked Hooper.

"What?" Hooper replied.

"What is that to *you!*" Jack replied, almost quoting several replies to similar questions posed to Aslan by Jill.

In the second instance, Hooper and Jack were discussing Malory's *Morte d' Arthur*, in which Lancelot sometimes explained his heroic actions as being motivated by a desire on his part of "win worship," which Hooper found a disappointing chink in Lancelot's character. "Without intending any embarrassment," Hooper writes, "I asked Lewis if he was ever aware of the fact that regardless of his intentions he was 'winning worship' from his books. He said in a low, still voice, and with the deepest and most complete humility I've ever observed in anyone, 'One cannot be too careful *not* to think of it.'"

THEY SAID . . .

"Lewis's writings are...graced with a clarity that almost takes your breath away. This, in combination with his powerful reason, makes it possible for his works on Christianity to be understood by nearly everyone, including some who are not easily convinced. We could mention as well Lewis's moral toughness, his charity, his love of God, and a wisdom which made him willing to be happy on God's terms."
—Walter Hooper, Introduction to C. S. Lewis's *The Weight of Glory*

Saint Clive

A plaque on a bench along a hiking trail above Belfast, Northern Ireland, is inscribed (in part):

C. S. Lewis (1898–1963)
From this favorite vantage point C. S. Lewis, saint and scholar from the County Down, enjoyed a view of the countryside and Belfast Lough after walking tours locally with his lifelong friend Arthur Greeves.

Though some might question the propriety of a government agency like a park department conferring sainthood on their area's favorite sons or daughters, many have been mentioning Jack and sainthood in the same breath for years. Though no backhanded compliment was intended, even Laura Miller's comments quoted previously allude to it by calling most Lewis scholarship hagiographic. (*Hagiography* literally means "holy writing" but is commonly used to mean biographical writings about saints.)

QUESTION

Was Jack a genius?

In a 2001 interview, stepson Douglas Gresham said, "Absolutely." He claimed remembering Jack asking him "to pick any book off his shelves,…pick a page and read a line and he would quote the rest of the page…He had this enormous capacity to remember everything he'd ever read."

Virtues

Speaking of Jack's exceptional "goodness," Walter Hooper put his finger on qualities many of those who knew Jack have described in generalities. On Jack's mirth, his being content to be happy as Christ wants his disciples to be happy, and his merriment, Walter speaks of these as "*causes* of the greatness of heart, his large intellect, and the most open charity I have ever found in anyone. He was a man, many of us have come to see, of common instincts combined with very uncommon abilities…I knew—I just *knew*—that no matter how long I lived, no matter who else I met, I should never be in the company of such a supremely good human being again."

Since the Anglican Church has declared only one new saint since its founding in the Reformation (though it recognizes Roman Catholic saints preceding the Reformation), it's not likely that Jack will be formally elevated any time soon. But one of the first qualifications for formally recognizing saints has long since pertained to Jack: widespread feelings of veneration among the faithful public for a man of great vision, moral character, and gifts suited to the teaching of the whole church.

Web Resources

Web Pages Referenced in This Book

Hypertext links to these pages can be found on Jon Kennedy's C. S. Lewis Web page, *www.nantyglo.com/cslewis.htm*.

C. S. Lewis Trail in East Belfast
✍ *http://dnausers.d-n-a.net/cslewis/brochure.html*

Web page on Siegfried and Brunhilde
✍ *http://larryavisbrown.homestead.com/files/Ring/Ring4_Twilight.htm*

Spirits in Bondage, full text online
✍ *www.anglicanlibrary.org/lewis/spirits*

Dom Bede Griffiths
✍ *www.bedegriffiths.com*

John Betjeman
✍ *www.johnbetjeman.com*

Web page on the Great Depression (1930s) in Great Britain
✍ *http://en.wikipedia.org/wiki/Great_Depression_in_the_United_Kingdom*

A calendar of Lewis's radio lectures
✍ *www.discovery.org/scripts/viewDB/index.php?command=view&program=CS%20Lewis%20and%20Public%20Life&id=519*

Eustace, the dragon, and spiritual reformation
✍ *www.salisburybible.org/narniadevos/1_Eustace%20the%20Dragon.pdf*

The Slip-Up Archive
✍ *www.slipups.com/items/19161.html*

Example article on content versus character education
✍ *www.findarticles.com/p/articles/mi_m1272/is_2711_133/ai_n6148294*

Sonderbooks (review of *The Horse and His Boy*)
✍ *www.sonderbooks.com/ChildrensFiction/horseandhisboy.html*

Critique of A. N. Wilson's biography
✍ *www.solcon.nl/arendsmilde/cslewis/reflections/e-definitivebiography.htm*

London fog (smog)
✍ *www.epa.gov/history/topics/perspect/london.htm*

"Narnia represents everything that is most hateful about religion" Polly Toynbee
✍ *www.guardian.co.uk/religion/Story/0,2763,1657759,00.html*

Dr. Bruce Edwards, Bowling Green State University, Ohio, on *Surprised by Joy*
✍ *http://personal.bgsu.edu/~edwards/surprised.html*

Our Own Silly Faces: C. S. Lewis on Psalms, by Stanley N. Rosenbaum
✍ *www.religion-online.org/showarticle.asp?title=1684*

Paraphrase of J. R. R. Tolkien remark about Walter Hooper
✍ *www.firstthings.com/article.php3?id_article=4512*

Chip Duncan interview with Douglas Gresham
✍ *www.duncanentertainment.com/interview_gresham.php*

Laura Miller, in *Salon,* "Oz vs. Narnia"
✍ *http://archive.salon.com/books/feature/2000/12/28/baum/index.html*

County Down plaque
✍ *http://en.wikipedia.org/wiki/Image:CSLewisPlaque.jpg*

An article on looking for Lewis's successor
✍ *www.firstthings.com/article.php3?id_article=4512*

Pages on Lewis Not Referenced in This Book

Source: Wikipedia: *http://en.wikipedia.org/wiki/C._S._Lewis*

Works by C. S. Lewis at Project Gutenberg
✍ *www.gutenberg.org/author/C.+S.+Lewis*

The Chronicle—British academic journal for C. S. Lewis and his circle
✍ *www.cslewischronicle.org*

C. S. Lewis Foundation
✍ *www.cslewis.org*

Marion E. Wade Center at Wheaton College—has the world's largest collection of Lewis's works and works about him
✎ *www.wheaton.edu/learnres/wade*

Taylor University, Upland, Indiana, has the world's largest private collection of C. S. Lewis first editions, letters, manuscripts, and ephemera—the Edwin W. Brown Collection
✎ *www.taylor.edu/academics/supportServices/csLewis*

Ancestry of C. S. Lewis
✎ *http://home.comcast.net/~smccaslin2/AncestryofC.S.Lewis.html*

The Northern Michigan C. S. Lewis Festival
✎ *www.cslewisfestival.org*

RapidNet.com—C. S. Lewis FAQ
✎ *www.rapidnet.com/~jbeard/bdm/exposes/lewis/cs-lewis.htm*

C. S. Lewis & The Inklings—Bruce Edwards's site, with resources on Lewis and friends
✎ *www.pseudobook.com/cslewis*

C. S. Lewis Blog—A blog of news and reflections on C. S. Lewis's life and work
✎ *www.pseudobook.com/cslewis/blog*

Into the Wardrobe—a Web site devoted to C. S. Lewis
✎ *http://cslewis.drzeus.net*

NarniaFans.com—C. S. Lewis news, database, and community
✎ *www.narniafans.com*

NarniaWeb.com—Narnia and C. S. Lewis news, resources, forum
✎ *www.narniaweb.com*

The Stone Table—the latest C.S. Lewis news, reviews, and community
✎ *www.thestonetable.com*

C. S. Lewis Chronicles—a compendium of information about Lewis
✎ *www.scriptoriumnovum.com/l.html*

C. S. Lewis Classics—a Web site by HarperCollins Publishers
✎ *www.cslewis.com*

C. S. Lewis at the Internet Speculative Fiction Database
✎ *www.isfdb.org/cgi-bin/ea.cgi?C.%20S.%20Lewis*

FindAGrave C. S. Lewis
✎ *http://findagrave.com/cgi-bin/fg.cgi?page=gr&GRid=1455*

Arend Smilde's C. S. Lewis Pages—Dutch and (mainly) English; several unique and hard-to-find texts and resources
✎ *www.solcon.nl/arendsmilde/cslewis*

Audio of C. S. Lewis speaking
✎ *www.bbc.co.uk/religion/religions/christianity/people/cslewis_16.shtml*

C. S. Lewis Society of California
✎ *http://lewissociety.org*

The Philippine Order of Narnians—A Filipino community of C. S. Lewis enthusiasts
www.filipinonarnians.org

C. S. Lewis at the Internet Book List
www.iblist.com/author349.htm

C. S. Lewis Hall, Christian private school in Austin, Texas
www.lewishall.org

Bibliography

Books by C. S. Lewis—Nonfiction

The Allegory of Love: A Study in Medieval Tradition (1936)

Rehabilitations and Other Essays (1939)—with two essays not included in *Essay Collection* (2000)

The Personal Heresy: A Controversy (1939, with E. M. W. Tillyard)

The Problem of Pain (1940)

A Preface to Paradise Lost (1942)

The Abolition of Man (1943)

Beyond Personality (1944)

Miracles: A Preliminary Study (1947, revised 1960)

Arthurian Torso (1948)—on Charles Williams's poetry

Mere Christianity (1952)—based on radio talks of 1941–1944

English Literature in the Sixteenth Century Excluding Drama (1954, reprinted 1975)

Major British Writers, Vol I (1954), contribution on Edmund Spenser

Surprised by Joy: The Shape of My Early Life (1955)—autobiography

Reflections on the Psalms (1958)

The Four Loves (1960)

Studies in Words (1960)

An Experiment in Criticism (1961)

A Grief Observed (1961)—first published under the pseudonym N. W. Clerk

Selections from Layamon's Brut (1963, editor G. L. Brook—introduction)

Prayer: Letters to Malcolm (1964)

The Discarded Image: An Introduction to Medieval and Renaissance Literature (1964)

Studies in Medieval and Renaissance Literature (1966)—not included in *Essay Collection* (2000)

Spenser's Images of Life (1967, editor Alastair Fowler)

Letters to an American Lady (1967)

Christian Reflections (1967)—essays and papers

Selected Literary Essays (1969)—not included in *Essay Collection* (2000)

Of Other Worlds (1982)—essays, with one essay not included in *Essay Collection*

Present Concerns (1986)—essays

All My Road Before Me: The Diary of C. S. Lewis 1922–27 (1993)

Essay Collection: Literature, Philosophy, and Short Stories (2000)

Essay Collection: Faith, Christianity, and the Church (2000)

Collected Letters, Vol. I: Family Letters 1905–1931 (2000)

Collected Letters, Vol. II: Books, Broadcasts, and War 1931–1949 (2004)

Collected Letters, Vol. III: Narnia, Cambridge, and Joy 1950–1963 (2007)

The Business of Heaven: Daily Readings from C. S. Lewis (1984, editor Walter Hooper)

Books by C. S. Lewis—Fiction

The Pilgrim's Regress (1933)

Space Trilogy
Out of the Silent Planet (1938)
Perelandra (1943)
That Hideous Strength (1946)

The Screwtape Letters (1942)

The Great Divorce (1946)

The Chronicles of Narnia
The Lion, the Witch, and the Wardrobe (1950)
Prince Caspian (1951)
The Voyage of the Dawn Treader (1952)
The Silver Chair (1953)
The Horse and His Boy (1954)

The Magician's Nephew (1955)
The Last Battle (1956)

Till We Have Faces (1956)

Screwtape Proposes a Toast (1961)—an addition to *The Screwtape Letters*

Letters to Malcolm: Chiefly on Prayer (1964)

The Dark Tower and Other Stories (1977)

Boxen: The Imaginary World of the Young C. S. Lewis (1985, editor Walter Hooper)

Books by C. S. Lewis—Poetry

Spirits in Bondage (1919)—published under the pseudonym Clive Hamilton

Dymer (1926)—published under pseudonym Clive Hamilton

Narrative Poems (1960, editor Walter Hooper)—includes *Dymer*

The Collected Poems of C. S. Lewis (1994, editor Walter Hooper)—includes *Spirits in Bondage*

Books and Articles about C. S. Lewis

John Beversluis. *C. S. Lewis and the Search for Rational Religion.* Eerdmans, 1985.

Humphrey Carpenter. *The Inklings: C. S. Lewis, J. R. R. Tolkien, Charles Williams and Their Friends.* George Allen & Unwin, 1978.

Joe R. Christopher and Joan K. Ostling. *C. S. Lewis: An Annotated Checklist of Writings about Him and His Works.* Kent State University Press, (1972).

James Como. *Branches to Heaven: The Geniuses of C. S. Lewis.* Spence, 1998.

———. *Remembering C. S. Lewis* (3rd edition of *C. S. Lewis at the Breakfast Table*). Ignatius, 2006.

Michael Coren. *The Man Who Created Narnia: The Story of C. S. Lewis.* Eerdmans Pub Co., 1996.

Colin Duriez. *Tolkien and C. S. Lewis: The Gift of Friendship.* Paulist Press, 2003.

Colin Duriez and David Porter. *The Inklings Handbook: The Lives, Thought, and Writings of C. S. Lewis, J. R. R. Tolkien, Charles Williams, Owen Barfield, and Their Friends.* Chalice Press, 2001.

Bruce L. Edwards. *Further Up and Further In: Understanding C. S. Lewis's The Lion, the Witch, and the Wardrobe.* Broadman and Holman, 2005.

———. *Not a Tame Lion: The Spiritual World of Narnia.* Tyndale, 2005.

————. *A Rhetoric of Reading: C. S. Lewis's Defense of Western Literacy.* Center for the Study of Christian Values in Literature, 1986.

————, editor. *C. S. Lewis: Life, Works, and Legacy.* 4 Vol. Praeger Perspectives, 2007.

————, editor. *The Taste of the Pineapple: Essays on C. S. Lewis as Reader, Critic, and Imaginative Writer.* The Popular Press, 1988.

Alastair Fowler. "C.S. Lewis: Supervisor." *Yale Review,* Vol. 91, No. 4 (October 2003).

Jocelyn Gibb, editor. *Light on C. S. Lewis.* Geoffrey Bles, 1965; Harcourt Brace Jovanovich, 1976.

Douglas Gilbert and Clyde Kilby. *C. S. Lewis: Images of His World.* Eerdmans, 1973, 2005.

Diana Pavlac Glyer. *The Company They Keep: C. S. Lewis and J. R. R. Tolkien as Writers in Community.* Kent State University Press, 2007.

David Graham, editor. *We Remember C.S. Lewis.* Broadman & Holman Publishers, 2001.

Roger Lancelyn Green and Walter Hooper. *C. S. Lewis: A Biography.* HarperCollins, 2002. Fully revised and expanded edition.

Douglas Gresham. *Jack's Life: A Memory of C. S. Lewis.* Broadman & Holman Publishers, 2005.

————. *Lenten Lands: My Childhood with Joy Davidman and C. S. Lewis.* HarperSanFrancisco, 1994.

William Griffin. *C. S. Lewis: The Authentic Voice.* formerly *C.S. Lewis: A Dramatic Life.* Lion, 2005.

Joel D. Heck. *Irrigating Deserts: C. S. Lewis on Education.* Concordia Publishing House, 2006.

David Hein. "A Note on C. S. Lewis's The Screwtape Letters." *The Anglican Digest* 49.2 (Easter 2007): 55-58. Argues that Lewis's portrayal of the activity of the Devil was influenced by contemporary events, in particular by the threat of a Nazi invasion of Britain in 1940.

David Hein and Edward Hugh Henderson, editors. *Captured by the Crucified: The Practical Theology of Austin Farrer.* T & T Clark/Continuum, 2004. A study of Lewis's close friend, the theologian Austin Farrer, this book also contains material on Farrer's circle, "the Oxford Christians," including C. S. Lewis.

Walter Hooper. *C. S. Lewis: A Companion and Guide.* HarperCollins, 1996.

————. *Through Joy and Beyond: A Pictorial Biography of C. S. Lewis.* Macmillan, 1982.

Alan Jacobs. *The Narnian: The Life and Imagination of C.S. Lewis.* HarperSanFrancisco, 2005.

Carolyn Keefe. *C. S. Lewis: Speaker & Teacher.* Zondervan, 1979.

Clyde S. Kilby. *The Christian World of C. S. Lewis.* Eerdmans, 1964, 1995.

W. H. Lewis, editor. *Letters of C. S. Lewis.* Geoffrey Bles, 1966.

Kathryn Lindskoog. *Light in the Shadowlands: Protecting the Real C. S. Lewis.* Multnomah Pub., 1994.

Susan Lowenberg. *C. S. Lewis: A Reference Guide 1972–1988.* Hall & Co., 1993.

Wayne Mardindale and Jerry Root. *The Quotable Lewis.* Tyndale House Publishers, 1990.

Markus Mühling. *A Theological Journey into Narnia: An Analysis of the Message Beneath the Text.* Vandenhoeck & Ruprecht, 2005.

Joseph Pearce. *C. S. Lewis and the Catholic Church.* Ignatius Press, 2003.

Thomas C. Peters. *Simply C.S. Lewis. A Beginner's Guide to His Life and Works.* Kingsway Publications, 1998.

Justin Phillips. *C. S. Lewis at the BBC: Messages of Hope in the Darkness of War.* Marshall Pickering, 2003.

Victor Reppert. *C. S. Lewis's Dangerous Idea: In Defense of the Argument from Reason.* InterVarsity Press, 2003.

George Sayer. *Jack: C. S. Lewis and His Times.* Macmillan, 1988.

Peter J. Schakel. *Imagination and the Arts in C. S. Lewis: Journeying to Narnia and Other Worlds.* University of Missouri Press, 2002.

————, editor. *The Longing for a Form: Essays on the Fiction of C. S. Lewis.* Kent State University Press, 1977.

————. *Reason and Imagination in C. S. Lewis: A Study of "Till We Have Faces."* Eerdmans, 1984.

Peter J. Schakel and Charles A. Huttar, editors. *Word and Story in C. S. Lewis.* University of Missouri Press, 1991.

Stephen Schofield. *In Search of C. S. Lewis.* Bridge Logos Pub., 1983.

Jeffrey D. Schultz and John G. West, Jr., editors. *The C. S. Lewis Readers' Encyclopedia.* Zondervan Publishing House, 1998.

G. B. Tennyson, editor. *Owen Barfield on C.S. Lewis.* Wesleyan University Press, 1989.

Richard J. Wagner. *C. S. Lewis and Narnia for Dummies.* Wiley Publishing, 2005.

Andrew Walker and Patrick James, editor. *Rumours of Heaven: Essays in Celebration of C.S. Lewis.* Eagle, 1998.

Chad Walsh. *C. S. Lewis: Apostle to the Skeptics.* Macmillan, 1949.

————. *The Literary Legacy of C. S. Lewis.* Harcourt Brace Jovanovich, 1979.

George Watson, editor. *Critical Essays on C. S. Lewis.* Scolar Press, 1992.

Michael White. *C.S. Lewis: The Boy Who Chronicled Narnia.* Abacus, 2005.

A. N. Wilson. *C. S. Lewis: A Biography.* W. W. Norton, 1990.

Index

THE EVERYTHING SERIES!

BUSINESS & PERSONAL FINANCE

Everything® Accounting Book
Everything® Budgeting Book
Everything® Business Planning Book
Everything® Coaching and Mentoring Book, 2nd Ed.
Everything® Fundraising Book
Everything® Get Out of Debt Book
Everything® Grant Writing Book
Everything® Guide to Foreclosures
Everything® Guide to Personal Finance for Single Mothers
Everything® Home-Based Business Book, 2nd Ed.
Everything® Homebuying Book, 2nd Ed.
Everything® Homeselling Book, 2nd Ed.
Everything® Improve Your Credit Book
Everything® Investing Book, 2nd Ed.
Everything® Landlording Book
Everything® Leadership Book
Everything® Managing People Book, 2nd Ed.
Everything® Negotiating Book
Everything® Online Auctions Book
Everything® Online Business Book
Everything® Personal Finance Book
Everything® Personal Finance in Your 20s and 30s Book
Everything® Project Management Book
Everything® Real Estate Investing Book
Everything® Retirement Planning Book
Everything® Robert's Rules Book, $7.95
Everything® Selling Book
Everything® Start Your Own Business Book, 2nd Ed.
Everything® Wills & Estate Planning Book

COOKING

Everything® Barbecue Cookbook
Everything® Bartender's Book, 2nd Ed., $9.95
Everything® Calorie Counting Cookbook
Everything® Cheese Book
Everything® Chinese Cookbook
Everything® Classic Recipes Book
Everything® Cocktail Parties & Drinks Book
Everything® College Cookbook
Everything® Cooking for Baby and Toddler Book
Everything® Cooking for Two Cookbook
Everything® Diabetes Cookbook
Everything® Easy Gourmet Cookbook
Everything® Fondue Cookbook
Everything® Fondue Party Book
Everything® Gluten-Free Cookbook
Everything® Glycemic Index Cookbook
Everything® Grilling Cookbook
Everything® Healthy Meals in Minutes Cookbook
Everything® Holiday Cookbook

Everything® Indian Cookbook
Everything® Italian Cookbook
Everything® Low-Carb Cookbook
Everything® Low-Cholesterol Cookbook
Everything® Low-Fat High-Flavor Cookbook
Everything® Low-Salt Cookbook
Everything® Meals for a Month Cookbook
Everything® Mediterranean Cookbook
Everything® Mexican Cookbook
Everything® No Trans Fat Cookbook
Everything® One-Pot Cookbook
Everything® Pizza Cookbook
Everything® Quick and Easy 30-Minute,
    5-Ingredient Cookbook
Everything® Quick Meals Cookbook
Everything® Slow Cooker Cookbook
Everything® Slow Cooking for a Crowd Cookbook
Everything® Soup Cookbook
Everything® Stir-Fry Cookbook
Everything® Sugar-Free Cookbook
Everything® Tapas and Small Plates Cookbook
Everything® Tex-Mex Cookbook
Everything® Thai Cookbook
Everything® Vegetarian Cookbook
Everything® Wild Game Cookbook
Everything® Wine Book, 2nd Ed.

GAMES

Everything® 15-Minute Sudoku Book, $9.95
Everything® 30-Minute Sudoku Book, $9.95
Everything® Bible Crosswords Book, $9.95
Everything® Blackjack Strategy Book
Everything® Brain Strain Book, $9.95
Everything® Bridge Book
Everything® Card Games Book
Everything® Card Tricks Book, $9.95
Everything® Casino Gambling Book, 2nd Ed.
Everything® Chess Basics Book
Everything® Craps Strategy Book
Everything® Crossword and Puzzle Book
Everything® Crossword Challenge Book
Everything® Crosswords for the Beach Book, $9.95
Everything® Cryptic Crosswords Book, $9.95
Everything® Cryptograms Book, $9.95
Everything® Easy Crosswords Book
Everything® Easy Kakuro Book, $9.95
Everything® Easy Large-Print Crosswords Book
Everything® Games Book, 2nd Ed.
Everything® Giant Sudoku Book, $9.95
Everything® Kakuro Challenge Book, $9.95
Everything® Large-Print Crossword Challenge Book
Everything® Large-Print Crosswords Book
Everything® Lateral Thinking Puzzles Book, $9.95

Everything® Literary Crosswords Book, $9.95
Everything® Mazes Book
Everything® Memory Booster Puzzles Book, $9.95
Everything® Movie Crosswords Book, $9.95
Everything® Music Crosswords Book, $9.95
Everything® Online Poker Book, $12.95
Everything® Pencil Puzzles Book, $9.95
Everything® Poker Strategy Book
Everything® Pool & Billiards Book
Everything® Puzzles for Commuters Book, $9.95
Everything® Sports Crosswords Book, $9.95
Everything® Test Your IQ Book, $9.95
Everything® Texas Hold 'Em Book, $9.95
Everything® Travel Crosswords Book, $9.95
Everything® TV Crosswords Book, $9.95
Everything® Word Games Challenge Book
Everything® Word Scramble Book
Everything® Word Search Book

HEALTH

Everything® Alzheimer's Book
Everything® Diabetes Book
Everything® Health Guide to Adult Bipolar Disorder
Everything® Health Guide to Arthritis
Everything® Health Guide to Controlling Anxiety
Everything® Health Guide to Fibromyalgia
Everything® Health Guide to Menopause
Everything® Health Guide to OCD
Everything® Health Guide to PMS
Everything® Health Guide to Postpartum Care
Everything® Health Guide to Thyroid Disease
Everything® Hypnosis Book
Everything® Low Cholesterol Book
Everything® Nutrition Book
Everything® Reflexology Book
Everything® Stress Management Book

HISTORY

Everything® American Government Book
Everything® American History Book, 2nd Ed.
Everything® Civil War Book
Everything® Freemasons Book
Everything® Irish History & Heritage Book
Everything® Middle East Book
Everything® World War II Book, 2nd Ed.

HOBBIES

Everything® Candlemaking Book
Everything® Cartooning Book
Everything® Coin Collecting Book
Everything® Drawing Book

Everything® Family Tree Book, 2nd Ed.
Everything® Knitting Book
Everything® Knots Book
Everything® Photography Book
Everything® Quilting Book
Everything® Sewing Book
Everything® Soapmaking Book, 2nd Ed.
Everything® Woodworking Book

HOME IMPROVEMENT

Everything® Feng Shui Book
Everything® Feng Shui Decluttering Book, $9.95
Everything® Fix-It Book
Everything® Green Living Book
Everything® Home Decorating Book
Everything® Home Storage Solutions Book
Everything® Homebuilding Book
Everything® Organize Your Home Book, 2nd Ed.

KIDS' BOOKS

All titles are $7.95

Everything® Kids' Animal Puzzle & Activity Book
Everything® Kids' Baseball Book, 4th Ed.
Everything® Kids' Bible Trivia Book
Everything® Kids' Bugs Book
Everything® Kids' Cars and Trucks Puzzle and Activity Book
Everything® Kids' Christmas Puzzle & Activity Book
Everything® Kids' Cookbook
Everything® Kids' Crazy Puzzles Book
Everything® Kids' Dinosaurs Book
Everything® Kids' Environment Book
Everything® Kids' Fairies Puzzle and Activity Book
Everything® Kids' First Spanish Puzzle and Activity Book
Everything® Kids' Gross Cookbook
Everything® Kids' Gross Hidden Pictures Book
Everything® Kids' Gross Jokes Book
Everything® Kids' Gross Mazes Book
Everything® Kids' Gross Puzzle & Activity Book
Everything® Kids' Halloween Puzzle & Activity Book
Everything® Kids' Hidden Pictures Book
Everything® Kids' Horses Book
Everything® Kids' Joke Book
Everything® Kids' Knock Knock Book
Everything® Kids' Learning Spanish Book
Everything® Kids' Magical Science Experiments Book
Everything® Kids' Math Puzzles Book
Everything® Kids' Mazes Book
Everything® Kids' Money Book
Everything® Kids' Nature Book
Everything® Kids' Pirates Puzzle and Activity Book
Everything® Kids' Presidents Book
Everything® Kids' Princess Puzzle and Activity Book
Everything® Kids' Puzzle Book
Everything® Kids' Racecars Puzzle and Activity Book
Everything® Kids' Riddles & Brain Teasers Book
Everything® Kids' Science Experiments Book
Everything® Kids' Sharks Book

Everything® Kids' Soccer Book
Everything® Kids' Spies Puzzle and Activity Book
Everything® Kids' States Book
Everything® Kids' Travel Activity Book

KIDS' STORY BOOKS

Everything® Fairy Tales Book

LANGUAGE

Everything® Conversational Japanese Book with CD, $19.95
Everything® French Grammar Book
Everything® French Phrase Book, $9.95
Everything® French Verb Book, $9.95
Everything® German Practice Book with CD, $19.95
Everything® Inglés Book
Everything® Intermediate Spanish Book with CD, $19.95
Everything® Italian Practice Book with CD, $19.95
Everything® Learning Brazilian Portuguese Book with CD, $19.95
Everything® Learning French Book with CD, 2nd Ed., $19.95
Everything® Learning German Book
Everything® Learning Italian Book
Everything® Learning Latin Book
Everything® Learning Russian Book with CD, $19.95
Everything® Learning Spanish Book with CD, 2nd Ed., $19.95
Everything® Russian Practice Book with CD, $19.95
Everything® Sign Language Book
Everything® Spanish Grammar Book
Everything® Spanish Phrase Book, $9.95
Everything® Spanish Practice Book with CD, $19.95
Everything® Spanish Verb Book, $9.95
Everything® Speaking Mandarin Chinese Book with CD, $19.95

MUSIC

Everything® Drums Book with CD, $19.95
Everything® Guitar Book with CD, 2nd Ed., $19.95
Everything® Guitar Chords Book with CD, $19.95
Everything® Home Recording Book
Everything® Music Theory Book with CD, $19.95
Everything® Reading Music Book with CD, $19.95
Everything® Rock & Blues Guitar Book with CD, $19.95
Everything® Rock and Blues Piano Book with CD, $19.95
Everything® Songwriting Book

NEW AGE

Everything® Astrology Book, 2nd Ed.
Everything® Birthday Personology Book
Everything® Dreams Book, 2nd Ed.
Everything® Love Signs Book, $9.95
Everything® Love Spells Book, $9.95
Everything® Numerology Book
Everything® Paganism Book
Everything® Palmistry Book
Everything® Psychic Book
Everything® Reiki Book
Everything® Sex Signs Book, $9.95

Everything® Spells & Charms Book, 2nd Ed.
Everything® Tarot Book, 2nd Ed.
Everything® Toltec Wisdom Book
Everything® Wicca and Witchcraft Book

PARENTING

Everything® Baby Names Book, 2nd Ed.
Everything® Baby Shower Book, 2nd Ed.
Everything® Baby's First Year Book
Everything® Birthing Book
Everything® Breastfeeding Book
Everything® Father-to-Be Book
Everything® Father's First Year Book
Everything® Get Ready for Baby Book, 2nd Ed.
Everything® Get Your Baby to Sleep Book, $9.95
Everything® Getting Pregnant Book
Everything® Guide to Pregnancy Over 35
Everything® Guide to Raising a One-Year-Old
Everything® Guide to Raising a Two-Year-Old
Everything® Guide to Raising Adolescent Boys
Everything® Guide to Raising Adolescent Girls
Everything® Homeschooling Book
Everything® Mother's First Year Book
Everything® Parent's Guide to Childhood Illnesses
Everything® Parent's Guide to Children and Divorce
Everything® Parent's Guide to Children with ADD/ADHD
Everything® Parent's Guide to Children with Asperger's Syndrome
Everything® Parent's Guide to Children with Autism
Everything® Parent's Guide to Children with Bipolar Disorder
Everything® Parent's Guide to Children with Depression
Everything® Parent's Guide to Children with Dyslexia
Everything® Parent's Guide to Children with Juvenile Diabetes
Everything® Parent's Guide to Positive Discipline
Everything® Parent's Guide to Raising a Successful Child
Everything® Parent's Guide to Raising Boys
Everything® Parent's Guide to Raising Girls
Everything® Parent's Guide to Raising Siblings
Everything® Parent's Guide to Sensory Integration Disorder
Everything® Parent's Guide to Tantrums
Everything® Parent's Guide to the Strong-Willed Child
Everything® Parenting a Teenager Book
Everything® Potty Training Book, $9.95
Everything® Pregnancy Book, 3rd Ed.
Everything® Pregnancy Fitness Book
Everything® Pregnancy Nutrition Book
Everything® Pregnancy Organizer, 2nd Ed., $16.95
Everything® Toddler Activities Book
Everything® Toddler Book
Everything® Tween Book
Everything® Twins, Triplets, and More Book

PETS

Everything® Aquarium Book
Everything® Boxer Book
Everything® Cat Book, 2nd Ed.
Everything® Chihuahua Book

Everything® Cooking for Dogs Book
Everything® Dachshund Book
Everything® Dog Book
Everything® Dog Health Book
Everything® Dog Obedience Book
Everything® Dog Owner's Organizer, $16.95
Everything® Dog Training and Tricks Book
Everything® German Shepherd Book
Everything® Golden Retriever Book
Everything® Horse Book
Everything® Horse Care Book
Everything® Horseback Riding Book
Everything® Labrador Retriever Book
Everything® Poodle Book
Everything® Pug Book
Everything® Puppy Book
Everything® Rottweiler Book
Everything® Small Dogs Book
Everything® Tropical Fish Book
Everything® Yorkshire Terrier Book

REFERENCE

Everything® American Presidents Book
Everything® Blogging Book
Everything® Build Your Vocabulary Book
Everything® Car Care Book
Everything® Classical Mythology Book
Everything® Da Vinci Book
Everything® Divorce Book
Everything® Einstein Book
Everything® Enneagram Book
Everything® Etiquette Book, 2nd Ed.
Everything® Guide to Edgar Allan Poe
Everything® Inventions and Patents Book
Everything® Mafia Book
Everything® Martin Luther King Jr. Book
Everything® Philosophy Book
Everything® Pirates Book
Everything® Psychology Book

RELIGION

Everything® Angels Book
Everything® Bible Book
Everything® Bible Study Book with CD, $19.95
Everything® Buddhism Book
Everything® Catholicism Book
Everything® Christianity Book
Everything® Gnostic Gospels Book
Everything® History of the Bible Book
Everything® Jesus Book
Everything® Jewish History & Heritage Book
Everything® Judaism Book
Everything® Kabbalah Book
Everything® Koran Book

Everything® Mary Book
Everything® Mary Magdalene Book
Everything® Prayer Book
Everything® Saints Book, 2nd Ed.
Everything® Torah Book
Everything® Understanding Islam Book
Everything® Women of the Bible Book
Everything® World's Religions Book
Everything® Zen Book

SCHOOL & CAREERS

Everything® Alternative Careers Book
Everything® Career Tests Book
Everything® College Major Test Book
Everything® College Survival Book, 2nd Ed.
Everything® Cover Letter Book, 2nd Ed.
Everything® Filmmaking Book
Everything® Get-a-Job Book, 2nd Ed.
Everything® Guide to Being a Paralegal
Everything® Guide to Being a Personal Trainer
Everything® Guide to Being a Real Estate Agent
Everything® Guide to Being a Sales Rep
Everything® Guide to Being an Event Planner
Everything® Guide to Careers in Health Care
Everything® Guide to Careers in Law Enforcement
Everything® Guide to Government Jobs
Everything® Guide to Starting and Running a Catering Business
Everything® Guide to Starting and Running a Restaurant
Everything® Job Interview Book
Everything® New Nurse Book
Everything® New Teacher Book
Everything® Paying for College Book
Everything® Practice Interview Book
Everything® Resume Book, 2nd Ed.
Everything® Study Book

SELF-HELP

Everything® Body Language Book
Everything® Dating Book, 2nd Ed.
Everything® Great Sex Book
Everything® Self-Esteem Book
Everything® Tantric Sex Book

SPORTS & FITNESS

Everything® Easy Fitness Book
Everything® Krav Maga for Fitness Book
Everything® Running Book

TRAVEL

Everything® Family Guide to Coastal Florida
Everything® Family Guide to Cruise Vacations
Everything® Family Guide to Hawaii
Everything® Family Guide to Las Vegas, 2nd Ed.
Everything® Family Guide to Mexico
Everything® Family Guide to New York City, 2nd Ed.
Everything® Family Guide to RV Travel & Campgrounds
Everything® Family Guide to the Caribbean
Everything® Family Guide to the Disneyland® Resort, California Adventure®, Universal Studios®, and the Anaheim Area, 2nd Ed.
Everything® Family Guide to the Walt Disney World Resort®, Universal Studios®, and Greater Orlando, 5th Ed.
Everything® Family Guide to Timeshares
Everything® Family Guide to Washington D.C., 2nd Ed.

WEDDINGS

Everything® Bachelorette Party Book, $9.95
Everything® Bridesmaid Book, $9.95
Everything® Destination Wedding Book
Everything® Elopement Book, $9.95
Everything® Father of the Bride Book, $9.95
Everything® Groom Book, $9.95
Everything® Mother of the Bride Book, $9.95
Everything® Outdoor Wedding Book
Everything® Wedding Book, 3rd Ed.
Everything® Wedding Checklist, $9.95
Everything® Wedding Etiquette Book, $9.95
Everything® Wedding Organizer, 2nd Ed., $16.95
Everything® Wedding Shower Book, $9.95
Everything® Wedding Vows Book, $9.95
Everything® Wedding Workout Book
Everything® Weddings on a Budget Book, 2nd Ed., $9.95

WRITING

Everything® Creative Writing Book
Everything® Get Published Book, 2nd Ed.
Everything® Grammar and Style Book
Everything® Guide to Magazine Writing
Everything® Guide to Writing a Book Proposal
Everything® Guide to Writing a Novel
Everything® Guide to Writing Children's Books
Everything® Guide to Writing Copy
Everything® Guide to Writing Graphic Novels
Everything® Guide to Writing Research Papers
Everything® Screenwriting Book
Everything® Writing Poetry Book
Everything® Writing Well Book